Lecture Notes in Computer Science   9264

Commenced Publication in 1973
Founding and Former Series Editors:
Gerhard Goos, Juris Hartmanis, and Jan van Leeuwen

More information about this series at http://www.springer.com/series/7410

Simone Fischer-Hübner · Costas Lambrinoudakis
Javier Lopez (Eds.)

Trust, Privacy and Security in Digital Business

12th International Conference, TrustBus 2015
Valencia, Spain, September 1–2, 2015
Proceedings

 Springer

Editors
Simone Fischer-Hübner
Karlstad University
Karlstad
Sweden

Javier Lopez
University of Malaga
Málaga
Spain

Costas Lambrinoudakis
University of Piraeus
Piraeus
Greece

ISSN 0302-9743   ISSN 1611-3349   (electronic)
Lecture Notes in Computer Science
ISBN 978-3-319-22905-8   ISBN 978-3-319-22906-5   (eBook)
DOI 10.1007/978-3-319-22906-5

Library of Congress Control Number: 2015946097

LNCS Sublibrary: SL4 – Security and Cryptology

Springer Cham Heidelberg New York Dordrecht London

Printed on acid-free paper

Springer International Publishing AG Switzerland is part of Springer Science+Business Media
(www.springer.com)

Preface

This book presents the proceedings of the 12th International Conference on Trust, Privacy and Security in Digital Business (TrustBus 2015), held in Valencia, Spain, September 1–2, 2015. The conference continued from previous events held in Zaragoza (2004), Copenhagen (2005), Krakow (2006), Regensburg (2007), Turin (2008), Linz (2009), Bilbao (2010), Toulouse (2011), Vienna (2012), Prague (2013), and Munich (2014).

The advances in the information and communication technologies (ICT) have raised new opportunities for the implementation of novel applications and the provision of high-quality services over global networks. The aim is to utilize this "information society era" to improve the quality of life for all citizens, disseminate knowledge, strengthen social cohesion, generate earnings, and finally ensure that organizations and public bodies remain competitive in the global electronic marketplace. Unfortunately, such a rapid technological evolution cannot be problem free. Concerns are raised regarding the lack of trust in electronic procedures and the extent to which information security and user privacy can be ensured.

TrustBus 2015 brought together academic researchers and industry developers, who discussed the state of the art in technology for establishing trust, privacy, and security in digital business. We thank the attendees for coming to Valencia to participate and debate the new emerging advances in this area.

The conference program included six technical papers sessions that covered a broad range of topics, from access control to trust and privacy issues in mobile environments, and from security and privacy in cloud systems to trust and reputation in pervasive environments. The conference attracted many high-quality submissions, each of which was assigned to four referees for review and the final acceptance rate was 37%.

We would like to express our thanks to the various people who assisted us in organizing the event and formulating the program. We are very grateful to the Program Committee members and the external reviewers, for their timely and rigorous reviews of the papers. Thanks are also due to the DEXA Organizing Committee for supporting our event, and in particular to Gabriela Wagner for her help with the administrative aspects.

Finally, we would like to thank Audun Jøsang for giving the invited keynote talk as well as all of the authors who submitted papers to the event and contributed toward an interesting set of conference proceedings.

September 2015

Simone Fischer-Hübner
Costas Lambrinoudakis
Javier Lopez

Organization

General Chair

Javier Lopez   University of Malaga, Spain

Program Committee Co-chairs

Simone Fischer-Hübner   Karlstad University, Sweden
Costas Lambrinoudakis   University of Piraeus, Greece

International Program Committee

Agudo, Isaac   University of Malaga (Spain)
Casassa Mont, Marco   HP Labs Bristol (UK)
Chadwick, David W.   University of Kent (UK)
Clarke, Nathan   Plymouth University (UK)
De Capitani di   Università degli Studi di Milano (Italy)
  Vimercati, Sabrina
Domingo-Ferrer, Josep   Universitat Rovira i Virgili (Spain)
Drogkaris, Prokopis   University of Piraeus (Greece)
Fernandez, Eduardo B.   Florida Atlantic University (USA)
Fernandez-Gago,   University of Malaga (Spain)
  Carmen
Ferrer, Josep L.   University of Balearic Islands (Spain)
Foresti, Sara   Università degli Studi di Milano (Italy)
Furnell, Steven   Plymouth University (UK)
Fuß, Jürgen   University of Applied Sciences Upper Austria (Austria)
Geneiatakis, Dimitris   Aristotle University of Thessaloniki (Greece)
Gritzalis, Dimitris   Athens University of Economics and Business (Greece)
Gritzalis, Stefanos   University of the Aegean (Greece)
Hansen, Marit   ULD - Independent Centre for Privacy Protection
                       Schleswig-Holstein (Germany)
Herrera-Joancomartí,   Universitat Autònoma de Barcelona (Spain)
  Jordi
Kalloniatis, Christos   University of the Aegean (Greece)
Karyda, Maria   University of the Aegean (Greece)
Katsikas, Sokratis   University of Piraeus (Greece)
Kesdogan, Dogan   University of Regensburg (Germany)
Kokolakis, Spyros   University of the Aegean (Greece)
Markowitch, Olivier   Université Libre de Bruxelles (Belgium)
Marsh, Stephen   University of Ontario, Institute of Technology (Canada)

Martinelli, Fabio	CNR (Italy)
Matyas, Vashek	Masaryk University (Czech Republic)
Megías, David	Universitat Oberta de Catalunya (Spain)
Mitchell, Chris	Royal Holloway, University of London (UK)
Mouratidis, Haralambos	University of Brighton (UK)
Olivier, Martin S.	University of Pretoria (South Africa)
Oppliger, Rolf	eSecurity Technologies (Switzerland)
Papadaki, Maria	Plymouth University (UK)
Pashalidis, Andreas	BSI (Germany)
Patel, Ahmed	Jazan University (Saudi Arabia) and Kingston University (UK)
Pernul, Guenther	University of Regensburg (Germany)
Piattini, Mario	University of Castilla-La Mancha (Spain)
Posegga, Joachim	University of Passau (Germany)
Rajarajan, Muttukrishnan	City University (UK)
Rizomiliotis, Panagiotis	University of the Aegean (Greece)
Rudolph, Carsten	Huawei (Germany)
Samarati, Pierangela	Università degli Studi di Milano (Italy)
Schaumueller-Bichl, Ingrid	University of Applied Sciences Upper Austria (Austria)
Schunter, Matthias	Intel Labs Europe (Germany)
Skarmeta, Antonio F.	University of Murcia (Spain)
Theocharidou, Marianthi	European Commission - Joint Research Centre (Italy)
Tjoa, A Min	Technical University of Vienna (Austria)
Tomlinson, Allan	Royal Holloway, University of London (UK)
Tsohou, Aggeliki	Ionian University (Greece)
Weippl, Edgar	SBA Research and Vienna University of Technology (Austria)
Xenakis, Christos	University of Piraeus (Greece)

External Reviewers

Bernal Bernabé, Jorge	Universidad de Murcia (Spain)
Blanco, Alberto	Universitat Rovira i Virgili (Spain)
Darra, Eleni	University of Piraeus (Greece)
Daud, Imran	Universitat Rovira i Virgili (Spain)
Iwaya, Leonardo Horn	Karlstad University (Sweden)
Kandias, Miltiadis	Athens University of Economics and Business (Greece)
Kunz, Michael	University of Regensburg (Germany)
Marín Pérez, Juan Manuel	Universidad de Murcia (Spain)
Ntantogian, Christoforos	University of Piraeus (Greece)
Pitropakis, Nikolaos	University of Piraeus (Greece)
Sabaté, Albert	Universitat Rovira i Virgili (Spain)
Sänger, Johannes	University of Regensburg (Germany)

Schillinger, Rolf	University of Regensburg (Germany)
Tsoumas, Bill	Athens University of Economics and Business (Greece)
Veshchikov, Nikita	Universite Libre de Bruxelles (Belgium)
Virvilis, Nikos	Athens University of Economics and Business (Greece)

Contents

Security and Privacy in the Cloud

Security Policies / Usability Issues

Privacy Requirements and Privacy Audit

Access Control

Attributes Enhanced Role-Based Access Control Model

Qasim Mahmood Rajpoot[1]([✉]), Christian Damsgaard Jensen[1], and Ram Krishnan[2]

[1] Department of Applied Mathematics and Computer Science, Technical University of Denmark, 2800 Kongens Lyngby, Denmark
{qara,cdje}@dtu.dk
[2] Department of Electrical and Computer Engineering, University of Texas at San Antonio, San Antonio, USA
ram.krishnan@utsa.edu

Abstract. Attribute-based access control (ABAC) and role-based access control (RBAC) are currently the two most popular access control models. Yet, they both have known limitations and offer features complimentary to each other. Due to this fact, integration of RBAC and ABAC has recently emerged as an important area of research. In this paper, we propose an access control model that combines the two models in a novel way in order to unify their benefits. Our approach provides a fine-grained access control mechanism that not only takes contextual information into account while making the access control decisions but is also suitable for applications where access to resources is controlled by exploiting contents of the resources in the policy.

Keywords: Context-aware access control · RBAC · Attributes · Content-Based access control · Role-permission explosion · Role-explosion

1 Introduction

RBAC [9] is the current standard access control model and has been a focus of research since last two decades. The RBAC paradigm encapsulates privileges into roles, and users are assigned to roles to acquire privileges, which makes it simple and facilitates reviewing permissions assigned to a user. It also makes the task of policy administration less cumbersome, as every change in a role is immediately reflected on the permissions available to users assigned to that role. A study [19] indicates that adoption of RBAC in commercial organizations is continuously increasing.

Due to the advent of pervasive systems, authorization control has become complex as access decisions may depend on the context in which access requests are made. The contextual information represents a measurable contextual primitive and may entail such information being associated with a user, object and environment [6]. For example, an access control policy may depend on the user's

© Springer International Publishing Switzerland 2015
S. Fischer-Hübner et al. (Eds.): TrustBus 2015, LNCS 9264, pp. 3–17, 2015.
DOI: 10.1007/978-3-319-22906-5_1

current location, the object being currently in a *specific state*, and the *time of day* when the access is requested. It has been recognized that RBAC is not adequate for situations where contextual attributes are required parameters in granting access to a user [16]. Another limitation of RBAC is that the permissions are specified in terms of object identifiers, referring to individual objects. This is not adequate in situations where a large number of objects in hundreds of thousands exist and leads to role-permission explosion problem. Moreover, in many applications, access to data is more naturally described in terms of its semantic contents [2], for example, in a rating system of movies, violent movies are restricted to audiences above a certain age, based on the movie contents.

A relatively new access control paradigm, ABAC [13,23] has been identified to overcome these limitations of RBAC [7]. ABAC is considered more flexible as compared to RBAC, since it can easily accommodate contextual attributes as access control parameters [16]. However, ABAC is typically much more complex than RBAC in terms of policy review, hence analyzing the policy and reviewing or changing user permissions are quite cumbersome tasks.

On one hand, both RBAC and ABAC have their particular advantages and disadvantages. On the other hand, both have features complimentary to each other, and thus integrating RBAC and ABAC has become an important research topic [7,12,14]. Also, NIST has announced an initiative [16] to integrate RBAC and its various extensions with ABAC in order to combine the advantages offered by both RBAC and ABAC. In this context, we proposed earlier the concept of an integrated RBAC and ABAC access control model [20]. In this paper, we extend it further by presenting the formal model for our Attribute Enhanced Role-Based Access Control model. We also present algorithms for two different ways in which access requests may be evaluated. Moreover, we analyze the properties of our model with the help of a scenario.

The model that we propose in this paper retains the flexibility offered by ABAC, yet it maintains RBAC's advantages of easier administration, policy analysis and review of permissions. In addition, our solution has the following key features: *a*) it allows to make context-aware access control decisions by associating conditions with permissions that are used to verify whether the required contextual information holds when a decision is made, *b*) it offers a content-based authorization system while keeping the approach role-oriented, in order to retain the advantages offered by RBAC. We achieve this by allowing to specify permissions using attributes of the objects rather than using only their identifiers.

The rest of the paper is organized as follows: Sect. 2 summarizes related work and compares our approach to prior work. In Sect. 3, we present the components of the proposed access control model while Sect. 4 presents a formal model and different possibilities in which a request may be evaluated. Section 5 discusses potential benefits offered by the proposed approach. We conclude the paper and identify future directions in Sect. 6.

2   Related Work

Kuhn et al. [16] announced a NIST initiative to incorporate attributes into roles in order to merge features of RBAC and ABAC. In response to this initiative,

Jin et al. [14] present first formal access control model called RABAC. They extend RBAC with user and object attributes and add a component called permission filtering policy (PFP). The PFP requires specification of filtering functions in the form of Boolean expression consisting of user and object attributes. Their solution is useful to address the role-explosion problem and as a result facilitates user role assignment. However, the approach does not incorporate environment attributes and is not suitable for systems involving frequently changing attributes, e.g., location and time. Also, our approach is significantly different in the sense that we make a fundamental modification in RBAC by using attributes of the objects in the permissions, addressing the issue of role-permission explosion, faced while using RABAC. Huang et al. [12] present a framework to integrate RBAC with attributes. The approach consists of two levels: underground and aboveground. The underground level makes use of attribute-based policies to automate the processes of user-role and role-permission assignment. The aboveground level is the RBAC model, with addition of environment attributes, constructed using attribute-based policies. Their work is different than ours in that it focuses on automated construction of RBAC. Xu and Stoller [22] focus on migration of RBAC-based systems to ABAC in order to avoid limitations of RBAC. They present a solution to mine attribute-based policies from an already configured RBAC model.

Several efforts have been reported which extend RBAC to include the context of access. Some of the key works in this area include environment roles [4], spatiotemporal RBAC [21] and context-aware RBAC [17]. However these approaches typically require creation of a large number of closely related roles, causing the role-explosion problem. Ge et al. [11], and Giuri et al. [10] focus on resolving the issue of role explosion by providing the mechanism of parametrized privileges and parametrized roles. However, the permissions in these solutions refer to objects using their identifiers. Few approaches propose a variant of RBAC categorizing the objects into groups or types in an attempt to resolve the role-permission explosion issue [5,15,18]. Grouping the objects allows to associate a single attribute with each object. The permissions are then specified using the group attribute – referred to as views in [15] and object classes in [5] – where each permission refers to a set of objects in that group. Moreover, as the number of object attributes grow, the number of groups increase exponentially. This makes task of policy administration cumbersome since for every new object to be added in the system it has to be associated with all those groups to which it belongs. Another area of research relevant to ours is content-based access control, where access to a resource is dependent on the information contained within the resource. Prior literature mainly uses attribute-based approaches to handle this requirement [1,2]. However, these approaches suffer from the ABAC limitations, discussed earlier. Using a combination of roles and attributes may help in simplifying the management and policy modification, as discussed in Sect. 5.

3   Overview of the Proposed Model

This section presents an overview of the proposed Attributes Enhanced Role-Based Access Control model (AERBAC). Figure 1 depicts our access control

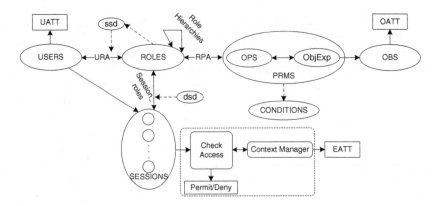

Fig. 1. Attributes enhanced role-based access control (AERBAC) model

model and its components. The entities users, roles, objects and operations have the same semantics as in RBAC. Users and objects in our model are associated with attributes too. We also incorporate the environment attribute to fully capture the situation in which access needs to be authorized. The dotted-box in Fig. 1 represents the modules of the architectural design to enforce this model. Below, we first describe the attributes and then discuss semantics of different components involved in AERBAC, including permissions, conditions, sessions and request evaluation.

Attributes: Attributes capture the properties of specific entities (e.g. user). We define an attribute function for each attribute that returns the value of that attribute. Each attribute is represented by a range of finite sets of atomic values. For example, the range of branch attribute is a set of names of branches semantically relevant for the application domain. *User attributes* capture the properties of the user who initiates an access request. Examples of user attributes are title, specialization, location, security clearance etc. *Object attributes* are used to define the properties of the resources protected by the access control policy. Examples of object attributes include type, status, location, time of object creation etc. *Environment attributes* capture external factors of the situation in which the access takes place. Temperature, occurrence of an incident, system mode or other information which not only pertains to a specific object or user, but may hold for multiple entities, are typically modeled as environment attributes.

An attribute may be either *static* or *dynamic*. The values of *static* attributes rarely change e.g. designation, department, type etc. On the other hand, *dynamic* attribute values may change frequently and unpredictably, so they may well change during the lifetime of a session. Examples of such attributes include officer in command, location, occurrence of an incident etc. They are also referred to as contextual attributes in the literature [6].

Permissions and Conditions: In contrast to the traditional approaches in RBAC, the permissions in AERBAC refer to objects indirectly, using their attributes. A permission refers to a set of objects sharing common attributes, e.g. type or branch, using a single permission, in contrast to separate permissions for each unique object. This is particularly relevant in those domains where several objects share common attribute values. This helps in significantly reducing the number of permissions associated with a role, while increasing the expressiveness and granularity of access control in a role-centric fashion.

In our proposed model, a permission consists of an object expression and an authorized operation on the object set denoted by the expression. Object expressions are formed using the attributes of objects. Each permission is associated with one or more conditions, which must be evaluated to be true in order for the user to exercise that permission. A condition associated with a permission may contain attributes of all entities including users, objects and environment. In some applications, it is required to compare user and object attributes – for example, in a bank, a manager of a branch is allowed to access only those accounts belonging to his own branch. The proposed model allows to perform such comparisons using conditions.

An example of a permission is: $p=$ ($(oType(o) = secret \land oStatus(o) = active)$, $read$) which states that a role having this permission can perform read operation on the objects denoted by the given object expression. Here $oType$ and $oStatus$ are object attribute functions that return the values of respective attributes for a given object. Suppose that the permission p is constrained by a condition $c= (uMember(u) = premium \land time\_of\_day() \leq uDuty\text{-}Expire(u))$ where $uMember$ and $uDutyExpire$ are user attribute functions that return the attribute values of a given user, whereas $time\_of\_day()$ is an environment attribute function. This condition implies that, in order to be granted the permission p, the user must be a premium user and time of access must be before the end of user's duty timing.

The Context Manager is responsible for propagating the updated values of dynamic attributes of the users, objects and environment. Depending on the application, some of these attribute values may also be provided by the user while placing an access request, however the application must ensure the authenticity of such information before using it in access decisions.

Session: A session contains a list of permissions associated with the roles activated by the user. As described earlier, the permissions are different from standard RBAC permissions in terms of referring to the objects using their attributes and being tied with the conditions that are evaluated every time a permission is to be exercised. Hence, the CheckAccess function needs to be re-defined.

Access request: An important consideration, in environments motivating the proposed approach, is that the user's request may also be based on the attributes of the objects. For instance, in a medical imaging application, a user might want to view all images containing specified characteristics e.g., objects with $type = tumor$ and $domain = hospital\text{-}nw$. For a user request to be granted, there must exist an object expression in the user's session that denotes the requested objects, and the condition tied to that object expression must be evaluated to be true. There are different possibilities in which such a request may be evaluated and we discuss them later in the paper (cf. Sect. 4.1).

Table 1. Sets and Functions used in AERBAC

- USERS, ROLES, OBS, and OPS (users, roles, objects and operations respectively)
- URA ⊆ USERS × ROLES, a many-to-many mapping of user-to-role assignment;
- SESSIONS, the set of sessions;
- user_sessions(u: USERS) → 2^{SESSIONS}, the mapping of user u onto a set of sessions;
- session_roles(s: SESSIONS) → 2^{ROLES}, the mapping of session s onto a set of roles. Formally: session_roles(s_i) ⊆ { r ∈ ROLES | (session_user(s_i), r) ∈ URA};
- avail_session_perms(s: SESSIONS) → 2^{PRMS}, the permissions available to a user in a session.

- UATT, OATT and EATT represent finite sets of user, object and environment attribute functions respectively.
- For each *att* in UATT ∪ OATT ∪ EATT, Range(*att*) represents the attribute's range, a finite set of *atomic* values.
- attType: UATT ∪ OATT ∪ EATT → {setType, atomicType}, specifies attributes as set or atomic valued.
- OBJ_EXP = Set of all object expressions formed using the language given in Table 2.
- COND = Set of all conditions formed using the language given in Table 2.
- PRMS = $2^{\text{(OPS × OBJ\_EXP)}}$, the set of permissions.
- RPA ⊆ ROLES × PRMS × COND
- Each attribute function in UATT, OATT and EATT returns either atomic or set values.

$$\forall ua \in \text{UATT}.\, ua : \text{USERS} \rightarrow \begin{cases} \text{Range(ua) if attType}(ua) = \text{atomicType} \\ 2^{\text{Range(ua)}} \text{ if attType}(ua) = \text{setType} \end{cases}$$

$$\forall oa \in \text{OATT}.\, oa : \text{OBS} \rightarrow \begin{cases} \text{Range(oa) if attType}(oa) = \text{atomicType} \\ 2^{\text{Range(oa)}} \text{ if attType}(oa) = \text{setType} \end{cases}$$

$$\forall ea \in \text{EATT}.\, ea \rightarrow \begin{cases} \text{Range(ea) if attType}(ea) = \text{atomicType} \\ 2^{\text{Range(ea)}} \text{ if attType}(ea) = \text{setType} \end{cases}$$

4   Formal AERBAC Model

In this section, we propose the formal model that incorporates the attributes of the user, object and environment into RBAC in a role-oriented fashion. We define the sets and functions used in AERBAC in Table 1. The upper part of the table shows the sets and functions defined in NIST RBAC which are also applicable to AERBAC. We provide further sets and functions needed for AERBAC in the lower part of the table. UATT, OATT and EATT represent sets of attribute functions for users, objects and environment, respectively. The notion we used for attribute representation is adapted from [13]. We use first order logic to make formal descriptions, and follow the convention that all unbound variables are universally quantified given as Range(att). Each attribute function returns

Table 2. Language to form object expressions and conditions

$\varphi ::= \varphi \wedge \varphi | \varphi \vee \varphi | (\varphi) |$ set setcompare set | atomic $\in$ set | atomic atomiccompare atomic
setcompare $::= \subset | \subseteq | \nsubseteq$
atomiccompare $::= < | = | \leq | \neq$

===

To define an object expression, set and atomic are as follows:

- set::= setoa(o:OBS) | ConsSet
- atomic::= atomicoa(o:OBS) | ConsAtomic
- setoa $\in$ {oa | oa $\in$ OATT $\wedge$ attType(oa) = setType}
- atomicoa $\in$ {oa | oa $\in$ OATT $\wedge$ attType(oa) = atomicType}

For condition specification, set and atomic are as follows:

- set::= setua (session_user(se)) | setoa(o:OBS) | setea() | ConsSet
- atomic::= atomicua (session_user(se)) | atomicoa(o:OBS) | atomicea() | ConsAtomic
- setua $\in$ {ua | ua $\in$ UATT $\wedge$ attType(ua) = setType }
- atomicua $\in$ {ua | ua $\in$ UATT $\wedge$ attType(ua)= atomicType }
- setoa $\in$ {oa | oa $\in$ OATT $\wedge$ attType(oa) = setType}
- atomicoa $\in$ {oa | oa $\in$ OATT $\wedge$ attType(oa) = atomicType}
- setea $\in$ {ea | ea $\in$ EATT $\wedge$ attType(ea) = setType}
- atomicea $\in$ {ea | ea $\in$ EATT $\wedge$ attType(ea) = atomicType}

---

either a set or an atomic value, determined based on the type of the attribute (i.e. attType). Attribute functions in UATT and OATT take as an argument a user and an object, respectively. Each attribute functions in EATT may or may not require an argument, depending on the attribute and the target system. For instance, in a banking system with multiple branches, an environment attribute function would require the branch name to return the value of an environment attribute, e.g., current-system-load, in that branch.

The role-permission assignment (RPA) relation captures permissions that are assigned to a role when a given set of conditions are fulfilled. Clearly, the permission set may change for a role if the conditions vary between requests. Permissions in AERBAC are specified using object expressions. The language to define an object expression and a condition is given in the first part of Table 2. The second part of the table specifies how instances of *set* and *atomic* may be formed to define an object expression and a condition. *ConsSet* and *ConsAtomic* are constant sets and atomic values. The object expressions may be specified using only attributes of the objects. While for specifying a condition, attributes of user, object and environment may be used. The function sesseion_user(se) is defined in NIST RBAC [9] that returns the user to whom a given session *se* belongs to.

4.1   Access Decisions

The main role of the access control mechanism is to verify whether a user u, requesting access to object o, using an operation op, is authorized to do so. As mentioned above, a user request can either explicitly specify an object, by listing its identifier, or can implicitly denote a set of objects using the attributes of the objects. If the user request is not for a specific object but rather a set of objects, the system must consider the given criteria to return the requested objects. Once a user submits an access request, the request is to be evaluated against the policy. The function checkAccess in RBAC needs to be modified such that it takes the user request as input, processes the request as per the format of a given request, and returns the result. In the following, we elaborate on evaluation of both identifier-based and attribute-based requests.

(a) Identifier-based request: In identifier-based request, the user specifies the identifier of the object to be accessed. The evaluation of such type of request is straight-forward. In this case, the input of the function checkAccess consists of a session se, an operation m, and an object obj. Recall that a permission consists of an object expression and an operation and is constrained by a condition. The checkAccess function returns true if and only if (i) there exists a permission p, in the *avail_session_perms* of session se, that contains an object expression which evaluates to true for obj, (ii) m matches op, and iii) the corresponding condition c evaluates to true.

(b) Attribute-based request: Using the second form of request, user may specify the attributes of the object in his/her request, rather than a unique identifier of the object. Specifying the object attributes in the request implies that the user wishes to access all those objects which have the specified attribute values. Below we discuss two possibilities to formulate and process such requests.

(b.1) Resource query: In this approach, user request contains an expression similar to the object expressions. An example user request could be: *Req = < se, (otype = secret ∧ odept = admin ∧ ostatus = inactive), write>* which states that the owner of the session se wishes to exercise the write operation on the objects denoted by the given object expression. The checkAccess function receives as input the access request *Req* and returns the authorized objects to the user, if request is granted, otherwise the request is denied. The given expression is converted to a query and the resulting objects are retrieved from the resource database. Next step is to find the applicable object expressions by matching the user's requested operation with the ones mentioned in the permission set existing in user's session. Once the object expressions are shortlisted, they are evaluated one-by-one for each object returned by the query. If an object expression and its corresponding condition evaluate to true for an object, the object is added into the list of authorized objects to be granted to the user. Finally, user is granted access to all those objects for which an object expression and its corresponding condition return true. Figure 2 presents algorithm for this approach. Since the object expressions are to be evaluated for each returned object, this approach may prove to be expensive in cases where several objects are returned by the query formed based on user's request.

Algorithm 1

Input: An access request: Req = <se, re, m >consisting of session identifier *se*, request expression *re*, and operation *m*.

Output: 1) Accept and return authorized objects, 2) Reject otherwise

Begin:

1: relevant_expressions = Φ;
2: object_set = Φ;
3: authorized_objects = Φ;
4: object_set = search_objects*(*re*);
5: **if** object_set $\neq \Phi$ **then**
6:     **for all** perm<object_exp, op>$\in$ avail_session_perms **do**
7:         **if** m = op **then**
8:             relevant_expressions $\leftarrow$ relevant_expressions $\cup$ object_exp;
9:         **end if**
10:     **end for**
11:     **for all** object $\in$ object_set **do**
12:         **for all** object_exp $\in$ relevant_expressions **do**
13:             **if** evaluate†(object_exp, object) **then**
14:                 **if** eval_cond‡(condition, object, session_user(*se*)) **then**
15:                     authorized_objects $\leftarrow$ authorized_objects $\cup$ object;
16:                     break;
17:                 **end if**
18:             **end if**
19:         **end for**
20:     **end for**
21: **end if**
22: **if** authorized_object $\neq \Phi$ **then**
23:     **return** authorized_objects;
24: **end if**
25: **return** Reject;

End

* search_objects(re) returns a set of objects existing in the resource database that are denoted by the constraints specified in expression *re*, in the request.

† evaluate(object_exp, object) returns TRUE if *object_exp* evaluates to true for the given *object*, else returns FALSE.

‡ eval_cond(condition, object, session_user(se)) returns TRUE if given *condition* evaluates to true for the given *object* attributes and the attributes of the user and the environment.

Fig. 2. Algorithm for access request evaluation using resource query

(b.2) Attribute values: An alternative strategy is to evaluate the user's request against the object expressions before retrieving the actual objects from the resource database. In this approach, rather than providing an expression, user specifies his/her access request by specifying the object attribute values of the desired objects. The checkAccess function receives as input the user request *Req*

and returns the objects denoted by object attribute values given in *Req*, if request is granted, otherwise the request is denied. To process user request, all

---

Algorithm 2

Input: An access request: Req = < se, obj_att_values, m> consisting of session identifier *se*, object attribute values *obj_att_values*, and operation *m*.
Output: 1) Accept and return authorized objects, 2) Reject otherwise
Begin:

1: relevant_expressions = Φ;
2: authorized_objects = Φ;
3: **for all** perm < object_exp, op > $\in$ avail_session_perms **do**
4:    **if** m = op $\wedge$ check_relevancy*(obj_exp, obj_att_values) **then**
5:       **if** evaluate† (object_exp, obj_att_values) **then**
6:          **if** eval_cond‡(condition, obj_att_values, session_user(se)) **then**
7:             authorized_objects = get_objects††(obj_att_values);
8:          **end if**
9:       **end if**
10:    **end if**
11: **end for**
12: **if** authorized_object $\neq$ Φ **then**
13:    **return** (Accept, authorized_objects)
14: **end if**
15: **return** (Reject)

End

* check_relevancy(object_exp, obj_att_values) returns TRUE if the given *object_exp* uses only those object attribute functions referred in *obj_att_values*
† evaluate(object_exp, obj_att_values) returns TRUE if the given *object_exp* evaluates to true when the object attribute functions are replaced with *obj_att_values*
‡ eval_cond(condition, obj_att_values, session_user(se)) returns TRUE if the given *condition* evaluates to true for the given object attributes and the attributes of the user and environment
†† get_objects(obj_att_values) returns a set of objects existing in the resource database that satisfy *obj_att_values*

Fig. 3. Algorithm for access request evaluation using attribute values

those object expressions existing in user's session are identified which use the attributes mentioned in the user's request and the operation specified in that permission matches with requested operation. Object expressions that include an attribute not specified by the user request are not relevant. Next, for each shortlisted object expression, the attribute functions in the object expression are given the user provided attribute values. For instance, if a user specifies the following object attribute in his/her request: *(otype = classified; odept = pg; ostatus = active)* and suppose we find an object expression as follows: *(otype(o) = classified $\wedge$ odept(o) $\subseteq$ {pg, ug, admin})*. Upon picking the values of the object attribute functions *otype* and *odept* from user given attribute values we get: *(classified = classified $\wedge$ pg $\subseteq$ {pg, ug, admin})* which would evaluate to true. As soon as an object expression and its corresponding condition return true, the user's request is granted and rest of the object expressions are ignored. When an expression returns true we form a query based on the object attribute values specified in the user request and the user is granted access to all those objects returned by the query. Algorithm for this approach is given in Fig. 3.

Note that we never evaluate an object expression which uses an object attribute not given in the user's request. This is because we replace the object attribute functions with the user given attribute values, hence any object expression involving those object attributes not given by the user cannot be evaluated. The query to get the authorized objects is formed using the object attributes mentioned in the user's request. Once an object expression returns true, this query may restrict the list of returned objects based on any additional attributes mentioned in the user's request. In the example above, the returned result is restricted based on additional object attributes *ostatus* which are mentioned in the user's request but does not exist in the expression which enables the request.

This approach is superior to resource query in terms of making an access decision by evaluating only the object expressions, without having to retrieve objects from the resource database. This is important, since many requests can be denied at this point without the overhead of object retrieval and condition evaluation. An obvious assumption made in this form of user request is that the multiple object attributes mentioned in the user request are always combined using logical conjunction operator.

5   Discussion

To illustrate the features of the proposed access control model, we present an example below, inspired from the online entertainment store example presented in [23]. Suppose an online entertainment store streams movies to subscribed users. Suppose, there are two different types of users; Adult and Juvenile. Adult users can view all movies while Juvenile can view only G-rated movies. Using the standard RBAC approach, clearly we need two roles to represent *Juvenile* and *Adult* users. In each role the permissions have to be specified using identifiers of the objects individual movies. Considering that there may exist thousands of movies in the database, referring each with its identifier would lead to role-permission explosion problem. To address this issue, AERBAC integrates roles and attributes in a novel way and uses the attributes of the objects in the permissions rather than identifiers of individual objects. Table 3 provides an example where permissions make use of object attributes. In this example, the role *Adult* is inherited by *Juvenile* role and hence inherits permissions assigned to *Juvenile* role.

In order to model multiple characteristics associated with user, object or environment, the number of roles in RBAC increase exponentially. Suppose we want to ensure that only premium users may view newly released movies and regular users may view newly released movies only during promotional periods. To represent these conditions in standard RBAC, we would need to create at least six roles: Adult_premium, Adult_promo, Adult_regular, Juvenile_premium, Juvenile_promo and Juvenile_regular, where Adult_promo

Table 3. Permissions in AERBAC

Role	Permissions
Adult	(view, (rating(m) = R))
Juvenile	(view, (rating(m) = G))

Table 4. Example configuration using AERBAC

Role	Permissions	Conditions
Adult	(view, (rating(m) = R ∧ release(m) = new))	(userType(u) = premium ∨ today ∈ PromoDates)
	(view, (rating(m) = R ∧ release(m) = old))	None
Juvenile	(view, (rating(m) = G ∧ release(m) = new))	(userType(u) = premium ∨ today ∈ PromoDates)
	(view, (rating(m) = G ∧ release(m) = old))	None

and Juvenile_promo roles would be available to users only during promotional periods. Configuring this using AERBAC, we need only two roles: Adult and Juvenile as we use attributes of objects in the permissions and other attributes in the condition corresponding to each permission. Table 4 provides the configuration of this scenario using the proposed approach.

Our motivation to integrate RBAC with attributes is to obtain advantages associated with both RBAC and ABAC, while addressing the limitations of RBAC and ABAC. Using a pure ABAC approach, in configuring situation such as above requires writing policy rules. When a user request needs to be evaluated, the relevant rules are identified using the attributes associated with requesting user, requested object and current environment. These shortlisted rules are then evaluated one-by-one unless we find a rule which allows the request. In contrast, our approach requires evaluation of only those object expressions which are associated with the roles activated by a user in his/her session. Note that this may significantly reduce the number of rules to be evaluated. Moreover, the user or environment attributes used in the conditions are evaluated only if an object expression evaluates to true for a given request. This is particularly useful in cases where user or environment attributes are dynamic and their current values are reported at the time of request evaluation. In our approach, such values would only need to be obtained if an object expression in the user's session returns true. This indicates that many user requests may be denied, just by evaluating object expressions, without obtaining the current values for user and environment attributes.

5.1   Merits of the Proposed Model

As discussed above, the object expressions and conditions that are to be evaluated against a user request are determined by the roles a user activates in a session. Imagine a user assigned to a senior executive role in an organization which has several privileges. For a user in this role, we might allow to access specific resources without giving any consideration to the time of request and location of user, for instance. This implies that there may be some attributes which are not relevant for a given role and hence the number of conditions and object expressions to be evaluated for that role may be reduced.

Compared to ABAC, our approach provides a systematic mechanism to evaluate a subset of policy rules which are determined based on the user's roles, yet retaining the advantages offered by RBAC including quick assignment and revocation of roles to users, reviewing of permissions assigned to a user or role, and reduced complexity of administration in large organizations. Moreover, we believe several limitations of the RBAC and ABAC approaches may be overcome using the approach we proposed. Below, we enlist some of these limitations and discuss how our approach overcomes these problems.

1- Fine-grained Access Control: RBAC provides a coarse-grained access control model where as many applications require a much finer-degree of granularity [8]. In order to satisfy the requirements posed by such applications, a large number of roles have to be created when pure RBAC is used. Using the proposed approach, we may provide a finer-grained access control mechanism without creating a large number of roles. As discussed in the example, we achieve this by associating conditions at permission level to check further attributes associated with a user and environment rather than granting a permission merely based on being a member of a role.

2- Context-aware Access: RBAC cannot easily handle dynamically changing attributes [7]. It typically does not support making contextual decisions unless many similar roles are created causing role-explosion problem. We provide a mechanism to incorporate these dynamically changing attributes in a role-centric manner yet without requiring to create a large number of roles. An important feature of our approach is checking the values of such attributes at the time of granting access rather than checking them at the time of session creation as done typically in RBAC.

3- Easy Auditing: When ABAC is used in a considerably large organization having a large number of policy rules, it may not be practically feasible to audit what permissions have been granted to a user. In ABAC, any combination of attributes may essentially grant an access and hence it requires to analyze all policy rules with an exhaustive enumeration of attributes used in each policy rule [7]. Our approach makes it simpler to audit what permissions may be granted to a user because of being role-centric while adding the flexibility and fine-grained access features offered by ABAC. When auditing for a particular position or employee, we need to consider only the policy rules given in the roles assigned to that position or employee.

4- Policy Modification Visualization: One of the issues in the ABAC approach is that the consequences of a newly added or removed policy rule are not easy to visualize [3]. It is not clear what set of users will be effected by a change in the policy. A change in policy essentially may affect those users who we wish to remain authorized to access a particular resource but they are no more authorized since a policy rule is removed. In our approach, it is relatively easy to visualize what is the impact of adding or removing a policy since policy specification is at the level of role. Therefore, a change in policy can effect only those users who are assigned to a role being modified.

6   Conclusion

In this paper, we proposed an access control model that integrates RBAC and ABAC bringing together the features offered by both models. In our model, the attributes may be associated with users, objects and environment allowing the request context to be considered in making access control decisions. Unlike traditional RBAC approaches, permissions in our model consist of operations and object expressions enabling content-based access control. We presented different request evaluation mechanisms that may be used by various applications depending on their requirements. We demonstrated the merits of the proposed model in the discussion section using a scenario. In the future, we plan to work on formally analyzing the properties offered by the proposed model as compared to existing access control model including ABAC and RBAC, and to develop an XACML profile of the proposed model. Further directions for future work include use of cache mechanisms to further expedite the access control decision process, to extend the model with continuous enforcement to deactivate a role or revoke a permission when context conditions fail to hold, and to include negative authorizations in the model.

Acknowledgments. The work of first two authors is supported by a grant from the Danish National Advanced Technology Foundation. The work of the third author is supported by a US National Science Foundation grant CNS-1423481.

References

1. Adam, N.R., Atluri, V., Bertino, E., Ferrari, E.: A content-based authorization model for digital libraries. IEEE Trans. Knowl. Data Eng. **14**(2), 296–315 (2002)
2. Bertino, E., Moustafa A.H., Walid A.G., Elmagarmid, A.K.: An access control model for video database systems. In: International Conference on Information and Knowledge Management, pp. 336–343. ACM (2000)
3. Best Practices in Enterprise Authorization: The RBAC/ABAC Hybrid Approach (EmpowerID). http://blog.empowerid.com/Portals/174819/docs/EmpowerID-WhitePaper-RBAC-ABAC-Hybrid-Model.pdf
4. Covington, M.J., Long, W., Srinivasan, S., Dev, A.K., Ahamad, M., Abowd, G.D.: Securing context-aware applications using environment roles. In: Symposium on Access Control Models and Technologies, pp. 10–20. ACM (2001)
5. Chae, J.H., Shiri, N.: Formalization of RBAC policy with object class hierarchy. In: Dawson, E., Wong, D.S. (eds.) ISPEC 2007. LNCS, vol. 4464, pp. 162–176. Springer, Heidelberg (2007)

6. Covington, M.J., Sastry, M.R.: A contextual attribute-based access control model. In: Meersman, R., Tari, Z., Herrero, P. (eds.) OTM 2006 Workshops. LNCS, vol. 4278, pp. 1996–2006. Springer, Heidelberg (2006)

7. Coyne, E., Weil, T.R.: ABAC and RBAC: scalable, flexible, and auditable access management. IT Prof. **15**(3), 14–16 (2013)

8. Fischer, J., Marino, D., Majumdar, R., Millstein, T.: Fine-grained access control with object-sensitive roles. In: Drossopoulou, S. (ed.) ECOOP 2009. LNCS, vol. 5653, pp. 173–194. Springer, Heidelberg (2009)

9. Ferraiolo, D.F., Sandhu, R., Gavrila, S., Kuhn, D.R., Chandramouli, R.: Proposed NIST standard for role-based access control. ACM Trans. Inf. Syst. Secur. (TISSEC) **4**(3), 224–274 (2001)

10. Giuri, L., Iglio, P.: Role templates for content-based access control. In: Workshop on Role-Based Access Control, pp. 153–159. ACM (1997)

11. Ge, M., Osborn, S.L.: A design for parameterized roles. In: Farkas, C., Samarati, P. (eds.) Data, Application Security and Privacy Conference. IFIP, vol. 144, pp. 251–264. Springer, Heidelberg (2004)

12. Huang, J., Nicol, D.M., Bobba, R., Huh, J.H.: A framework integrating attribute-based policies into RBAC. In: Symposium on Access Control Models and Technologies, pp. 187–196. ACM (2012)

13. Jin, X., Krishnan, R., Sandhu, R.: A unified attribute-based access control model covering DAC, MAC and RBAC. In: Cuppens-Boulahia, N., Cuppens, F., Garcia-Alfaro, J. (eds.) DBSec 2012. LNCS, vol. 7371, pp. 41–55. Springer, Heidelberg (2012)

14. Jin, X., Sandhu, R., Krishnan, R.: RABAC: role-centric attribute-based access control. In: Kotenko, I., Skormin, V. (eds.) MMM-ACNS 2012. LNCS, vol. 7531, pp. 84–96. Springer, Heidelberg (2012)

15. Kalam, A.A.E., Baida, R.E., Balbiani, P., Benferhat, S., Cuppens, F., Deswarte, Y., Miege, A., Saurel, C., Trouessin, G.: Organization based access control. In: 4th International Workshop on Policies for Distributed Systems and Networks. IEEE (2003)

16. Kuhn, D.R., Coyne, E.J., Weil, T.R.: Adding attributes to role-based access control. IEEE Comput. **43**, 79–81 (2010)

17. Kulkarni, D., Tripathi, A.: Context-aware role-based access control in pervasive computing systems. In: Symposium on Access Control Models and Technologies, pp. 113–122. ACM (2008)

18. Moyer, M.J., Abamad, M.: Generalized role-based access control. In: International Conference on Distributed Computing Systems, pp. 391–398. IEEE (2001)

19. O'Connor, A.C., Loomis, R.J.: Economic Analysis of Role-Based Access Control. NIST Report (2010)

20. Rajpoot, Q.M., Jensen, C.D., Krishnan, R.: Integrating attributes into role-based access control. In: Samarati, P. (ed.) DBSec 2015. LNCS, vol. 9149, pp. 242–249. Springer, Heidelberg (2015)

21. Ray, I., Toahchoodee, M.: A spatio-temporal role-based access control model. In: Barker, S., Ahn, G.-J. (eds.) Data and Applications Security 2007. LNCS, vol. 4602, pp. 211–226. Springer, Heidelberg (2007)

22. Xu, Z., Stoller, S.D.: Mining attribute-based access control policies from RBAC policies. In: 10th International Conference and Expo on Emerging Technologies for a Smarter World (CEWIT), pp. 1–6. IEEE (2013)

23. Yuan, E., Tong, J.: Attributed Based Access Control (ABAC) for Web Services. In: International Conference on Web Services. IEEE (2005)

Ontology-Based Delegation of Access Control: An Enhancement to the XACML Delegation Profile

Malik Imran Daud[(✉)], David Sánchez, and Alexandre Viejo

UNESCO Chair in Data Privacy,
Department of Computer Science
and Mathematics, Universitat Rovira I Virgili,
Avda. Països Catalans, 26, 43007 Tarragona, Spain
{malikimran.daud,david.sanchez,
alexandre.viejo}@urv.cat

Abstract. Delegation of access control (i.e. transferring access rights on a resource to another tenant) is crucial to efficiently decentralize the access control management in large and dynamic scenarios. Most of the delegation methods available in the literature are based on the RBAC or ABAC models. However, their applicability can be hampered by: (i) the effort required to manage and enforce multiple roles for each delegatee (i.e. access roles and delegated roles) and (ii) the efforts required to specify constraints for the enforcement of the delegated roles or policies. Moreover, the performance of these methods decreases proportionally as the number of users increase. To tackle these issues, we propose an ontology-based delegation framework that enhances the standard XACML delegation profile by modeling the delegation logics in an ontological way. By means of the ontology, the operations of delegation, verification and revocation of access rights can be performed on the workflow generated by instantiating the ontology classes and their interrelations according to the entities involved in the delegation. By exploiting these workflows, we propose a cost-effective algorithm that performs delegation operations without involving any human intervention.

Keywords: Security · Access control · Delegation · ABAC · XACML · Ontology

1 Introduction

In the field of information security, access control management is a method to manage the access to the resources based on the identity of the users [1]. Delegation is one of the mechanisms to manage access control in a flexible way [2], wherein, users can transfer their access rights to other entities on a particular resource. Most of the delegation mechanisms are based on the role-based access control (RBAC) model [3], where access rights are delegated in the form of roles. Few models rely on the attribute-based access control (ABAC) model [4] for delegation, where delegation is managed by using policies instead of roles.

© Springer International Publishing Switzerland 2015
S. Fischer-Hübner et al. (Eds.): TrustBus 2015, LNCS 9264, pp. 18–29, 2015.
DOI: 10.1007/978-3-319-22906-5_2

XACML delegation profile [5] is one of the delegation mechanisms that is based on the ABAC model. In this mechanism, access rights on the resources are delegated in the form of policies. In the XACML profile, reduction is a process that is performed to validate the authenticity of the issuer of the policy. In this process, a graph of policies is generated as a result of each access request for a resource, which contains the hierarchy of the delegated policies. To generate a policy graph, the attributes of the *access request* are searched (i.e. the delegatee and requested resource) within the policy delegated to the requester and, then, edges between that policy and its delegated policy nodes are created by matching the attributes of the entities within the hierarchy of the delegated policies (attributes are the delegatee and its delegator). Then, the path of the graph, which connects the owner of a resource and the requester with all the intermediate delegators, is checked in order to verify the authenticity of the delegated policy of the requester. As a result, decisions are made in the form of permit or deny access to the resource.

In this approach, the method to evaluate an access request, that is, generating a policy graph and finding attributes within all policies for each *access request,* is a costly solution in terms of performance. Figure 1 illustrates a graph generated as a result of access request. The connection between the delegated policies represents the flow of the delegation, whereas the edges determine the delegation decision, that is, the policy permits (PP) the delegation or denies (DP) it to the other policy.

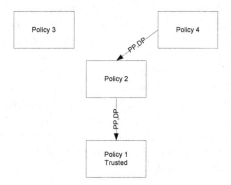

Fig. 1. XACML delegation graph [5]

In the XACML delegation profile, the delegated policies defined by the delegators on a common resource are maintained in a policy set. Thus, to process an access request for a resource, this policy set is searched to find the required policies in order to generate a flow of delegation in the graph of policies. This can result in a serious performance overhead in a large scale environment dealing with a large number of delegatees during the following actions: (i) searching within a large number of delegated policies on an access request, and (ii) generation of the graph on each access request. Moreover, the delegation graph is connected to the trusted policy, which differentiates with other policies with the omitted policy issuer element, and there is no mechanism to validate this trusted policy as the fields can easily be forged.

1.1   Contributions

To tackle these issues, in this paper we propose an ontology-based delegation frame-work that enhances the standard XACML delegation profile by modeling the delegation logics in an ontological way. In contrast to previous methods [6–8], the specification of constraints or authorization rules for each delegator and delegatee to enforce delegation is not required; instead the proposed system automatically manages delegation by using suitable algorithms (i.e. delegation and verification). This is attained by a formal representation of the delegation workflow, which is made by instantiating an ontology modeling the entities and their interrelations that are involved in the delegation process. Moreover, it does not require generating rules or policy graphs for each access request for a resource; instead the request is validated through the interrelations of the entities. Furthermore, in order to build trust, each workflow of the delegation is originated by the trusted policy that is digitally signed by the owner of the resource. We next summarize the main contributions of our work:

- We propose an ontology that models the entities involved in the delegation process, which includes subjects (i.e., delegators or delegatees), objects (resources or services), policies (document that translate delegated privileges) and their interrelations. This ontology facilitates to keep a track of who is delegating, what privileges on a resource are being delegated and also provides an intuitive solution to verify the attributes of the actors involved in the delegation.
- In contrast to the methods that verify the delegator's authority through roles [9], our system automatically verifies the authority through the attributes of the entities and the policy of the delegator by following the interrelations of the entities (represented as instances of the ontology) that lead to the trusted policy.
- Contrary to [8, 10], our system does not require the specification of rules, but it automatically enforces delegation and verifies the delegated authority by using a simple algorithm. In addition, our proposal does not require any additional rules to implement the delegated policies; instead, it automatically implements a delegated policy that combines the normal access policy and the delegated policy and also resolves possible policy conflicts.

The rest of the paper is organized as follows. Section 2 presents our ontology-based delegation framework. Section 3 provides a discussion on the scalability and performance of the proposed system. Section 4 includes related works. Finally, Sect. 5 provides the conclusions and presents some lines of future work.

2   Ontology-Based Delegation Framework

We have extended the XACML delegation profile by modeling and incorporating an ontology to model the access control and delegation workflow; this provides two main benefits: (i) it is easy and intuitive to implement, since it clearly defines the semantics (i.e. knowledge) of the delegation process, and (ii) the relations between the entities can be defined and interpreted in an automatic way [11]. This ontology models the knowledge related to the delegation process according to the entities involved in it (i.e. delegators, delegatees and resources) and their interrelations. According to this, the actual entities involved in a particular delegation process are instances of the generic classes modeled in the ontology and their interrelations represent the workflow of the delegation. Therefore, to evaluate an *access request* for a resource, the authority of the delegator, who has issued a policy to the requester, is verified by examining the instance interrelations (which include the delegators' hierarchy, the delegatee and the delegated resource) instead of finding entities within the policies. With this mechanism, the request attributes are only matched with the instances of the entities and their policy is checked just once to get their related rules. By doing so, it avoids the overhead of repeatedly examining each policy set (in order to find entities involved in the delegation) and then generating a policy graph for each access request (as done in the XACML profile). Moreover, it is also an intuitive way to validate the attributes of a policy with the attributes of the entity instances (attributes can be the identities of the delegator and the delegatee and their privileges).

In our model, a user can be assigned two types of policies (as shown in Fig. 2): (i) an *access policy* (a policy defined for a particular user in order to allow or deny the access to a given resource) and (ii) an *administrative policy* (a policy that enables a user to issue access policies or delegated policies to other users). For example, in the access policy defined in Fig. 2(a), the administrator allows user *Alice* to use the services of *printer-1*, whereas in the administrative policy in Fig. 2(b), the administrator also delegates the possibility to issue policies on the same resource (*access or administrative policies*) to the users of the *employee* category. In the *rule* attribute, the delegator can define limitations on the delegation in order to grant a limited access on a given resource. Moreover, the owner of the resource can limit the delegation (i.e. the number of times or levels a resource can be delegated) by setting a value of an attribute of the policy, which is reduced at each delegation level and added to the *policy set* of the delegatee. The access rights cannot be further delegated if the attribute value reaches zero.

a) Access Policy   b) Administrative Policy   c) Access Request

Fig. 2. Examples of policies and access request

The policies defined by the delegator for the different users on the same resource are managed in a document called a *policy set*. A *policy set* is a document written by an issuer, which contains several policies (*access or administrative policies*) and may have different rules for users on a common resource. In the XACML profile, a *policy set* is maintained with respect to the resource that contains the policies of all the delegators sharing privileges on a common resource. In contrast to XACML, in our model, each beneficiary of the delegation maintains a separate *policy set* for its resource in a distributed way. As a result of an *access request*, only those policies are checked according to the interrelations that are managed by the required delegators. For example, if a delegator *Alice* is managing two resources, then she maintains two *policy sets* of the delegated policies; as a result of an *access request* by the delegatee, only Alice's *policy set* (managed for intended resource) will be examined. The benefits of this approach are: (i) decentralizing the *policy sets*, (ii) incorporating delegation for distributed environment, and (iii) improving the process of verification of the delegation authority.

2.1 Modeling ABAC as an Ontology

In ABAC, there are three main entities that are involved in managing access control: *subjects, objects* and *policies*. Subjects are the owners of the resources and can control the access to their resource objects (e.g. data, services, applications or network resources) by writing *access policies* for other users. In these policies, the access rights on the resource objects are managed by defining policy rules for other subjects. The subjects and the objects are identified by their attributes, which are also used for taking authorization decisions in order to manage access rights. During the authorization, the policy rules are evaluated against the attributes of the subjects and the objects, and access decisions are taken based on this evaluation. In order to automatically manage the workflow of the delegation process, the attributes of the policies (shown in Fig. 2(a) and (b)) can be used to create interrelations within the entities by modeling them as ontology classes and their properties.   ·

In the same way, subjects can delegate their access rights to others by using attributes of the entities and by defining delegation policies. Therefore, we can define a delegation workflow between subjects, objects and policies by modeling them in the ontology and, based on the workflow, we can also make delegation and authorization decisions. Hence, in our ontology, the entity types are represented as classes. The relationships among the entities are represented by directed edges that show a dependency between classes that are either a subclass or a property of the classes. Figure 3 depicts the proposed ontology that models the knowledge of the delegation process (i.e., entities and interrelationships).

The *entity* abstract class is the root of the ontology, which has three subclasses: *subject, object* and *policy*. A subject is an entity that may require access to the resource in order to accomplish her task; in general, that entity can be an organization, an employee, a department, or it can be any software-computing service. Therefore, subjects can be generally classified into two subclasses i.e. *user* and *service*. The *user* class models all types of subjects (mentioned above) except services, which are modeled in the *service* class. The attributes of the *user* class may vary depending on the type of the subject. For example, if a subject is an organization, then attributes can be the identifier of the organization, the organization name etc.; for a department, the attributes can be the department identifier, the department name or the organization it belongs to. Similarly, the services provided are modeled in *service* class. A *service* is a subclass of the *subject* class because it may also require resources in order to deliver its services and these services are identified and managed by their attributes (e.g. the service identity, the name of service or the provider of the service).

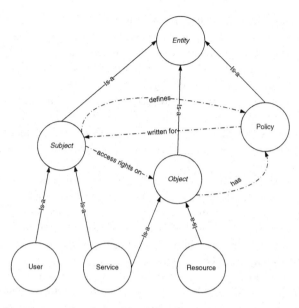

Fig. 3. Ontology representing the entities and interrelationships involved in delegation

Subjects (e.g. users or services) can have or can define *access rights on* resources, which are modeled as *objects*. The relationship between the *subject* and the *object* classes are defined as ontological properties. *Objects* can be hardware resources (e.g. storage space, servers, etc.) or software resources (e.g. a web application, web service, etc.). Hardware resources are modeled as *resources* and they are managed by *subjects*, who are the owners. On the other hand, software resources are modeled as *services* that are also a subclass of the *object* class. Thus, *service* is a class that is inherited by both of the *subject* and the *object* classes, because, a service is treated as *subject* when it requires an access to the resources in order to accomplish its task and it is treated as an *object* when a user requires it as a service. The system can easily manage *service* instances according to their classification (i.e. as *subject* or *object*) from their attributes and their related policies, because a policy contains information about who is delegating to whom and what resources.

The *subject* and the *object* classes are linked to the *policy* class through their respective properties. In order to control the access, the subject *defines* policies for others to manage access rights on their resources (i.e. *object*). In practice, the attributes of subjects and objects are used in the *policy* class, and the access rights are delegated by defining related rules. The attributes of the *policy* class are same as mentioned in Fig. 2. The policy of the owner is different from the policies of other delegators, that is, this policy contains an attribute that is digitally signed by the owner and considered a *trusted policy*, which can be verified during the access request.

Ontology-Based Representation of the Delegation Workflow. The ontology presented in Fig. 3 can be instantiated to represent the workflow of the delegated access rights. To do so, instances of the entity classes (i.e. delegators, delegatees and their policies) are created, and the delegation interrelations are managed based on their properties. In order to delegate access rights, each instance of the *subject* class, provided that it has delegation privileges, maintains a separate *policy set* that is stored in the local repository of the delegator and it is represented with the policy instance and linked to the instances of the delegatee *objects*.

An example of the delegation workflow generated through the proposed ontology is presented in Fig. 4. In this example, a *Dept1* (i.e. an instance of the *user* subclass) is the owner of two services (*Service-1* and *Service-2*) that are the instances of the *object* subclass *Service*. *Dept1* delegates its privileges on both services to the users *Alice, Bob* and *Alex* (who are also *subjects*) by defining policy sets *P1* and *P2* respectively. *Alice* and *Bob* share access rights on *Service-1* and have a common policy set *P1*, whereas *Dept1* maintains a separate policy *P2* for the user *Alex* with who shares access rights on *Service-2*. The policy set *P1* contains an *access policy* for *Alice* and an *administrative policy* for *Bob,* whereas, the policy set *P2* only contains an *access policy* for *Alex*. As a result of the *access policies, Alice* and *Alex* can only access *Service-1* and *Service-2* respectively (but cannot further delegate access rights); on the contrary, *Bob* is authorized to access and also to further delegate access rights to other users (due to *administrative policy*). In another level of delegation, *Bob* further delegates the access rights on *Service-1* to the users *Ted* and *Fred* by specifying a *policy set P4.*

For each delegation, the system creates instances of the entities involved in the delegation and links them automatically with each other as it is shown in Fig. 4. From this representation, the privileges of each accessing entity can be verified. In addition, the privileges of the delegation authority, who has issued her *access policy*, can also be validated from the delegation workflow.

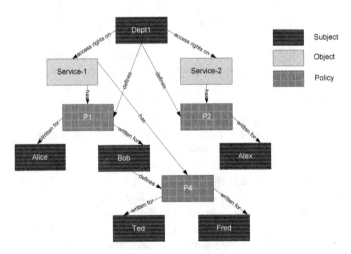

Fig. 4. Ontology-Based representation of the delegation workflow

2.2 Workflow of the System

As shown in the previous section, during each delegation, instances of the involved entities are created together with the interrelations between the delegator and the delegated resource according to the knowledge modeled in the ontology; this forms a graph like workflow among the instances (as shown in Fig. 4). Then, as a result of a user's *access request*, the user's privileges are assessed and the authenticity of the issuer of the policy (who has issued the user's *access policy*) is verified through the workflow generated from the ontology. To do so, the attributes of the *access request*, as shown in Fig. 2(c), are validated with the attributes of its immediate *access policies* through the policy instance linked with the requestor. If the attributes are matched, the system initiates an *administrative request* and the authenticity of the issuer of the policy is verified. To do so, the attributes of the issuer are verified from the delegator instances that are linked with the target *access policy*. Then, a chain of the *administrative policies* is generated at each level of the delegation to verify the authority at each level from the workflow graph (because each policy is issued by its predecessor delegator that also needs verification). As a result, a permit response is generated and access to the resource is granted in case the flow of the delegation is originated from the owner of the resource and a denial of access otherwise. Moreover, a policy is considered authentic if the hierarchy of policies leads to the trusted policy (a policy that is digitally signed and verified by the owner of the target resource or service) and there are no further policies connected to it in the workflow.

In the same way, a delegator, at any level of delegation, can revoke delegated privileges by generating a simple *revoke request*. Consequently, a chain of policies is verified (backward chaining beginning from the request initiator) and, if the request is genuine, all subsequent delegations are revoked by simply deleting instances from the workflow generated from the ontology.

```
Algorithm 1:    AccessRequest (subject requestor, object resource)
 1:    subject_instance ← subject_requestor
 2:    delegator_verified=false
 3:    while owner of object_resource is not found do
 4:            get policy instance written for subject_instance
 5:            read policy rule
 6:            if rule is 'permit' then
 7:                 subject_instance ← get delegator instance that de-
                    fined policy instance
 8:                 delegator_verified= true;
 9:            else
10:                  Deny Access
11:                  delegator_verified=false
12:                  if delegator_verified is 'false' then
13:                      end iteration in line 3
14:                  end if
15:            end if
16:    end while
17:    if owner found and delegator is verified then
18:        signature ← verify owner's signature using her public key
19:        if signature is valid then
20:            Grant Access
21:        else    Deny Access
22:        end if
23:    else    Deny Access
24:    end if
```

The above process is formalized in Algorithm-1, which is invoked to verify the access rights of the requestor and to validate the delegator's authority that has granted the access rights. Line 1 determines the instance of the requestor from the workflow. Then, the access privileges of this requestor are determined (in line 5) from the policy stored locally in the database through the policy instance determined in line 4. Once the requestor has privileges (line 6), represented in the form of policy rule on the requested resource, then the authority of the delegator is verified. To do so, line 7 determines the instance of the delegator from the workflow. The same process is repeated (lines 3-14) for the chain of delegators until the owner of the resource is found in the workflow. Then, the signature of the owner is verified in lines 18-22 and access is granted to the resource provided the owner has digitally signed the policy and the delegator is verified.

2.3 Policy Conflicts

In the studied scenario, there can be the following situations in which two policies contradict the rules of each other:

1. A user has *access policies* issued by two different subjects on a common resource, where one policy permits the access to the resource while the other one denies it.
2. A user has two policies issued by two different subjects on a common resource, where one policy contains an *access policy* that only allows her to access to the resource, whereas the other policy contains an *administrative policy* that delegates access rights to issue policies on the same resource.

The policy conflicts mentioned above are automatically handled by the system without requiring any additional constraints or rule specifications. Conflict resolution is achieved by comparing the precedence of the issuers of the policies, that is, the delegation precedence of the conflicting delegators is determined from the delegation workflow. The preceding delegator is given a higher priority for the implementation of her policy because the upper level entities delegate privileges and can revoke them for the subsequent delegators. In case the delegators have same precedence level, the strictest rule of the policies of the delegators is implemented (e.g., denial dominates over permit). Notice that the determination of the precedence of the policy issuers does not incur any extra cost, since it can be determined from the delegation level attribute (discussed in Sect. 2) of the policies of the delegators.

3 Performance Analysis

As mentioned in Sect. 2, the proposed model improves the XACML delegation profile in following three ways: (i) better management of the policies, (ii) intuitive ontology-based generation delegation workflows (iii) more efficient policy search while processing an access request. In order to quantify the efficiency improvement of the policy search, in this section we analyze and compare the computational complexity of the standard XACML profile with respect to our proposal.

In the XACML profile, on each *access request*, the system searches all the policies in a given policy set to get the policy of the requester and, in order to verify the authority, the credentials of the *access request* are matched with the elements of the policies. Therefore, in the worst case, the search requires to compare M policies (i.e. $O(M)$) and the verification of the authority requires matching M policies to generate the policy graph, which is also $O(M)$; thus, the overall cost of this process is $O(2M)$.

In contrast, our system can directly get the policy of the requester from the delegation workflow (which associates policies with the corresponding requester instance), which is a constant cost ($O(1)$). Then, the authority of the delegator can be verified by following the workflow that, in the worst case, would take $\log_n N$ matches, where n is the number of delegator nodes who have delegated policies to the instance being verified, and N is the number of delegators in the delegation chain of the resource. As a result, the cost of our proposal is $O(\log_n N)$. Thus, as the number of delegators increases, this N becomes smaller then M, which proves that the proposed system results in performance gain over the XACML profile.

4 Related Work

Several researchers have addressed the issues of access control management by proposing solutions that rely on delegation mechanisms. Most of these solutions [6–8, 12] have extended the role-based access control (RBAC) model [3] to incorporate delegation, wherein roles are delegated to other users in order to grant access privileges. In contrast, few models [13, 14] rely on attribute-based access control (ABAC) model [4] for delegation, where delegation is served by using policies instead of roles. ABAC is a better model than RBAC in terms of scalability (i.e. number of users), flexibility (i.e. easy to implement in a large scale environment) and better access control management (i.e. delegation by simply associating attributes to other users) [15, 16].

In the following, we discuss delegation frameworks that rely on the ABAC model, and specifically on the XACML profile, for delegation of access privileges. Xu et al. [13] proposed a delegation model based on the XACML standard and also extended this standard by introducing roles as the attributes of the users (by using roles as attributes of the policy extends ABAC with the capabilities of the RBAC model). In this method, roles are assigned to the delegators in order to enable them to delegate privileges that can further be delegated to other users. In this mechanism, the authority of delegators is verified from the role hierarchy that is generated as a result of each resource request, which can be an expensive solution in terms of performance (i.e. searching each role and plotting their graph on each request). In XACML based approach [14], a delegator can delegate limited privileges by defining a policy, and the system creates a new policy by updating an existing policy of a delegatee. In order to enforce delegation, a locally maintained system performs authorization of delegated policies. However, this system is customized for a specific application (i.e. account management) and cannot serve in large scale environment that has a large number of users.

Even though ontologies have been used to manage access control, ontology-based delegation of access rights have not been properly considered so far. For example, Choi et al. [17] proposed ontology-based context-aware access control model that manages context information of the users in an ontological way. The access decisions are made through the semantic analysis of the access rights of the service provider and the users. In this model, the access request of the user is analyzed and the access decision is made based on the context information of user's authentication and its access rights managed in form of security policy for a given resource. In this approach, separate policies are maintained for the administrator (i.e. service provider) and the user. However, this may not be feasible for the delegation of access rights as a delegatee will have to maintain two policies, which are administrative policy being delegator of inherited access rights and the delegated policy being delegated. This may result in policy conflict, which will require special handling.

5   Conclusions and Future Work

In this paper, we proposed an access control delegation framework that enhances the XACML delegation profile by intuitively modeling the delegation process as an ontology-based workflow. Contrary to the XACML profile, the policies of the delegators are self-managed. As a result, only those policies that are related to the intended delegators and delegatees are analyzed, thus reducing the cost of searching entities within the policies. Moreover, it does not require generating a graph on each *access request* because the delegation workflow is automatically generated (by instantiating the ontology classes for the subject, object and policy) on each transfer of privileges by the delegator.

As future work, we plan to implement this framework in real and complex systems in which the delegation of access control has a prominent importance. For example, Cloud computing, in which the access to the outsourced resources should be managed for heterogeneous entities located at different places, and Social Networks, where users can delegate the access to their resources (e.g. messages, images, etc.) according to the attributes of their contacts and to revoke them accordingly. For this purpose, our general ontology can be extended to incorporate the entities and attributes involved in those platforms and delegation management algorithms can be tailored to implement their casuistry.

Acknowledgements and Disclaimer. This work was partly supported by the European Commission under FP7 project Inter-Trust and H2020 project CLARUS, by the Spanish Ministry of Science and Innovation (through projects CO-PRIVACY TIN2011-27076-C03-01 and ICWT TIN2012-32757) and by the Government of Catalonia (under grant 2014 SGR 537). This work was also made possible through the support of a grant from Templeton World Charity Foundation. The opinions expressed in this paper are those of the authors and do not necessarily reflect the views of UNESCO of the Templeton World Charity Foundation.

References

1. Ferraiolo, D.F., Kuhn, R.D., Chandramouli, R.: Role-Based Access Control, 2nd edn. Artech House Inc, Norwood (2007)
2. Wang, Q., Li, N., Chen, H.: On the security of delegation in access control systems. In: Jajodia, S., Lopez, J. (eds.) ESORICS 2008. LNCS, vol. 5283, pp. 317–332. Springer, Heidelberg (2008)

3. Sandhu, R.S., Coyne, E.J., Feinstein, H.L., Youman, C.E.: Role-based access control models. Computer **29**, 38–47 (1996)
4. Hu, V.C., Ferraiolo, D., Kuhn, R., Schnitzer, A., Sandlin, K., Miller, R., Scarfone, K.: Guide to Attribute Based Access Control (ABAC) Definition and Considerations. NIST Special Publication (2014)
5. XACML v3.0 Administration and Delegation Profile Version 1.0, vol. 3.0. OASIS (2009)
6. Ruan, C., Varadharajan, V.: Dynamic delegation framework for role based access control in distributed data management systems. Distrib. Parallel Databases **32**, 245–269 (2014)
7. Sohr, K., Kuhlmann, M., Gogolla, M., Hu, H., Ahn, G.-J.: Comprehensive two-level analysis of role-based delegation and revocation policies with UML and OCL. Inf. Softw. Technol. **54**, 1396–1417 (2012)
8. Wainer, J., Kumar, A., Barthelmess, P.: DW-RBAC: a formal security model of delegation and revocation in workflow systems. Inf. Syst. **32**, 365–384 (2007)
9. Ahn, G.-J., Mohan, B., Hong, S.-P.: Towards secure information sharing using role-based delegation. J. Netw. Comput. Appl. **30**, 42–59 (2007)
10. Wainer, J., Kumar, A.: A fine-grained, controllable, user-to-user delegation method in RBAC. In: Proceedings of the Tenth ACM Symposium on Access Control Models and Technologies, pp. 59–66. ACM, Stockholm (2005)
11. Carminati, B., Ferrari, E., Heatherly, R., Kantarcioglu, M., Thuraisingham, B.: A semantic web based framework for social network access control. In: Proceedings of the 14th ACM Symposium on Access Control Models and Technologies, pp. 177–186. ACM, Stresa (2009)
12. Gusmeroli, S., Piccione, S., Rotondi, D.: A capability-based security approach to manage access control in the internet of things. Math. Comput. Model. **58**, 1189–1205 (2013)
13. Xu, M., Wijesekera, D.: A role-based XACML administration and delegation profile and its enforcement architecture. In: Proceedings of the 2009 ACM Workshop on Secure Web Services, pp. 53–60. ACM, Chicago (2009)
14. Seitz, L., Rissanen, E., Sandholm, T., Firozabadi, B.S., Mulmo, O.: Policy administration control and delegation using XACML and Delegent. In: 2005 The 6th IEEE/ACM International Workshop on Grid Computing, p. 6 (2005)
15. Coyne, E., Weil, T.R.: ABAC and RBAC: scalable, flexible, and auditable access management. IT Prof. **15**(3), 14–16 (2013)
16. Priebe, T., Dobmeier, W., Kamprath, N.: Supporting attribute-based access control with ontologies. In: 2006 The First International Conference on Availability, Reliability and Security ARES 2006, p. 8 (2006)
17. Choi, C., Choi, J., Kim, P.: Ontology-based access control model for security policy reasoning in cloud computing. J. Supercomput. **67**, 711–722 (2014)

Trust and Reputation in Pervasive Environments

VISIO: A Visual Approach for Singularity Detection in Recommendation Systems

Alessandro Colantonio[1], Roberto Di Pietro[2,3], Marinella Petrocchi[3], and Angelo Spognardi[3(✉)]

[1] Bay 31, Zug, Switzerland
alessandro@bay31.com
[2] Bell Laboratories, Alcatel-Lucent, Paris, France
roberto.di_pietro@alcatel-lucent.com
[3] IIT-CNR, Pisa, Italy
{marinella.petrocchi,angelo.spognardi}@iit.cnr.it

Abstract. Reviews are a powerful decision-making tool for potential new customers, since they can significantly influence consumer purchase decisions, hence resulting in financial gains or losses for businesses. In striving for trustworthy review systems, validating reviews that could negatively or positively bias new customers is of utmost importance. To this goal, we propose VISIO: a visualization based representation of reviews that enables quick analysis and elicitation of interesting patterns and singularities. In fact, VISIO is meant to amplify cognition, supporting the process of singling out those reviews that require further analysis. VISIO is based on a theoretically sound approach, while its effectiveness and viability is demonstrated applying it to real data extracted from Tripadvisor and Booking.com.

1 Introduction

Consulting online reviews before the purchase of services and products has become a common practice in the last years. When people want to buy a product, they often surf the WEB to find opinions of other customers about that product. Reviews can remarkably influence users' purchase decisions: if most reviews are positive, people are inclined to buy the product; on the contrary, negative reviews will almost certainly bias the user to look for alternatives. The financial consequences are easy to figure out. Unfortunately, this fact strongly induces the submission of fake opinions to review systems, with the main intent of twisting product perception [9].

To tackle this issue, assessment processes have been developed, mostly implemented by review system owners, to actively monitor and verify the appropriateness of users' reviews, based on identification and subsequent analysis of suspicious posts. The responsibility for periodically removing "biased" reviews based

---

This research has been partially supported by the MIB (My Information Bubble) project of *Registro.it*.

S. Fischer-Hübner et al. (Eds.): TrustBus 2015, LNCS 9264, pp. 33–47, 2015.
DOI: 10.1007/978-3-319-22906-5_3

on their appropriateness, rests with the system owner. This fostered a rich literature about deceptive opinions and reviews [1,12,20,22]. However, proposed solutions to this problem can be still considered in their infancy. For instance, one aspect that hinders reviews analysis is the large number of reviews available. We observed that the hotel-reviewing website Booking.com have more than one million reviews submitted during the last year just for hotels in New York.

The richness of data and the intrinsic complexity of review analysis naturally calls for closely coupled human-machine interaction. A way to bridge this gap is to resort to *visual analytics* — the science of analytic reasoning facilitated by interactive visual interfaces [18]. This paper proposes a visual approach for singularity detection in recommendation systems. To the best of our knowledge, none of the existing approaches to spot anomalous reviews leverages a visual representation of the reviews themselves. It is worth noting that we do not aim at replacing existing techniques; rather, our idea is to complement them, by providing VISIO (VIsual Singularity IdentificatiOn), a "visual workbench" for review analysts. Our proposal is mainly inspired by the visual approach developed in the context of role mining for access control [3]. We adapted those results to implement a novel methodology for review analysis. Other than being rooted on sound theory, VISIO is also accompanied by an extensive experimental campaign that confirm the quality and viability of our solution.

The remainder of this paper is as follows: Sect. 2 describes the general problem of graphically representing data in a matricial form. The viability of adopting matrices to display reviews is then demonstrated with an application to real cases in Sect. 3, by analyzing reviews extracted from Tripadvisor and Booking.com. Section 4 reports on work related to detecting anomalous reviews. Finally, Sect. 5 provides concluding remarks.

2   Matrix-Based Representation

This paper is based on the general assumption that visual representations of data can actually amplify cognition, leading to optimal analysis results. Various data mining and machine learning methods have been used to automatically analyze the data in several fields. Although these approaches have proven their usefulness in many practical applications, they may not be perfect under all analysis scenarios. Analysts often have to provide their knowledge to iteratively refine the methods. It is usually difficult to understand and interpret the findings in an intuitive and meaningful manner. To address these challenges, *visual analytics* has been developed in recent years through a proper combination of automated analysis with interactive visualizations [17].

To our knowledge, there is a lack of visual approaches that can help owners (and consumers) of review systems to actively monitor and verify the appropriateness of users' reviews. The problem that we are willing to address is thus offering a graphical way to effectively *navigate* existing reviews in a system, showing at glance what it would take a lot of data, processing and time to expound.

Among all possible graphical representations, we focus on *binary matrices*. Such matrices occur in several fields, such as bioinformatics and computational biology, access control, ecology, paleontology, and information retrieval, to cite a few [3, 14, 16]. A *(binary) matrix-based visualization* consists of a two-dimensional graphical representation of a (binary) matrix, where rows, columns, and cells have assigned a meaning depending on the particular field of application. The main problem to address when depicting a matrix is identifying a *proper sorting of rows and columns*. In fact, it can be proven that rearranging rows and columns properly allows to highlight the main patterns embedded in the represented data [3]. More generally, the matrix visualization problem can be reduced to the identification of the row/column sorting that best visualizes a given collection of discovered patterns.

In this scenario, the most recent contribution about binary matrix representation is represented by [3]. The authors adopted such a graphical representation for access control systems, where rows and columns correspond to users and permissions, and each cell is "on" when a certain user has a certain permission granted. One of the objectives in access control is finding *roles*, that is groups of users that have the same set of permissions granted. In other data mining contexts, these patterns are also referred to as *tiles* [5], *biclusters* [15], or *(closed) itemsets* [23]. By changing the sorting of users and permissions, the authors of [3] demonstrated that it is possible to visually highlight patterns as sets of consecutive cells that are "on". Moreover, a proper matrix sorting allows to naturally deduce patterns from the matrix by only visually inspecting it. Finally, a visual representation can highlight potential exceptions within data in an effective manner.

To identify the best row/column sorting for binary matrices, [3] propose a fast algorithm referred to as ADVISER (*Access Data VISualizER*), which is able to provide a compact representation of patterns embedded in binary data. In particular, the algorithm reorders rows and columns of the binary matrix independently, minimizing the "visual fragmentation" of main patterns in the resulting representation.

The remainder of this paper focuses on applying the same techniques, and in particular the use of the algorithm ADVISER, to provide a matrix representation for reviews. As we will see, this enables quick analysis and elicitation of interesting patterns and singularities.

3   Visual Analysis of Reviews

In this section, we describe how a matrix-based representation of reviews can be leveraged to identify interesting patterns and singularities. We first discuss how to translate a list of reviews into a matrix, and later we propose some types of analysis that can be performed by using the resulting matrix. In particular, we will present:

- The meaning of rows, columns, and cells in the case of data extracted from a review system, pointing out a few basic observations that can be made through a simple visual inspection of the matrix. (Sect. 3.1)

- How the matrix can be used to compare reviews from two different platforms—in our case, Tripadvisor and Booking.com. (Sect. 3.2)
- How the matrix can help to analyze reviews that have been manually removed (either by system owners or by reviewers themselves). Indeed, we suppose that reviews could be withdrawn by reviewers that have posted them, or evicted (after some time that they have been published) by the owner of the recommended service/product, e.g., when inappropriate. (Sect. 3.3)
- How to further analyze the outcome of a data mining algorithm by providing a matrix representation of it. We will first data-mine groups of reviewers that recommended the same set of hotels in Tripadvisor. Then, we will pick up the "clusters" with high rating variance and similar review dates and represent them in the matrix. (Sect. 3.4)

It is worth noting that, despite the concrete application of the proposed techniques and methodology, they are general enough to enjoy an high degree of adaptability to other (different) contexts, where quality of reviews are at stake.

3.1   Matrix Representation of Reviews

The basic step of our approach is specifying how to construct a matrix-based visualization out of review data. To this aim, we extracted real data from Tripadvisor[1] and Booking.com[2] websites. To keep the size of dataset reasonably small, we decided to focus on one city at a time. We downloaded data for hotels in New York, Rome, Paris, Rio de Janeiro, and Tokyo. Due to space limitation, however, in the following we will only report on reviews about hotels in New York. Indeed, the type of patterns and singularities that we identified for the city of New York can also be observed in other cities.

Figure 1(a) shows a matrix representation of Tripadvisor's data. It represents all the reviews that can be accessed on the website at the date of the 26th of June 2014 for hotels in New York. The extracted dataset consists of a list of reviews, where for each review we have: user ID, hotel name, review date, review text, rating value (from 1 to 5). The oldest review dates back to August 27, 2001, whereas the newest that we extracted comes from June 25, 2014. We discarded reviews from user ID "Anonymous" since it represents users of the platform http://www.daodao.com—the Chinese version of Tripadvisor—where all reviewers are indifferently gathered in this single virtual user. The resulting dataset is made up of 365,196 reviews provided by 320,374 Tripadvisor's registered users that reviewed 389 hotels.

After downloading such a dataset, we proceeded to generate several matrix representation of it, striving to find out the most meaningful and manageable one. The first representation that we tested was a matrix where rows represent reviewers, columns represent hotels, and cell colors represent the rating provided by the given user for the given hotel. However, the resulting matrix was quite

---

[1] http://www.tripadvisor.com.

[2] http://www.booking.com.

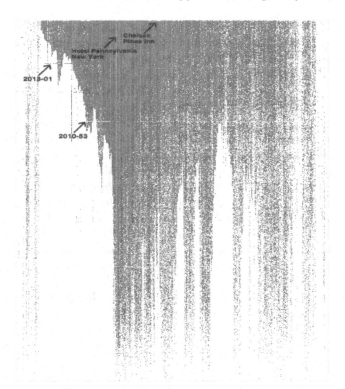

(a) **Tripadvisor** reviews from August 27, 2001 to June 25, 2014 for hotels in New York. Each row of the matrix represents a week, sorted from top to bottom in reverse chronological order. Columns represent hotels, sorted according to the algorithm ADVISER. A cell is "filled" when there is at least one review for the given hotel in the given week; cells are yellow when the average rating for the corresponding in the given week is 1 star (the lowest), whereas red cells means an average rating of 5 stars (the highest). The white space indicates no reviews at all. A few annotations in the picture highlight a few singularities further discussed in Section 3.1.

(b) **Booking.com** reviews from May 10, 2012 to July 11, 2013, hotels in New York. Similar to Figure (a), rows are weeks, columns hotels, and cells indicate the rating value.

Fig. 1. Matrix representation of **Tripadvisor** and **Booking.com** reviews

large and, most importantly, very sparse (i.e., no clear evidence of "clusters", that is groups of users reviewing the same set of hotels). Indeed, the fact that 320,374 users provided 365,196 reviews means *per se* that most of them are single-review users.

After a few attempts, we resorted to the initial representation above described where, instead of mapping reviewers to rows, we adopted weeks. The result is what can be seen in Fig. 1(a). Each row of the matrix represents a week, sorted from top to bottom in reverse chronological order. Columns represent hotels, sorted according to the algorithm ADVISER described in Sect. 2. A cell is "filled" when there is at least one review for the given hotel in the given week; cells are yellow when the average of all ratings for the hotel (column) in the given week (row) is 1 star (the lowest), whereas red cells means an average rating of 5 stars (the highest). The white space indicates no reviews at all. We used chronological order for rows instead of the one provided by ADVISER because in this way we can easily come up with considerations about review trends during the time. The default sorting provided for rows by ADVISER attempts to put together weeks that have similar reviews. However, as it can be seen in Fig. 1(a), reviews progressively increased over the time. Therefore, ADVISER is not able to identify weeks with similar reviews. As for columns, ADVISER automatically sorts hotels according to number, starting period, and frequency of reviews, putting the most reviewed hotels in the middle.

The matrix-based representation shows at glance what it would take a lot of data, processing and time to expound. The very first fact to observe is about trends. One can clearly see that from 2001 (bottom) to 2014 (top) several hotels progressively joined Tripadvisor, some of them being reviewed constantly (i.e., "filled" columns), others sporadically (i.e., columns with several "holes").

Cell col-ours enable another dimension of analysis. Vertical "lines" with the same color display hotels with the worst and best reviews in the city. For instance, in Fig. 1(a) we highlighted "Hotel Pennsylvania New York", which is at the bottom of Tripadvisor's hotel ranking (position N° 380 out of 454 hotels in New York in October 2014). In fact, that hotel has got many negative (yellow) reviews since the starting of Tripadvisor's service. On the other hand, "Chelsea Pines Inn" is a top-of-the-ranking hotel (position N° 1), resulting in a vertical red line in the matrix. Notice also that most hotels have an homogeneous rating during time (always high, always low, or always fluctuating). In no case there is a clear improvement trend (i.e., a vertical line that progressively goes from yellow to red during the time).

A big power of matrix-based representation is the inherent ability to reveal patterns. For instance, Fig. 1(a) highlights two "anomalous" weeks. The first week of 2013 (annotated with "2013-01" in the picture) shows some reviews for a group of hotels that have most of their reviews concentrated much later in the year. Another case is the last week of 2010 (annotated with "2010-53" in the picture) where a large set of hotels have no reviews at all. Finally, other hotels have very sparse reviews during a certain period of time (identifiable with sporadic "dots" in Fig. 1(a)), but starting from a certain date on, they get constant and continuous reviews from people.

Identifying the exact meaning of the above occurrences in the data is out of the scope of this paper. What we would like to stress is how a matrix representation can easily point out those cases by just resorting to visual inspection.

The subsequent analyst's task is to push further the analysis by leveraging her domain expertise as well as matching patterns with additional meta-data that could be at the disposal of the review system owner. It is worth mentioning that all the results discussed before can certainly be obtained with a combination of data mining and statistical analysis techniques. However, queries should be known in advance, and multiple techniques should be applied. The real advantage of this graphical representation is thus having a single "tool" that allow for multiple considerations of different nature.

Figure 1(b) shows the matrix representation of data from Booking.com. Unfortunately, the dataset is not as rich as the one from Tripadvisor since reviews older than one year are not provided by the system. In this case, we have reviews from October 10, 2012 to July 11, 2013, a set of 489 reviewed hotels, resulting to a total of 1,023,806 reviews—by also considering the shorter time frame, Booking.com has a far much higher number of reviews than Tripadvisor. We could apply the same type of considerations made for Fig. 1(a) also in this case, but we omit the detailed analysis due to space limitation.

3.2   Comparison of the Two Review Platforms

In this section, we leverage matrix representation to highlight differences in the two platforms Tripadvisor and Booking.com. Figure 2 summarizes the result. First of all, we identified the subset of hotels that have reviews in both systems. We used a naïve string matching to identify hotels existing in both datasets, resulting to 171 hotels in common (that is, 44 % of Tripadvisor's hotels, and 35 % of Booking.com's) for the period October 10, 2012-July 11, 2013—the time frame in which the two datasets overlap. Figure 2(a) represents reviews for such a set of hotels in Tripadvisor in the given time frame, while Fig. 2(b) is the subset of Booking.com.

As pointed out in Sect. 4, there are several ways to compare reviews. One example is [11], where the authors compared Expedia.com with Tripadvisor by examining differences in the distribution of reviews for a given hotel between the two platforms. They exploited the characteristics of a hotel's neighbors; unfortunately, we were not able to use the same data since they are not publicly available.[3] Therefore, instead of adopting existing comparison approaches from the literature and replicating them visually, we propose something novel. Again, we compared weeks of reviews by computing the differences between the two matrices. In other words, we analyzed weeks where certain hotels had reviews in one platform but not in the other one. Figure 2(c) shows reviews provided only in Tripadvisor. It can be seen as the matrix of Fig. 2(a) "minus" the matrix of Fig. 2(b)—obtained by removing a cell when it is present in both matrices. Figure 2(d) depicts hotels reviewed only in Booking.com for the given weeks. Figure 2(e) shows weeks where both platforms contain reviews for the same hotels; in this case the meaning of colors slightly changes: a yellow cell means that there is no difference between the rating provided in the two platforms, whereas red means conflicting reviews.

---

[3] The authors of [11] used data from STR: www.str.com.

(a) Reviews in Tripadvisor for hotels in common between the two platforms

(b) Reviews in Booking.com for hotels in common between the two platforms

(c) Reviews in Tripadvisor and *not* in Booking.com

(d) Reviews in Booking.com and *not* in Tripadvisor

(e) Shared reviews in Booking.com and Tripadvisor

Fig. 2. Differences between reviews in Tripadvisor and Booking.com. Figures (d) and (c) show hotels that received reviews only in one of the two platforms for the given weeks. Figure (e) displays differences between the two platforms—yellow means no difference, red means opposite reviews (Color figure online).

The main observation is that there are hotels mostly reviewed in one system and not in the other one. Those are represented by vertical lines in Fig. 2(c) and (d). Interestingly, such a set of hotels is more distinct in Fig. 2(d) than in Fig. 2(c)—Fig. (d) shows hotels that are almost exclusively reviewed in Booking.com. In Tripadvisor there is no hotel that is exclusive for this platform—no contiguous vertical lines in Fig. 2(c). Note also that in both Fig. 2(c) and (d) cells are mainly red, which means that the differences between the two platforms is mainly made up of positive ratings.

Finally, Fig. 2(e) highlights the difference in terms of rating. A cell is red or yellow when the corresponding hotel has a review in both Tripadvisor and Booking.com for the given week. Yellow means a matching (i.e., low or high rating in both platforms), while red means a conflict (i.e., low rating in one platform and high in the other). Overall, we can observe a matching between the two platforms, with however some conflicts that could be further investigated by an analyst.

3.3   Analysis of Removed Reviews

Some recommendation systems allow for review removal. Reviews could be manually removed by system owners when they consider them inappropriate. In other cases, reviews could be directly declined by reviewers, or rejected by the owner of the recommended service/product since inappropriate.

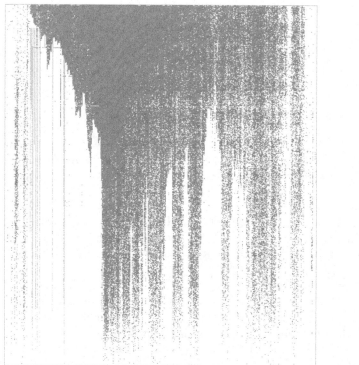

(a) Dark blue cells display reviews existing on Tripadvisor at the date of June 20, 2014. Light blue cells are reviews that disappeared from the website after September 10, 2013.

(b) Only reviews disappeared after September 10, 2013

Fig. 3. Differences between two "snapshots" of Tripadvisor taken on September 10, 2013 and June 20, 2014

In the following, we analyze removed reviews in Tripadvisor by leveraging our matrix-based approach. We performed a full extraction of data from Tripadvisor in two different dates: the first one on September 10, 2013, the second one on June 20, 2014. Figure 3 graphically summarizes the differences. Figure 3(a) displays removed reviews in light-blue. Compared to Fig. 1(a), we can neatly see two different cases: (1) there are certain hotels that no longer have reviews prior

Fig. 4. An example of removed reviews. No hotels with more than 10 removed reviews. No hotels with single-removed-review users.

to a certain date (represented by long, vertical light-blue lines in the picture); (2) there are very sparse removed reviews (represented by small light-blue dots in the matrix). Figure 3(b) depicts only removed reviews so that we can visualize sparse reviews more clearly.

Several questions arise from the visual inspection of Fig. 3. The first one is why those hotels have all the reviews before a certain date removed. The second question is what is the rationale behind the "sparsely removed" reviews. Again, only an analyst can provide further insights by leveraging her domain expertise arguments. As for the second point, though, we can offer more insight by providing an additional matrix that can highlight specific cases in a better way. For example, we could look for single users that provided biased reviews or groups of users that potentially colluded (see Sect. 4), hence justifying a removal by Tripadvisor. Such cases can be easily identified in Fig. 4. It represents a subset of removed reviews, where we further removed hotels with more than 10 reviews removed—namely, the long vertical lines. This time, each row represents a single reviewer, columns are still hotels, and cells indicate a review. Both rows and columns are sorted with the algorithm ADVISER. Horizontal lines represent users that have multiple reviews removed.

Figure 4 does not show any group of colluding users that reviewed the same hotels as they would be represented with an horizontal "strip" of cells. The figure highlights with a red circle one user who had 3 reviews removed. Table 1 is a "zoom" on what this user actually reviewed. Interestingly, the user submitted 6 reviews overall: 3 for the "Casablanca Hotel Times Square", all extremely positive (not reported in this paper, but still online); and, *at the same 3 dates* (namely, 2011-01-15, 2012-04-13, 2013-01-04), 3 reviews for the hotels listed in

Table 1. One example of user with multiple reviews removed. At the same three dates reported in this table, the user also provided a highly positive review for "Casablanca Hotel Times Square". Interestingly, the three hotels are relatively close to Casablanca H.T.S.. The third hotel is very close to a subway station, so there certainly are some lies in the review.

Hotel	Review	Date	Rating	Distance from Casablanca HTS
Library Hotel	I stayed at this hotel after staying at *its sister hotel The Casablanca*. The staff were courteous, but the hotel was noisy [. . .] *I would recommend The Casablanca over the Library Hotel.*	2011-01-15	★ ★ ★	0.7 mi
Hotel Giraffe	Stayed for 5 nights. Location is good, but hotel in general is plain sloppy. Guest computer is riddled with malware and bugs. [. . .] My stay was just not as I thought it would be.	2013-01-04	★ ★ ★	0.7 mi
Hotel Elysee	I was so disappointed in this hotel. It is very tired and in desperate need of sound proofing. [. . .] I moved to *their sister hotel, the Casablanca* – I had stayed there before and wish I had booked the Casablanca for all 9 nights of my trip to New York. I also found the location quite a way out – *a fair walk from the subway* etc.	2012-04-13	★★	1.4 mi

Table 1. The user clearly provided a negative review to hotels in the table in favor of "Casablanca Hotel Times Square". We do not know the reason why Tripadvisor decided to remove those reviews, but this behavior sounds odd indeed—raising un-answered questions.

3.4 Analysis of Rating and Date Variance

This section discusses how to adopt the matrix representation to visualize patterns resulting from data mining algorithms. In particular, similar to the previous section where we identified "biased" reviews being removed, now we still want to point out biased reviews, but among non-removed reviews. The steps are the following:

1. We run a closed itemset mining algorithm (e.g., [23]) to identify all groupings of at least 2 users that reviewed the same 2 or more hotels. There are 15,934 closed itemsets with a minimum of 2 users × 2 hotels in the data we extracted from Tripadvisor.
2. Among the previous patterns, we identified those that have low variance of dates and high variance of rating. The rationale is that groups of users that collude probably submit their reviews in the same, short time frame and provide opposite rating for different hotels.

We identified a very limited number of patterns that matched the second constraint. Table 2 reports one of them, where two users rated the same two hotels the same day. Figure 5 depicts all the users that reviews those two

Table 2. A couple of users that moved from one hotel to another. All the 4 reviews have been submitted exactly the same day, namely June 27, 2010.

	New York Inn (rated 1 star by both users)	*The GEM Hotel SoHo* (rated 5 stars by both users)
SolVoyce	"When me and my boyfriend booked the place, we read the reviews but thought that it really can't be that bad. Oh lord, were we wrong. If you read this and are thinking about making a reservation for the New York Inn – don't!"	"Me and my boyfriend were in New York for five nights and had made reservations for a room in Midtown. The hotel was the worst you could ever imagine with bedbugs, mice etc. . . "
MagneSweden	"I have traveled all over the world. I've been staying at hotels in Europe, China, Africa and USA, both big and small, and New York Inn is by far the worst hotel I've ever stayed at. Even small hostels on the chinese countryside were better."	"The Gem is truly a gem. It is located in Soho, close to two subway stations and many restaurants."

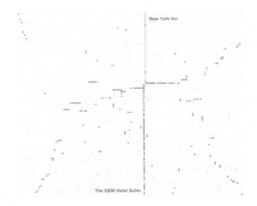

Fig. 5. Two hotels, one with high rating values, the other one poor rating values. In the middle of the picture a review overlap can be seen. It represents a special case of a couple moving from one hotel to the other since they were unhappy of the first hotel, as described in Sect. 3.4

hotels—rows are users, columns hotels, light blue indicates rating 1–3, dark blue rating 4–5. By reading the comments of Table 2 it can be easily deduced that the two users are likely engaged, and they moved from "New York Inn" to "The GEM Hotel SoHo" since they were unhappy with the first hotel. Notice in Fig. 5 that "New York Inn" has a low average rating, whereas "The GEM Hotel SoHo" is highly rated. Therefore, this pattern of reviews is unlikely to be illicit, and thus it should not be removed.

4   Related Work

In the last years, following the spreading of online social platforms, Academia has shown a growing interest towards recommendation systems and a flourishing literature exists on deceptive reviews. David and Pinch [4] started describing the most common practice of abuse of online review and recommendation systems.

A large part of the literature focuses on the detection of opinion spam by means of text analysis and machine learning. Jindal and Liu [6] were among the first authors that propose to study the differences between email spam and opinion spam, analyzing some manually-labeled comments on the popular online store Amazon.com. Li et al. [8] adopted machine learning algorithms to evaluate opinion spam from Epinion website. Starting from a labeled corpus of reviews, the authors train a fake-review detector and use such tool to evaluate all the reviews of a same reviewer and eventually prove an indication on whether the reviewer is a spammer. Ott et al. [13] followed another approach, deliberately building a gold standard of fake and genuine opinions, thus evaluating their linguistic characteristics for detection purposes.

Another approach for discovering fake reviews consists on searching groups of colluding users. GroupTie [22], for example, examines the similarity of user groups that rate the same apps in the Chinese Apple's Store. The authors consider several elements to evaluate the similarity of users, like the set and the ratings of the evaluated apps, the time of their rating and the impact of their ratings on the app final rating. How the opinions deviate the rating of Irish restaurants in Tripadvisor is also considered in [21]. Similarly, in [12], the authors use a frequent itemset mining approach joined to several behavioral models to detect reviewer groups on the reviews of Amazon. The Copycatch [1] algorithm is used to find suspicious Page Likes on Facebook, observing the graph structure of the social network, to detect "lockstep" behavior of user groups, considering the time at which groups of users can perform actions together. Another mechanism that uses graph properties for spam detection is proposed in [20], where the authors analyze the www.resellerratings.com website using a particular kind of graph made of reviewers, review and stores. The properties of such graph make the authors able to evaluate the reliability of the stores, the trustworthiness of the reviews and the honesty of the users.

Another discussed phenomenon that was identified is the so called "astroturfing" [10], in which an interested entity (like a firm or a political party) pushes for online contents, making them to resemble as originated from grassroots: this practice allows to influence the public opinion using fake (i.e. sponsored) contents, like forum or blog posts, reviews or articles, that mimic genuine and spontaneous ones, in order to support (or smear) a company or a political decision. One of the methods proposed to detect astroturfing considers that often the campaigns are originated leveraging crowdsourcing services like Amazon Mechanical Turk, Rapidworkers.com or Microworkers.com. The authors of [19] studied the Zhubajie and Sandaha Chinese crowdturfing sites, in order to analyze their campaigns, also evaluating the effectiveness, by running their own campaigns. The authors of [7] try to link the users that take part to astroturfing campaigns to their profiles on Twitter. With this solution, the authors recognize three types of "crowdturfers" (professional, casual and middle) and exploit the obtained model to differentiate them with regular users. In [2], instead, this differentiation is conducted using behavioral patterns and semantic analysis. The authors start from a dataset of manually labeled comments to news articles, containing fake comments posted by paid posters.

We highlight that the main advantage of adopting a visual approach lies in strengthening the "human" side of a human-machine interaction. Putting humans in the loop allows for a better correlation of human knowledge with low-level data. In fact, it is not always possible to translate additional knowledge into structured data. Moreover, visualization enables the analyst to visually mine data, without recurring to any data mining or machine learning algorithms, but just by means of human reasoning. It is also worth noting that data mining results (obtained with any of the methods cited in this section) may also be represented by means of binary matrices, as illustrated in Sect. 3.4.

5   Conclusions

This paper introduced VISIO, a VIsual Singularity IdentificatiOn approach to the problem of singularity detection in recommendation systems. The paper provided several contributions: we have highlighted how to interpret raw review data as input to binary matrices that are the basis for the visualization and we have showed the effectiveness and quality of the proposed solution over an extensive experimental campaign over real data extracted from Tripadvisor and Booking.com. Further, the exposed techniques and methodologies, other than being rooted on sound theory, are general enough to be adopted and adapted to other fields as well. While the proposed approach is not a definitive answer to the vexed issue of detecting misleading reviews, we believe that the novel approach introduced by VISIO paves the way for further contributions in the area of visual analytics applied to recommendation systems.

Acknowledgements. The authors warmly thank Vittoria Cozza for her support to the realization of this work.

References

1. Beutel, A., Xu, W., Guruswami, V., Palow, C., Faloutsos, C.: Copycatch: stopping group attacks by spotting lockstep behavior in social networks. In: WWW 2013, Rio de Janeiro, Brazil, pp. 119–130 (2013)
2. Chen, C., Wu, K., Srinivasan, V., Zhang, X.: Battling the Internet water army: detection of hidden paid posters. In: ASONAM 2013, Niagara, ON, Canada, pp. 116–120 (2013)
3. Colantonio, A., Di Pietro, R., Ocello, A., Verde, N.V.: Visual role mining: a picture is worth a thousand roles. IEEE Trans on Knowl. Data Eng. **24**(6), 1120–1133 (2012)
4. David, S., Pinch, T.: Six degrees of reputation: the use and abuse of online review and recommendation systems (originally published in March 2006). First Monday (2006). http://firstmonday.org/ojs/index.php/fm/article/view/1590
5. Geerts, F., Goethals, B., Mielikäinen, T.: Tiling databases. In: Suzuki, E., Arikawa, S. (eds.) DS 2004. LNCS (LNAI), vol. 3245, pp. 278–289. Springer, Heidelberg (2004)

6. Jindal, N., Liu, B.: Opinion spam and analysis. In: WSDM 2008, pp. 219–230. ACM (2008)
7. Lee, K., Tamilarasan, P., Caverlee, J.: Crowdturfers, campaigns, and social media: tracking and revealing crowdsourced manipulation of social media. In: ICWSM 2013, Cambridge, Massachusetts, USA (2013)
8. Li, F., Huang, M., Yang, Y., Zhu, X.: Learning to identify review spam. In: IJCAI 2011 - Volume Three, Barcelona, Catalonia, Spain, pp. 2488–2493 (2011)
9. Liu, B.: Sentiment Analysis and Opinion Mining. Synthesis Lectures on Human Language Technologies. Morgan & Claypool Publishers, San Rafael (2012)
10. Lyon, T.P., Maxwell, J.W.: Astroturf: interest group lobbying and corporate strategy. J. Econ. Manag. Strategy 13(4), 561–597 (2004)
11. Mayzlin, D., Dover, Y., Chevalier, J.: Promotional reviews: an empirical investigation of online review manipulation. Am. Econ. Rev. 104(8), 2421–2455 (2014). http://www.aeaweb.org/articles.php?doi=10.1257/aer.104.8.2421
12. Mukherjee, A., Liu, B., Glance, N.S.: Spotting fake reviewer groups in consumer reviews. In: WWW 2012, Lyon, France, pp. 191–200 (2012)
13. Ott, M., Choi, Y., Cardie, C., Hancock, J.T.: Finding deceptive opinion spam by any stretch of the imagination. In: Proceedings of 49th Annual Meeting of the Association for Computational Linguistics: Human Language Technologies-Volume 1, pp. 309–319 (2011)
14. Puolamäki, K., Fortelius, M., Mannila, H.: Seriation in paleontological data using Markov Chain Monte Carlo methods. PLoS Comput. Biol. 2(2), e6 (2006)
15. Santamaria, R., Theron, R., Quintales, L.: BicOverlapper: a tool for bicluster visualization. Bioinformatics 24(9), 1212–1213 (2008)
16. Shmulevich, I., Zhang, W.: Binary analysis and optimization-based normalization of gene expression data. Bioinformatics 18(4), 555–565 (2002)
17. Sun, G., Wu, Y., Liang, R., Liu, S.: A survey of visual analytics techniques and applications: state-of-the-art research and future challenges. J. Comput. Sci. Technol. 28(5), 852–867 (2013)
18. Thomas, J.J., Cook, K.A.: A visual analytics agenda. IEEE Comput. Graph. Appl. 26(1), 10–13 (2006)
19. Wang, G., Wilson, C., Zhao, X., Zhu, Y., Mohanlal, M., Zheng, H., Zhao, B.Y.: Serf and turf: crowdturfing for fun and profit. In: WWW 2012, Lyon, France, pp. 679–688 (2012)
20. Wang, G., Xie, S., Liu, B., Yu, P.S.: Review graph based online store review spammer detection. In: ICDM 2011, pp. 1242–1247. Vancouver, BC, Canada (2011)
21. Wu, G., Greene, D., Smyth, B., Cunningham, P.: Distortion as a validation criterion in the identification of suspicious reviews. In: Proceedings of 1st Workshop on Social Media Analytics, pp. 10–13. ACM (2010)
22. Xie, Z., Zhu, S.: Grouptie: toward hidden collusion group discovery in app stores. In: WiSec 2014 (2014)
23. Zaki, M.J., Hsiao, C.-J.: Efficient algorithms for mining closed itemsets and their lattice structure. IEEE Trans. Knowl. Data Eng. 17(4), 462–478 (2005)

Hidden in Plain Sight. SDP-Based Covert Channel for Botnet Communication

Zisis Tsiatsikas[1]([✉]), Marios Anagnostopoulos[1], Georgios Kambourakis[1], Sozon Lambrou[1], and Dimitris Geneiatakis[2]

[1] Department of Information and Communication Systems Engineering,
University of the Aegean, Karlovassi, Greece
{tzisis,managn,gkamb}@aegean.gr
[2] Electrical and Computer Engineering Department,
Aristotle University of Thessaloniki, 541 24 Thessaloniki, Greece
dgeneiat@auth.gr

Abstract. Covert channels pose a significant threat for networking systems. In this paper, we examine the exploitation of Session Description Protocol (SDP) information residing in Session Initiation Protocol (SIP) requests with the aim to hide data in plain sight. While a significant mass of works in the literature cope with covert communication channels, only a very limited number of them rely on SIP to realize its goals. Also, none of them concentrates on SDP data contained in SIP messages to implement and evaluate such a hidden communication channel. Motivated by this fact, the work at hand proposes and demonstrates the feasibility of a simple but very effective in terms of stealthiness and simplicity SIP-based covert channel for botnet Command and Control (C&C). As a side contribution, we assess the soundness and the impact of such a deployment at the victim's side via the use of two different types of flooding attacks.

Keywords: SIP · Botnet · Covert channel · C&C · SDP

1 Introduction

During the last decade, VoIP services have exhibited a remarkable expansion. As a matter of fact, recent reports [1] indicate that IP multimedia communication services gain ground against the Public Switched Telephone Network (PSTN) ones. This is because VoIP services provide more flexible and inexpensive models, and thus they gradually dominate the market. Among others, multimedia session establishment and management constitutes a fundamental operation in VoIP networks. Nowadays, Session Initiation Protocol (SIP) has been adopted as the prevalent signaling protocol for handling multimedia sessions over the Internet and 3rd Generation partnership Project (3GPP) realms. On the downside, SIP is inherently susceptible to different kinds of attacks [2,3]. One of them lies in its exploitation as a covert channel. Adversaries usually employ covert channels

© Springer International Publishing Switzerland 2015
S. Fischer-Hübner et al. (Eds.): TrustBus 2015, LNCS 9264, pp. 48–59, 2015.
DOI: 10.1007/978-3-319-22906-5_4

aiming to communicate information over legitimate data flows. In fact, the text-based nature of SIP fosters such types of attacks. An adversary could easily craft specific parts of the message in order to deliver data with special meaning over legitimate SIP requests. The only requirement for such an attack would be to conform to SIP syntax, otherwise the message parser module at the receiver side would possibly drop the request as malformed.

So far, SIP-based covert channels are scarcely addressed in the literature, and to our knowledge, no implementation exists. That is, the majority of the existing works concentrates on the applicability of information hiding techniques in VoIP-related protocols in general. This includes SIP, Real Time Protocol (RTP) and RTP Control Protocol (RTCP). The delivered channels may be used in a variety of ways, aiming to establish secret paths of communication. In this paper, we examine the feasibility of exploiting SIP as a Command and Control (C&C) covert channel aiming to deliver commands to a SIP botnet and launch attacks. The main contributions of this paper are summarized as follows:

- We present a simple but powerful in terms of stealthiness covert communication protocol to exchange botnet C&C messages over SDP data in SIP requests.
- We evaluate the effectiveness of the covert channel by controlling several bots and launching two different Denial of Service (DoS) type of attacks.
- An assessment of the attack impact in terms of resource consumption at the victim side is also included.

The rest of the paper is structured as follows. Section 2 provides an overview of session establishment in SIP-based networks. It also presents background information for botnet networks and an overview of the threat model. Section 3 briefly describes the proposed architecture and details on the protocol used for realising the covert C&C channel. Section 4 evaluates the impact of the attack in terms of CPU, memory and network utilization at the victim's side. Similar work in the literature is addressed in Sect. 5. The last section draws a conclusion and gives pointers to future work.

2 Preliminaries

2.1 SIP Architecture

This section briefly describes the basic SIP architecture, including message structure, the involved entities, and the process of session establishment. The two endpoints, namely the caller and calee also referred to as User Agents (UA), have to send a REGISTER request to a SIP Registrar in order to declare their presence in the service provider or to update their contact information. The latter entity is responsible for gathering and storing registration data into a database to provide location service. Whenever a user wishes to start a session, she sends an INVITE request to the local SIP proxy. The latter retrieves the calee's information from

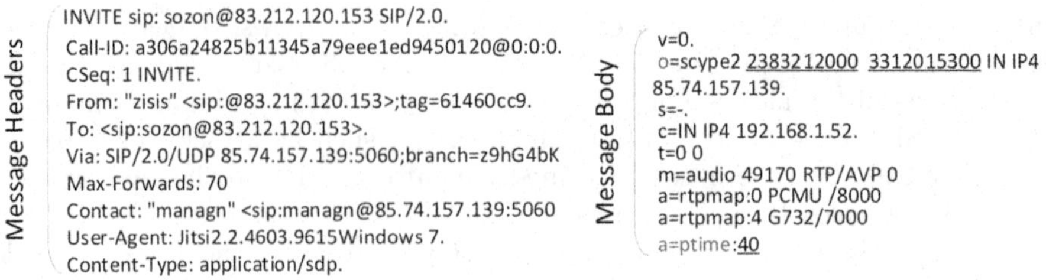

Message Headers

INVITE sip: sozon@83.212.120.153 SIP/2.0.
Call-ID: a306a24825b11345a79eee1ed9450120@0:0:0.
CSeq: 1 INVITE.
From: "zisis" <sip:@83.212.120.153>;tag=61460cc9.
To: <sip:sozon@83.212.120.153>.
Via: SIP/2.0/UDP 85.74.157.139:5060;branch=z9hG4bK
Max-Forwards: 70
Contact: "managn" <sip:managn@85.74.157.139:5060
User-Agent: Jitsi2.2.4603.9615Windows 7.
Content-Type: application/sdp.

Message Body

v=0.
o=scype2 2383212000 3312015300 IN IP4
85.74.157.139.
s=-.
c=IN IP4 192.168.1.52.
t=0 0
m=audio 49170 RTP/AVP 0
a=rtpmap:0 PCMU /8000
a=rtpmap:4 G732/7000
a=ptime:40

Fig. 1. A typical SIP INVITE message

the location server and forwards the message to it. Either the caller or the calee are able to terminate an ongoing session anytime by sending a BYE request.

A SIP message comprizes of several headers and a message body. It is text-based and presents similar structure to that of HTTP. Figure 1 depicts a typical INVITE request. As observed from the figure, the various headers contain information related to the sender and the recipient of the message, and also the communication path. Also, as seen in the figure, such a message is comprized of two parts; the left one containing the various headers, and the message body describing streaming media initialization parameters. The latter part is built following the SDP standard format [4]. Given the text nature of the message an adversary could straightforwardly manipulate the data contained in the SIP headers or SDP descriptors with the aim to build a covert channel over the legitimate information. Note that if this is done in a SIP-oriented (natural) way, the channel has many changes of going undetected. However, as explained further down, care must be taken in order not to alter important information that are required by the peers or the proxies to establish communication. Moreover, any manipulation in the various headers or parameters must be syntactically neutral; otherwise, the message could be dropped by the receiver's message parser. One may also think of encrypting the parts of the message to be used as the covert channel carrier. This however would require the provision of some key management process, and more importantly, will attract the attention of network defenses. So, the idea here is to hide the (C&C in our case) information in plain sight by simply mimicking the values contained in the fields of a normal SIP message.

2.2 Botnet Architectures

A botnet can be considered as a network consisting of infected and compromized computers, called bots, zombies or slaves, which are controlled by an attacker known as the botmaster or bot-herder. A bot agent obeys every command received by its botmaster ordering it to initiate or terminate an attack. Botnets pose a serious threat to the Internet, since they are capable of disrupting the normal operation of services, networks and systems at will of their botmaster. For instance, botnets could be used for launching Distributed DoS (DDoS) attacks [5], sending spam emails on a massive scale, performing identity theft, distributing malware or even copyrighted material, and so forth.

Perhaps the most vital demand for maintaining control of the entire botnet is the ability for a bot to constantly stay in touch with its C&C infrastructure through a reliable and undetectable covert channel. That is, a bot will not be able to receive new instructions if the C&C cannot be located, and continue to probe the vanished C&C in vain. In this direction, botmasters employ a number of techniques to not only minimize the probability of bots losing contact with their C&C infrastructure, but also to render their botnet more agile to hijacking and stoppage attempts. Depending on how the bots are remotely controlled by their master, i.e., how the C&C channel is structured, one is able to classify them into centralized, decentralized or hybrid architectures.

The centralized infrastructure is based on the client-server model, where all bots are directly connected with one or few C&C servers. These servers undertake to coordinate the bots and instruct them to take action. Although a centralized botnet exhibits optimum coordination and rapid dissemination of commands, it also poses a single point of failure. From the moment the C&C server is detected and deactivated the entire botnet is turned off. Usually, a bot-herder conveys its command through a well-known protocol. This way, she is able to hide the C&C traffic into a legitimate one. As a rule of thumb, the communication channels in this approach are based on HTTP or IRC protocol [6]. In the first case, the communication is disguised inside the normal Web network traffic as the usage of Web is allowed in most networks, including corporate ones. On the other hand, in IRC-based architecture the bots are connected to IRC channels and waiting for commands from the bot-herder. Of course, the messages on the IRC channel are in an obfuscated custom dialect, e.g., encrypted or hashed to avoid disclosure. In our case, a centralized infrastructure is employed, where one or more SIP proxies are responsible for dispatching the commands to bots. Furthermore, we are not based on the aforementioned protocols, but rather we utilize SIP as a covert channel. Although, centralized approach seems easily detectable, the botmaster is capable of evading defence mechanisms by applying fluxing techniques. As explained further down, fluxing allows the aspiring botmaster to frequently change the IP and/or the domain name of the proxy.

Alternatively, a decentralized architecture may be selected to carry out the C&C mechanism. In this approach, there is not a central C&C server, but rather the various bots communicate with each other via Peer-to-Peer (P2P) protocols. In other words, the bots behave as C&C server and client at the same time. Therefore, if any of the bots is tracked down and deactivated, there are no implications to the robustness of the entire network [7]. The hybrid architecture combines the advantages of both the centralized and decentralized ones. That is, in this setting, the bot agents exhibit diverse functionalities. Some of them, temporarily undertake the C&C server role, with the aim to coordinate the botnet and disseminate the instructions, while the others wait for commands before springing to action [8].

2.3   Threat Model

As already pointed out, various vulnerabilities have been presented so far in the literature concerning SIP [2,3,9]. The formulation of a threat model in our case has to do with adversaries who try to capitalize on SIP as a covert channel. We consider two different cases depending on who controls the SIP Registrar with which the bots need to be registered.

In the first one, the botmaster controls the Registrar, e.g., she is the owner of this server or she has compromized it in some way. As a result, the botmaster is able of registering users with the SIP proxy. This way she solves the problem of randomly assigning and updating usernames to the bots. Moreover, she is capable of further eliminating the chances of getting detected by applying IP and Domain Fluxing to the SIP proxy without significant modification to the proposed architecture. In the case of IP flux, the botmaster would regularly alter the IP address pertaining to the Fully Qualified Domain Name (FQDN) of SIP Registrar by owning or controlling a group of PCs dedicated to that purpose. On the other, by applying domain fluxing, she continuously modifies and associates multiple FQDNs to the SIP Registrar. For example, every day, the botmaster could assign a new domain name to the SIP Registrar. These names might be generated by a hash function taking as input the current global date and a secret string. With the same way, the various bots could produce the domain name of a specific day.

The second scenario is the opposite of the former, i.e., the botmaster does not control the Registrar. In this case, the easiest workaround for the botmaster is to register the bots and herself to a SIP public service provider. A list of such providers is included in [10]. However, the problem of assigning usernames in this case may not be so trivial. The botmaster and consequently the bots must know which usernames are still available (not taken by other users). This requires either a public directory or a P2P protocol for sharing and updating a list which contains the already assigned usernames. Another more straightforward solution lies in exploiting SIP protocol requests to determine if a UA is alive. For example, an OPTIONS request could be used by the botmaster (or a bot) to identify if a username has already been assigned to another user. According to SIP RFC [11], this request is used by a UA for identifying the capabilities either of another UA or a SIP proxy. Therefore, one could take advantage of this functionality to build a list of the already occupied usernames. A third option is for the botmaster to assign totally randomly generated usernames for the bots, but this may attract the attention of the proxy administrator. Such a list can be shared between the botmaster and each bot beforehand. Generally, it can be argued that the more realistic the usernames the less the chances of being detected as malicious.

In our case, we assume that the Registrar is in the possession of the botherder. We also hypothesize that the bots have been installed in the host machines following an infection. Nonetheless, this infection phase remains out of scope of this work.

3   Architecture and Operation

3.1   SIP as a Covert Channel

To create a SIP-based covert channel one needs to choose specific parts of the message and use them as data carriers. In fact, several SIP headers or SDP descriptors contained in, say, a SIP request can be used to bear information with special meaning to the communicating parties. In any case, the selection must fulfil the next two requirements. On the one hand, it must be syntactically correct, otherwise the message will be most likely dropped by the parsing process. On the other, it must preserve the communication information at least regarding to the sender and the SIP proxy. Otherwise, the message may never be delivered correctly.

In this work, we concentrate on fields contained in the message body of a SIP request where the literature seems to be quite incomplete. As already pointed out and depicted in the right part of Fig. 1, this part of the message follows the SDP data format. Precisely, these pieces of data contain information related to the media parameters of a session and are comprized of 5 mandatory and 15 optional fields [4]. We make use of only two descriptors namely as $<o>$ and $<a=ptime>$. The first one is mandatory while the second is optional. The $<o>$ descriptor carries information in regards to the session originator and it is composed of 5 fields. Among them, the first and the last one point out the username and the IP address of the caller ("skype2" in Fig. 1), while the second and the third indicate a unique session id and the session version. The fourth field is a text string bearing the type of the network ("IN" (Internet) in the normal case). The creation of session id and version fields are up to the creating tool. The RFC [4] suggests that both these parameters must receive numerical string values of at least 10 digits each created based on a Network Time Protocol (NTP) [12] format timestamp in order to ensure uniqueness. Also, RFC states that the $<a=ptime>$ descriptor bears the length of time in milliseconds represented by the media in a packet. So, for example, any decimal value representing time in milliseconds is considered normal. The selected fields are shown in red in Fig. 1. The interested reader who wishes to get a deeper understanding of SDP can refer to the corresponding RFC [4].

For exploiting the above mentioned fields aiming to deliver a covert channel over legitimate SIP messages one has to set specific values. Table 1 summarizes these values in the context of this work. As observed from the table, the protocol relies on three simple commands related to the type, the parameters, and the execution and termination of an attack. That is, the $a=ptime:<packet\ time>$ descriptor can receive three values 20, 30 and 40. The first one triggers the UA to extract attack parameters and wait for further commands. The other two values correspond to the initiation and termination of the attack respectively. As shown in the table, the second and the third fields of the $<o>$ descriptor bear the first and the second half of the victim's IPv4 accordingly. In the example given in Fig. 1, the second and the third values of this descriptor are equal to 2383212000 and 3312015300 respectively. So, the IP address can be extracted by a bot as

Table 1. Description of C&C protocol messages (character X corresponds to a single digit of the victim's IPv4 address, and Z refers to a digit used for another command or it is zero-padded)

Descriptor	Field	Value	Hidden Message
<o>	sess-id	33XXXXXXZZ	First half of Victim's IP
<o>	sess-version	33XXXXXXZZ	Second half of Victim's IP
<o>	sess-version	ZZZZZZZZ00	SYN Flood attack
<o>	sess-version	ZZZZZZZZ11	PING Flood attack
a=ptime:<packet time>	-	20	Save attack parameters &wait
a=ptime:<packet time>	-	30	Launch attack
a=ptime:<packet time>	-	40	Stop attack

follows: Assuming a quad-dotted notation, the first two digits of each 10 digit number represent the number of digits that this half of the address is consisted of. In the example, the first two values of session id are 2 and 3 leading the bot to extract the first half of the IP address, i.e., 83.212. In the same manner, session version starts with 33, thus allowing the bot to extract the remaining half 120.153. The last two digits of the second field of session version instruct the bot about the type of the attack. Specifically, a value of 00 means a SYN flooding, while 11 designates a PING one. Special care has been taken for these values to appear as perfectly legitimate ones. To do so, both session id and version numbers are appropriately padded with zeros to reach 10 digits, which is the minimum length suggested by the SDP RFC [4].

Keep in mind that the selected SDP descriptors receive values that correspond to fields which do not affect the session establishment, and thus the covert channel remains functional. In this way, a botmaster is able to hide messages in plain sight without being exposed. On the downside, the use of one optional descriptor for the creation of the covert channel adds 10 extra bytes per message. However, it can be safely argued that this presents a negligible increase in the network traffic to be noticed by the underlying defense mechanisms. Even for a large population of bots, where the botmaster needs to send one SIP request per bot, this augmentation shall be in the order of some tenths of kilobytes (e.g., for 10,000 bots it would be ≈98 kilobytes).

It should be stressed out that the aforementioned descriptors and fields are not the only ones that can be exploited for secretly communicating information between the two ends. Several other selections and combinations are possible. However, each of them should be done in such a way that will attract the minimum attention. For instance, the k= descriptor is to be avoided because its use is not recommended by the RFC [4]. Also, the employment of a large number of SDP optional fields for the needs of the covert channel would not only raise suspicions, but also augment the volume of each SIP request. On the other hand, the information carried by the a=ptime:<packet time> descriptor in our protocol could be moved to the padded segment of the <o> descriptor as given above.

Another point of interest here is that the architecture is fully dynamic because it can be used both by static and mobile UAs. That is, due to SIP intrinsic operation, each bot is reachable from virtually anywhere. As explained in Sect. 2, the IP of the Registrar may change but the bots can become aware of this shift via a domain fluxing scheme or otherwise by extending the C&C instruction repertoire. The reader would likely notice that the communication protocol between the bot master and the bots is one-way. That is, a bot does not send any messages toward its bot-herder. Actually, from the botmaster's point of view, this is not really a problem; as she is in control of the SIP registrar she always knows which bot is alive (i.e., has been registered with the Registrar). On the other hand, one can anticipate that this approach also contributes in keeping the communication channel as hidden as possible. Putting it another way, the less information are transmitted towards a single receiver (the bot-herder) the less the chances of revealing the channel.

4 Evaluation

4.1 Test-Bed Setup

In order to evaluate the effectiveness of the C&C covert channel we created a test-bed depicted in Fig. 2. We used 7 SIP UAs, one of which was used as the Botmaster and the rest as bots. The SIP UA were developed in JAVA language using the JAIN-SIP library [13]. Each UA runs on an Intel i3 3.3 GHz processor with 4 GB of RAM. The well-known SIP proxy Kamailio [14] has been employed in the cloud as both a SIP server and Registrar. The server machine was equipped with 1 GB of RAM. Finally, the victim's machine was running on an Intel Pentium 4 2.8 GHz processor having 1 GB of RAM available.

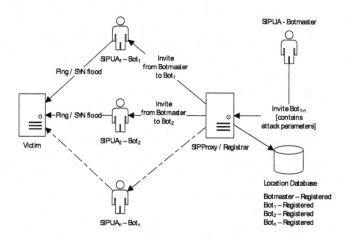

Fig. 2. Deployed test-bed and generic attack scenario

We created six different scenarios each one employing a variant number of attack threads launched by each bot. We released both PING and SYN flooding assaults, each one with different number of attack threads. The first three scenarios correspond to a SYN flooding attack, while the rest to a PING one. For SYN flooding we used correspondingly 5, 15 and 30 attack threads per bot, while for PING 30, 80 and 160. This increased number of attack threads in the second type of attack was used in an effort to augment the impact of this particular attack. This is because a SYN flood is generally more powerful in contrast to a PING one. We used this simulation methodology aiming to grab a better understanding of the attack impact, especially when its volume augments. We employed three metrics to estimate the fallout of each type of attack on the victim's machine; network bandwidth utilization, memory consumption, and CPU usage.

4.2   Results

Figures 3 and 4 present snapshots of the received network traffic and CPU usage at the victim side under a SYN and PING flood attack respectively. From the left figure, one can easily observe that as the number of attack threads per bot remains low, the incoming traffic at the victim's side presents moderate fluctuations. On the downside, when the number of threads increases significantly the incoming traffic doubles. For example, when the threads per bot become equal to 30 the network volume doubles reaching 6MB/sec.

Figure 4 depicts CPU usage at the target machine for a different number of PING flooding threads. It is well perceivable that as the number of threads per bot increases, the CPU utilization percentage augments notably. For example, when the number of the attack threads per bot is set to 30 the CPU usage reaches a maximum value equal to 25 %. On the other hand, when the number of threads per bot are sextupled (180), CPU usage reaches a peak value of 30 %.

Regarding the memory consumption at the victim's side, we perceived a worst case increment of ≈100 % (from 12 % to 24 %) in the case of PING flooding, and ≈118 % (from 22 % to 48 %) for the SYN one.

5   Related Work

This section succinctly reports on works that have been presented in the literature so far regarding this particular topic. In the following, we group them into three categories. The first one includes a single contribution that relies on SIP to convey botnet singaling. The second embraces two works that identify SIP messages as possible carriers of spurious data. The last focuses on the use of RTP as a means of covert communication.

Regarding the first category, the authors in [15] present a SIP-driven botnet. They rely on the well-known Storm botnet by encapsulating its P2P traffic (based on the Overnet Protocol) over SIP. They develop a test-bed composed of 30 bots claiming that the generated message rate resembles that of Storm's one.

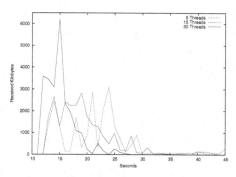
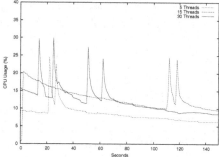

Fig. 3. Network Utilization at victim's side under a SYN flood attack

Fig. 4. CPU Usage at victim's side under a PING flood attack

They correctly observe that their proposal introduces a significant overhead due to the use of SIP as the botnet's conveyor mechanism. This is caused by the need of continuously maintaining permanent connection paths between the various entities. Opposed to that, we simply exploit specific descriptors of the SDP data included in, say, a SIP INVITE request without further stressing the infrastructure.

To our knowledge, until now two works have been presented investigating the potential exploitation of SIP as a covert channel. In [16] the authors survey various steganographic techniques aiming to hide data in legitimate traffic of various networking protocols. They also address this potential for SIP, and for both message body and SDP data. Nevertheless, their analysis is at a high-level only without presenting any real implementation or results. This is in contrast to our work where we capitalize on SDP data to deliver C&C messages. The authors in [17] exploit 3 randomly generated strings included in SIP messages in order to create a covert channel. They rely in chaos theory aiming to analyze and reconstruct the random numbers included in the Call-ID header and the various Tags of a SIP message. This is undertaken by means of a time series analysis.

As already mentioned, the last category of works concentrate on RTP-based covert channels. The authors in [18] make use of four different data hiding algorithms at the RTP layer in order to assess the feasibility of covert channels in VoIP. Their approach is assessed in terms of bit error rates under the G.729 compression algorithm. Similar techniques at the RTP layer has been investigated by works in [19] and [20]. In the first one, the authors propose to build a covert channel over specific unused fields in RTP and RTCP by using steganography. Moreover, they introduce a method which relies on the intentional delay of packets for communicating data secretly. In [20] the authors create a covert channel over IP/UDP/RTP packets aiming to either to improve IP Telephony security or change the behavior of existing protocols such as RTCP one. They propose two packet payload types characterized as either security or informational. They claim that their protocol is capable of ensuring authentication and integrity not only for the voice and its sender, but also for authenticating protocol parameters, including both the security and informational payloads.

6   Conclusions

This paper elaborates on the exploitation of SIP as a covert channel for building botnet C&C. We demonstrate that with little effort an aggressor is able to tinker with SDP data contained in SIP requests aiming to convey spurious information secretly. This is also done in an straightforward and simple way, perfectly in line with SIP/SDP standards, and without raising any suspicions or causing the messages to be dropped by the receiver as malformed. From a network defense view point, little can be done; the messages seem completely legitimate, they are sent only sporadically and do not augment the network traffic significantly (i.e., 10 additional bytes per bot is perceived). So, even deep and continuous packet inspection at the application or other layer would not reveal something suspicious. The only effective counteraction is to monitor SIP transactions for requests without a matching response. But on the other hand, this mismatch occurs for legitimate SIP transactions quite often too, thus it is to be assumed that it will cause a high false alarm rate at the proxy-side IDS. Overall, we argue that the simplest and more innocuous the covert channel the less the possibility of detecting it. As a secondary contribution, we provide results about the feasibility of such a covert C&C deployment by implementing two kinds of flooding attacks executed by the bots.

We are currently working on enriching C&C with more options for the botmaster. An idea is to find a way to dynamically change the pattern of communication, that is, the places (message headers or descriptors) where the bytes with special meaning are put. This way, the detection of the covert channel would become even harder. On the downside, upon change, this pattern must be communicated to the bot population. A second interesting issue to consider is the possibility of botnet partitioning. That is, in view of what has been discussed in the latter half of Sect. 2.3, having some bots registered to a given public provider and the rest to another one(s). In this case, every bot needs to be informed to which Registrar (domain or IP) must register with, and the botmaster needs to keep and update a list of {*bot-username, Registrar-domain-name*} for being able to correctly dispatch the Invites. This naturally implies an extension of the covert channel to communicate a "Registrar shift" message to the bots.

Acknowledgements. This paper is part of the 5179 (SCYPE) research project, implemented within the context of the Greek Ministry of Development-General Secretariat of Research and Technology funded program "Excellence II / Aristeia II", co-financed by the European Union/European Social Fund - Operational program "Education and Life-long Learning" and National funds.

References

1. Mohr, C.: Report: Global voip services market to reach 137 billion by 2020, November 2014. http://www.tmcnet.com/channels/hosted-softswitch/articles/ 393593-report-global-voip-services-market-reach-137-billion.htm
2. Keromytis, A.D.: A comprehensive survey of voice over ip security research. IEEE Commun. Surv. Tutorials **14**(2), 514–537 (2012)
3. Geneiatakis, D., Dagiuklas, T., Kambourakis, G., Lambrinoudakis, C., Gritzalis, S., et al.: Survey of security vulnerabilities in session initiation protocol. IEEE Commun. Surv. Tutorials **8**(3), 68–81 (2006)
4. Handley, M. et al.: Sdp: session description protocol. RFC 4566, US (2006)
5. Anagnostopoulos, M., Kambourakis, G., Kopanos, P., Louloudakis, G., Gritzalis, S.: Dns amplification attack revisited. Comput. Secur. **39**, 475–485 (2013)
6. Silva, S.S.C., Silva, R.M.P., Pinto, R.C.G., Salles, R.M.: Botnets: a survey. Comput. Netw. **57**(2), 378–403 (2013)
7. Wang, P., Wu, L., Aslam, B., Zou, C.C.: A systematic study on peer-to-peer botnets. In: IEEE ICCCN 2009, pp. 1–8, August 2009
8. Wang, P., Sparks, S., Zou, C.C.: An advanced hybrid peer-to-peer botnet. IEEE Trans. Dependable Secure Comput. **7**(2), 113–127 (2010)
9. Geneiatakis, D., Kambourakis, G., Lambrinoudakis, C., Gritzalis, T.S.: A framework for protecting a sip-based infrastructure against malformed message attacks. Comput. Netw. **51**(10), 2580–2593 (2007)
10. Sip service providers and carriers (2015). http://www.cs.columbia.edu/sip/ service-providers.html
11. Rosenberg, J., et al.: Sip: session initiation protocol. IETF RFC 3261, US (2002)
12. Mills, D.: Network time protocol (version 3) specification, implementation. RFC 1305, US (1992)
13. O'Doherty, P., Ranganathan, M.: JAIN SIP Tutorial - Serving the Developer Community, Technical report (2003)
14. Kamailio the open source sip server (2014). http://www.kamailio.org/w/
15. Berger, A., Hefeeda, M.: Exploiting sip for botnet communication. In: IEEE NPSec 2009, pp. 31–36, October 2009
16. Mazurczyk, W., Szczypiorski, K.: Covert channels in sip for voip signalling. In: Jahankhani, H., Revett, K., Palmer-Brown, D. (eds.) Global E-Security. CCIS, vol. 12, pp. 65–72. Springer, Heidelberg (2008)
17. Zhao, H., Zhang, X.: Sip steganalysis using chaos theory. In: IEEE CMCSN 2012, pp. 95–100, July 2012
18. Takahashi, T., Lee, W.: An assessment of voip covert channel threats. In: IEEE SecureComm 2007, pp. 371–380, September 2007
19. Mazurczyk, W., Szczypiorski, K.: Steganography of VoIP streams. In: Meersman, R., Tari, Z. (eds.) OTM 2008, Part II. LNCS, vol. 5332, pp. 1001–1018. Springer, Heidelberg (2008)
20. Mazurczyk, W., Kotulski, Z.: Covert channel for improving voip security. In: Pejaś, J., Saeed, K. (eds.) Advances in Information Processing and Protection, pp. 271–280. Springer, US (2007)

The Design of a Configurable Reputation Service

Channel Hillebrand and Marijke Coetzee[(✉)]

Academy for Computer Science and Software Engineering,
University of Johannesburg, Johannesburg, South Africa
channel.hillebrand@gmail.com, marijkec@uj.ac.za

Abstract. Novel trust and reputation models are frequently proposed by the research community to suit the needs of a specific environment. From the plethora of models that are available, it becomes difficult to know which features can be combined in general-purpose models suitable for commercial use. In order to address this problem, the focus of recent research on trust and reputation systems has been on the identification of common features in order to enable reuse. Organizations who need to use a reputation system within their application domain have to custom build it, which may be challenging for novice developers. This paper defines a strategy to develop a configurable SaaS reputation service that has the ability to support common features, but at the same time accommodate the unique requirements of a variety of online communities. A domain analysis reveals common features that can be arranged and re-organized using variability modeling to enable a SaaS providers to support the configuration of a SaaS reputation service.

Keywords: Reputation · Reuse, configurable · SaaS · Variability modeling

1 Introduction

Centralized online reputation systems [1] are used by established online ecommerce web sites and social web platforms to aid users to build trust and reputation in their communities. For example, eBay [2], a trading platform that supports transactions between strangers from any part of the world, would not have become successful without the trust instilled into the eBay community, resulting from the honesty and good behaviour encouraged by eBay's reputation mechanisms. Reputation systems are custom created for each new web site, often by developers who may not familiar with the inherent complexities and nuances. Though the functional and other requirements of the reputation systems of eBay, Amazon [5] and Digg [4] differ, there are many common features that they share.

The creation of a well-designed reputation system is not easy [3, 6]. As there are no off-the-shelf reputation system components to integrate into application environments, a need exists for pre-built, sophisticated reputation system components to support the successful deployment of applications. In this regards, Moyano et al. presented a pluggable reputation framework for social-cloud applications that application developers can adapt to their environments [33]. Recently, a business model for software

© Springer International Publishing Switzerland 2015
S. Fischer-Hübner et al. (Eds.): TrustBus 2015, LNCS 9264, pp. 60–70, 2015.
DOI: 10.1007/978-3-319-22906-5_5

applications namely Software as a Service (SaaS) has emerged which lowers the development and deployment costs of applications [7]. The challenge is to support a reputation service with a single code base, but to accommodate unique features of tenant organizations by configuring features. As SOA (Service-oriented Architectures) and SaaS are very closely related architectural models [8], BPM (Business Process Modelling) can be used to deliver configurable SaaS applications by specifying the order in which services are invoked [9]. However, there are challenges to be addressed as a SaaS provider needs to define all common process definitions, and maintain variations as required by tenants. Variability modelling, used in software product line engineering, can enable the application of variability in service-oriented SaaS applications [9].

The contribution of this paper is to propose the design of a configurable reputation service as a SaaS solution to accommodate the different needs of organizations. Next, a reputation service is introduced and its requirements described. A background on SaaS configuration and customization is given and a SaaS design strategy is presented, based on recent research. The design of a configurable reputation service is presented following the design strategy, by presenting a domain analysis, service composition model and variability model. Finally, the paper is concluded.

2   Requirements for a Configurable Reputation Service

A reputation service is defined as a software as a service (SaaS) application. A cloud provider hosts the reputation service and rents it to customers called tenants, whose users access the application over the internet [10]. As the reputation service needs to be composable with the applications of tenants, machine-to-machine interactions are supported with either SOAP [11] or REST [12] calls. Figure 1 gives two tenants A and B, their users and applications that consume the reputation service. The focus of the design of a SaaS-based reputation service is to serve large numbers of tenants and their users using one instance of the reputation system. However, every tenant is unique and adjustments to components of the reputation system may be required [13].

Multi-tenancy requires configuration data for each tenant, created by the administrators of the tenant using a configuration tool, as shown in Fig. 1. Thus a designer configures the reputation service by setting up configuration files. When users invoke the reputation system via their application, configuration files are retrieved by the reputation service to provide a customized SaaS application and all the while maintaining the context of interactions per tenant and user. Requirements for a reputation service was previously identified by the authors [36]. This research now extends these requirements with new requirements to address the design features of a reputation service.

- *Support for common features* - The reputation service should support software functions and features that are common among a large number of service consumers to support a high level of re-use.
- *Configurability* – The reputation service should be able to support unique features of tenants.

Next, the nature of configurability, how it can be provided, and a design strategy is described.

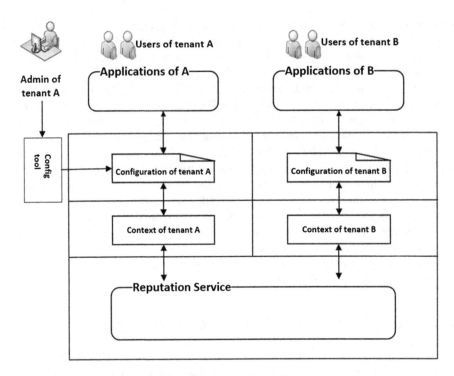

Fig. 1. Reputation service architecture

3 SaaS Application Configuration

When considering the configuration of a SaaS application, the terms customization and configuration are frequently used interchangeably. Configuration does not requires source code changes but rather addresses the setting of parameters, changing of application functions by adding data fields, drop-down lists or buttons, and changing business rules. On the other hand, customization involves source code changes to the SaaS reputation service to create functionality, making it more expensive for both SaaS vendors and clients [13, 15, 16]

Configuration objects in SaaS are divided into three classes namely the user interface, work flow and access control [17]. As a reputation services supports machine-to-machine interfaces, the configuration of the user interface is not considered by this research, but rather the machine interface. The workflow describes a service composition addressing activities and rules that are specific to the organization, which can be switched, added or re-ordered to change application behavior.

Research on the configuration of SaaS applications is still in its infancy. Popular methodologies such as object-orientation do not support SaaS software engineering tasks such as modeling common features and variability [18]. In this regard, service oriented architecture (SOA) can support the realization of SaaS applications as it supports the definition of new composite applications out of an existing set of services.

By composing a SaaS application, configuration of software can be done by re-ordering individual services [18]. Service configuration can be supported by variability modeling techniques from software product line engineering (SPL) [35]. Commonality and variability of a software product line is defined to create applications tailored to the specific needs of different customers. A variability model describes the dynamic configurations of the service composition in terms of activation or deactivation of features. In order to be able to perform variability modeling, a technique to implement the variability model is needed such as feature modeling [19]. Current research in software engineering [14, 15, 18, 20–22, 34] enables the configuration of SaaS applications by modelling variability. The reputation service developer needs a strategy to enable tenants to configure the reputation service to suit their needs without changing the SaaS application source code [22], described next.

3.1 SaaS Configuration Strategy

A strategy to design a configurable reputation service is performed at design-time. The final result is a configured service composition that activates features required by a specific tenant using a set of pre-defined options.

The following steps are defined:

1. Perform a domain analysis to define a service composition that includes all common components and features required to ensure a high level of reusability.
2. Create a variability model that describes the possible variants needed in a service composition.
3. Deploy the variability model by linking features to service operations so that they can be dynamically activated or deactivated when a particular configuration of the service composition is reached.

4 Reputation Service Configuration Strategy

The steps of the SaaS configuration strategy is now applied to create a configurable the reputation service by focusing on the design of centralized online reputation systems [1] to fit the architecture of cloud-based applications. This research does not present a new reputation model, but rather attempts to integrate current research to create a reputation service that is generic in nature, but is configurable.

4.1 Domain Analysis

A reputation system collects, aggregates and distributes information about an entity, to be used to portray and predict [23, 24] that entity's future behaviour. Information is provided to the reputation system by a person such as a rater (evaluator), or another system. A target is the entity for which the rater provides information and may be a product, transaction or even a blog. The analysis and review of reputation system components, with the aim of identifying reusable components, taxonomies and meta-models has been the focus of recent research [1, 26–31]. The main components of a reputation system are input, processing, output and feedback [1]. These components and their related set of possible features that may be configured are described next. Some features can be represented by a list of options, making them easily configurable, where other are more complex and represent a section of code that is executed.

Input: Two collection methods can be used to gather information from sources namely *direct and indirect collection* [26, 27, 29]. The *set of raters* [1, 27] who are eligible to do evaluations must be determined by the reputation systems' regulations. For example, a reputation system may allow people to leave reviews anonymously or may require of a rater to register before leaving a review. The *representation of reputation information* [1, 26–31] is the format employed to describe, exchange and interpret reputation information. Commonly used types of information are [25] binary (boolean values), discrete (discrete integer values), continuous (floating point number), and string (textual form), allowing a wide range of data to be maintained. The *set of rating criteria* [26] needs to be defined to give a better and more complete view of a reputation object. Both single- and multiple-criteria can be defined. Finally, before reputation information is passed to the processing component, it needs to be *prepared* to be valid and of high integrity using e.g. data transformation and normalization.

Processing: The processing component is the central part of the reputation service that takes collected reputation information and generates a reputation score as output [1, 26–31]. *Protection against malicious entities* [31] needs to be implemented to prevent unfair ratings and bad behaviour. Protection can be implemented with methods such as behavioural analysis and the management of the reliability of the buyer or seller by considering the monetary value of a transaction. Information needs to be *filtered and weighted* before it is aggregated [28, 30]. Finally, when performing *aggregation*, many types of computations are needed [1, 26–31]. Firstly, the target rating algorithm need to be executed using simple algorithms, such as summation, average or percentage [1] or more advanced algorithms, such as, Bayesian systems and fuzzy models [29]. The credibility of the rater is determined by a rater credibility algorithm, generally using simple algorithms such as average and summation and feedback aggregation algorithms aggregate feedback ratings, commonly with summation and averaging [1].

Output: After reputation scores are computed they are stored and distributed to relevant participants [1, 26–31]. T*ransaction history* can be managed by storing the time that are rating was made at. *Aging* of information must be applied as old information losses its relevancy [1, 31]. *Distribution* controls who can get reputation information and the manner in which they can access it. *Granularity of reputation information* is addressed by the level of detail presented. An overall reputation should be presented in a concise and comparable format by giving time scales and descriptive dimensions.

Feedback Loop: The feedback loop is very often an optional component added to a reputation system [1] following the same flow (input, processing and output) as the reputation system where targets are the reviews. The *feedback loop function* detects dishonest and improper reviews. Amazon lets end users rate reviews as 'helpful' or 'not helpful', increasing the rater's credibility score with each 'helpful' vote. In C2C environments sellers may also rate buyers, which means that the rating given by the target (seller) influences the credibility of the raters (buyer). The *feedback collection channel* collects feedback from end users directly through web pages. *The set of feedback providers can be* both end users and targets. End users can vote 'helpful' or 'not helpful' whereas in C2C marketplaces, buyers and sellers can rate each other. The rating made by the seller can be seen as the feedback to the buyer. Restrictions can be made on the set of raters. The *feedback loop level* allows multiple replies to the feedback [1].

This domain analysis reveals a number of features that should commonly be present in a reputation service. The ability to support different combinations of these features is firstly addressed by defining a service composition for a reputation service, defined next.

Reputation Service - Service Composition Model.   Features that can be implemented as services or simply as configurable options are identified from the domain analysis and listed in Table 1. Services and options belonging to the Feedback component have been placed with the Input, Processing and Output components. Together

Table 1. Configurable services and options

Component	Services	Configuration options
Input	Collect direct experiences	Set of targets
	Passive gathering	Set of raters
	Active gathering	Rating and reputation score representation
	Collect indirect experiences	Rating criteria
	Collect feedback	Sources of reputation (indirect experiences)
	Anonymous entities	Set of feedback providers
	Registered entities	Feedback representation
	Data transformation	
	Data normalization	
Processing	Malicious entity protection	Transaction amount threshold
	Behavioural analysis	Behavioural thresholds
	Management of reliability	Reliability thresholds
	Filter information	Filter settings
	Discount function	Discount function settings
	Calculate target reputation	Target algorithm settings, thresholds
	Calculate feedback	Feedback algorithm settings, thresholds
	Calculate rater credibility	Rater credibility algorithm settings, thresholds
Output	Age data	Decay thresholds
	Store transaction history	Timelines
	Process granularity	Distribution settings
	Send reputation information	Feedback loop level
	Send feedback information	

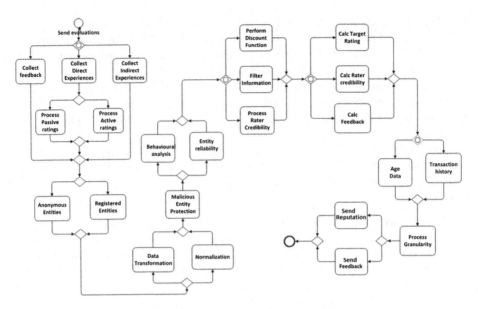

Fig. 2. BPM reputation service composition

these features can be used to create a configurable reputation service. The configuration of internal cloud hosting features such as availability is not considered here.

A BPM service composition is defined at design time, as shown in Fig. 2, using the set of identified services. The computation of reputation is a sequential process that starts when a rater evaluates a product, and ends when final scores are distributed and stored. It should be noted that the reputation workflow attempts to incorporate the most general features that should be present in a centralized reputation service, but should by no means be seen as a complete solution.

4.2   Variability Model

A variability model is now created to describe the variants according to which a configuration can be done, where variability is defined as the ability to change or customize a system [20]. A feature is an application functionality that can be included by the designer of a tenant in an application. For this purpose, a variability model describes the dynamic configurations of the service composition in terms of activation or deactivation of features [22]. The variability model has variation points such as *Collect Direct Experiences* that express decisions leading to different variants (*Passive Gathering* and *Active Gathering*) at runtime as shown in Fig. 3.

The variability model is implemented as a feature model, where features are hierarchically linked in a tree structure using variability relationships such as optional, mandatory, and alternatives [19]. There is only one root feature on which all the other features depend, with primitive features as the leaves and compound features as the interior nodes. Features in grey, shown in Fig. 3, give a current configuration of the

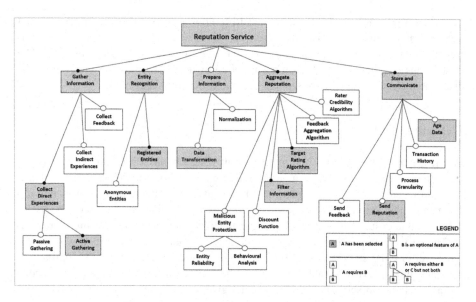

Fig. 3. Feature model for the reputation service

system as they are active. Features in white are inactive. The legend on the bottom right of Fig. 3 give variant rules. The feature model shown here by greyed features supports a very simple reputation system with the most common features that can be found in a reputation system. First, direct experiences are collected in an active manner. Registered entities are allowed to provide evaluations to the system. Data is transformed and filtered, before the target rating algorithm is executed. Finally, data is aged when it is stored and reputation scores are published.

The selection of features from the feature model cannot sufficiently support the definition of a reputation service as more options are set via a configuration file. For example, the representation of data or the definition of rating criteria needs to be set additionally by the designer of the tenant. In order to configure the reputation service, tenants need to choose the variants that should be part of their application. For this purpose a tool is needed to present them with all possible configuration options in order to bind the variability of the reputation service.

It is important to note that it is not possible to give a complete specification of a system by using features because they are not independent from each other. If features are added or removed, they may impact other features. An additional set of rules to manage the propagation of features needs to be created.

4.3   Deployment Based on Variability Model

After the binding of the reputation service variability, the application must be deployed [14]. Variability descriptors need to be transformed into WS-BPEL process models to guide the customization [34]. The feature model, mapped from the BPMN process is now mapped to WS-BPEL. For each variability point in a variability descriptor a BPEL scope is defined and inside the scope a BPEL flow activity is generated. Additional rules and algorithms for variability descriptors used in the reputation service application templates is needed to ensure that only valid configurations are generated [22]. The result is that each tenant application is supported by a WS-BPEL process that executes all features chosen, and is exposed via generated machine interfaces.

5   Conclusion

This research makes a contribution to current research on reputation reusability by presenting a design strategy for a configurable reputation service. A domain analysis, based on recent research on reputation components, defines common features that are found in online centralized reputation systems, as well as features that may optionally be included to ensure a higher level of sophistication to applications carrying more risk.

The focus of this research is to create a generic reputation service that will have a high level of reuse in commercial settings, to be rented out to tenants. An approach is presented on how variability modeling can be used as a guide to implement a configurable reputation service. A feature model gives developers a view of configurable services that can be modified, together with a list of possible configuration options that can be set. It should be noted that services such as the transformation of data should be designed in such a manner as to be able to accommodate configurable options such as the choice of data representation.

To the best of our knowledge, this is the first attempt at creating a configurable SaaS reputation service. Future work will address the refinement of the framework by integrating the feature model with service composition using a toolset to automate the definition of configurable workflows. Experimentation may reveal configuration dependencies that are critical to consider and features that are more appropriate to configure.

Acknowledgement. The support of SAP P&I BIT Mobile Empowerment and the National Research Foundation (NRF) under Grant number 81412 and 81201 towards this research is hereby acknowledged. Opinions expressed and conclusions arrived at are those of the authors and not necessarily to be attributed to the companies mentioned in this acknowledgement.

References

1. Liu, L., Munro, M.: Systematic analysis of centralized online reputation systems. Decis. Support Syst. **52**(2), 438–449 (2012). ISSN 0167-9236
2. www.eBay.com
3. Hui, X.-A., Saeedi, M., Sundaresan, N., Shen, Z.: From lemon markets to managed markets: the evolution of ebay's reputation system. Working paper, Ohio State University (2014)
4. www.Digg.com
5. www.Amazon.com
6. Farmer, R., Glass, B.: Building Web Reputation Systems, 1st edn. Yahoo! Press, USA (2010)

7. Braithwaite, F., Woodman, M.: Success dimensions in selecting cloud software services. In: 37th EUROMICRO Conference on Software Engineering and Advanced Applications (2011)
8. Laplante, P.A., Jia, Z., Voas, J.: What's in a name? Distinguishing between SaaS and SOA. IT Prof. **10**, 46–50 (2008)
9. Mietzner, R., Leymann, F., Papazoglou, M.P.: Defining composite configurable saas application packages using SCA, variability descriptors and multi-tenancy patterns. In: Internet and Web Applications and Services (ICIW), pp. 156–161 (2008)
10. Schroeter, J., Mucha, P., Muth, M., Jugel, K., Lochau, M.: Dynamic configuration management of cloud-based applications. In: Proceedings of the 16th International Software Product Line Conference (SPLC 2012), vol. 2, pp. 171–178. ACM, New York (2012)
11. Gudgin, M., Hadley, M., Mendelsohn, N., Moreau, J.-J., Nielsen, H.F.: SOAP version 1.2 (2003). http://www.w3.org/TR/soap12-part1/
12. Fielding, R.T., Taylor, R.N.: Principled design of the modern web architecture. ACM Trans. Internet Technol. **2**(2), 115–150 (2002)
13. Sun, W., et al.: Software as a service: configuration and customization perspectives. In: Congress on Services Part II, SERVICES-2, pp. 18–25. IEEE, 23–26 September 2008
14. Mietzner, R., Metzger, A., Leymann, F., Pohl, K.: Variability modeling to support customization and deployment of multi-tenant-aware Software as a Service applications. In: ICSE Workshop on Principles of Engineering Service Oriented Systems, PESOS 2009, pp. 18–25, 18–19 May 2009
15. Tsai, W.T., Sun, T.: SaaS multi-tenant application customization. In: Proceedings of the 2013 IEEE Seventh International Symposium Service-Oriented System Engineering, pp. 1–12, March 2013
16. Bezemer, C.P., Zaidman, A., Platzbeecker, B., Hurkmans, T., Hart, A.: Enabling multi-tenancy: an industrial experience report. In: Proceedings of 2010 IEEE International Conference on Software Maintenance, pp. 1–8, September 2010
17. Al-Shardan, M.M., Ziani, D.: Configuration as a service in multi-tenant enterprise resource planning system. Lect. Notes Softw. Eng. **3**(2), 95–100 (2015)
18. La, H.J., Kim, S.D.: A systematic process for developing high quality SaaS cloud services. In: Jaatun, M.G., Zhao, G., Rong, C. (eds.) Cloud Computing. LNCS, vol. 5931, pp. 278–289. Springer, Heidelberg (2009)
19. Kang, K., Cohen, S., Hess, J., Novak, W., Peterson, S.: Feature-oriented domain analysis (FODA) feasibility study. Technical report CMU/SEI-90-TR-021. Software Engineering Institute, Carnegie Mellon University, November 1990. http://www.sei.cmu.edu/library/abstracts/reports/90tr021.cfmKeeney
20. Mietzner, R., Metzger, A., Leymann, F., Pohl, K.: Variability modeling to support customization and deployment of multi-tenant-aware software as a service applications. In: ICSE Workshop on Principles of Engineering Service Oriented Systems (2009)
21. Ghaddar, A., Tamzalit, D., Assaf, A., Bitar, A.: Variability as a service: outsourcing variability management in multi-tenant SaaS applications. In: Ralyté, J., Franch, X., Brinkkemper, S., Wrycza, S. (eds.) CAiSE 2012. LNCS, vol. 7328, pp. 175–189. Springer, Heidelberg (2012)
22. Alférez, G.H., Pelechano, V., Mazo, R., Salinesi, C., Diaz, D.: Dynamic adaptation of service compositions with variability models. J. Syst. Softw. **91**, 24–47 (2014). ISSN 0164-1212
23. Resnick, P., Zeckhauser, P.: Trust among strangers in internet transactions: empirical analysis of eBay's reputation system. Adv. Microeconomics Res. Ann. **11**, 127–157 (2002)

24. Ruohomaa, S., Kutvonen, L., Koutrouli, E.: Reputation management survey. In: The Second International Conference on Availability, Reliability and Security, ARES 2007, pp. 103–111 (2007)
25. Jøsang, A., Ismail, R., Boyd, C.: A survey of trust and reputation systems for online service provision. Decis. Support Syst. **43**(2), 618–644 (2007)
26. Mármol, F.G., Pérez, G.M.: Towards pre-standardization of trust and reputation models for distributed and heterogeneous systems. Comput. Stan. Interfaces **32**(4), 185–196 (2010)
27. Noorian, Z., Ulieru, M.: The state of the art in trust and reputation systems: a framework for comparison. J. Theor. Appl. Electron. Commer. Res. **5**(2), 97–117 (2010)
28. Sänger, J., Pernul, G.: Reusability for trust and reputation systems. In: Zhou, J., Gal-Oz, N., Zhang, J., Gudes, E. (eds.) Trust Management VIII. IFIP AICT, vol. 430, pp. 28–43. Springer, Heidelberg (2014)
29. Hendrikx, F., Bubendorfer, K., Chard, R.: Reputation systems: a survey and taxonomy. J. Parallel Distrib. Comput. **75**, 184–197 (2015). ISSN 0743-7315
30. Vavilis, S., Petković, M., Zannone, N.: A reference model for reputation systems. Decis. Support Syst. **61**, 147–154 (2014). ISSN 0167-9236
31. Costagliola, G., Fuccella, V., Pascuccio, F.A.: Towards a trust, reputation and recommendation meta model. J. Vis. Lang. Comput. **25**(6), 850–857 (2014). ISSN 1045-926X
32. Liang, Z., Shi, W.: Performance evaluation of rating aggregation algorithms in reputation systems. In: Collaborative Computing: Networking, Applications and Worksharing, San Jose, CA (2005)
33. Moyano, F., Gago, M.C.F., Lopez, J.: A framework for enabling trust requirements in social cloud applications. Requir. Eng. **18**(4), 321–341 (2013)
34. Mietzner, R., Leymann, F.: Generation of BPEL customization processes for SaaS applications from variability descriptors. In: Proceedings of the 2008 IEEE International Conference on Services Computing, vol. 2, pp. 359–366. IEEE Computer Society, Washington, DC (2008)
35. Pohl, K., Böckle, G., van der Linden, F.: Software Product Line Engineering: Foundations, Principles and Techniques. Springer, Heidelberg (2005)
36. Hillebrand, C., Coetzee, M.: Moving reputation to the cloud. SAIEE Afr. Res. J. **105**(2) (2014)

Trust and Privacy Issues in Mobile Environments

Attacking GSM Networks as a Script Kiddie Using Commodity Hardware and Software

Christoforos Ntantogian[1(✉)], Grigoris Valtas[1], Nikos Kapetanakis[1],
Faidon Lalagiannis[1], Georgios Karopoulos[2], and Christos Xenakis[1]

[1] Department of Digital Systems, University of Piraeus, Piraeus, Greece
{dadoyan, xenakis}@unipi.gr,
{gregbaltas, nickkap, flalagiannhs}@ssl-unipi.gr
[2] Department of Informatics and Telecommunications,
University of Athens, Athens, Greece
gkarop@di.uoa.gr

Abstract. With the emergence of widely available hardware and software tools for GSM hacking, the security of cellular networks is threatened even by script kiddies. In this paper we present four different attacks in GSM networks, using commodity hardware as well as open source and freely available software tools. All attacks are performed using a common DVB-T TV tuner, which is used as a sniffer for the GSM radio interface, as well as an Arduino combined with a GSM shield that is used as a software programmable mobile phone. The attacks target both mobile users and the network, ranging from sniffing the signaling traffic to tracking and performing denial of service to the subscribers. Despite the script kiddie style of the attacks, their consequences are critical and threaten the normal operation of the cellular networks.

Keywords: Mobile networks · GSM hacking · Script kiddie · Software Defined Radio · Arduino

1 Introduction

Today, Long Term Evolution (LTE) is being deployed in all regions, and subscriptions for this technology are predicted to reach 2.6 billion by 2019 [1]. Despite the proliferation and rapid migration to 4G networks, mainly in developed markets, GSM remains the dominant cellular technology in many countries. In fact GSM-only subscriptions represent the largest share of mobile subscriptions today [5]. As most new LTE devices are backwards compatible to GSM, the latter will not be replaced, but rather complement 3G and 4G connectivity, operating as a fallback mechanism.

The security of GSM networks has been extensively analyzed in the literature. Many works have pinpointed the fact that the GSM security is based on some arbitrary trust assumptions that malicious actors can violate and attack both mobile users and the network [2]. However, a common limitation of the previous works lies to the fact that the discovered vulnerabilities and attacks were presented and analyzed in a theoretical manner, thus their feasibility is questionable. This can be attributed to the closed nature of the GSM industry players including the phone manufacturers, baseband vendors and infrastructure equipment suppliers, which do not release specifications of their products.

© Springer International Publishing Switzerland 2015
S. Fischer-Hübner et al. (Eds.): TrustBus 2015, LNCS 9264, pp. 73–86, 2015.
DOI: 10.1007/978-3-319-22906-5_6

Additionally, the hardware and software to perform practical experiments to GSM networks were very expensive or they were available only to mobile operators to assess their network. This situation was beneficiary for the mobile operators, since they were not pressured to enhance their provided level of security despite the discovered vulnerabilities.

In the last years, radio communications systems based on Software Defined Radio (SDR) as well as open-source micro controller boards have been emerged, allowing anyone to perform experiments in GSM networks in a cost-effective and flexible manner. These low-cost and widely available hardware/software systems can become a powerful tool at the hands of malicious actors, introducing an asymmetric threat to mobile operators, since anyone, including script kiddies, can use them to disrupt the normal operation of a mobile network. Driven by this observation, this paper presents four different attacks in GSM networks using commodity hardware as well as open source and freely available software tools. The main equipment of our test bed is a common DVB-T TV tuner [15], which is used as a sniffer to the GSM radio interface, as well as an Arduino [6] combined with a GSM shield that is used as a software programmable mobile phone. The above testbed allowed us to perform a variety of attacks targeting the Mobile Station (MS) and the mobile operator. The performed attacks are:

1. Retrieve sensitive data (identities and keys) from the SIM card with the aim of identifying potential issues regarding the security configuration of the mobile operators in Greece.
2. Sniff, capture and analyze paging requests and derive useful observations regarding traffic load, security policies and the number of roaming subscribers for the Greek mobile operators.
3. Perform a stealthy Denial of Service (DoS) attack to a targeted MS. The result of this attack is that the victim MS cannot receive legitimate phone calls, without noticing any suspicious activity.
4. Track MS with a granularity of a cell coverage area.

The simplicity yet effectiveness of our attacks depicts that no security mechanisms are implemented to prevent, block or even monitor malicious activities in cellular mobile networks. We believe that security mechanisms, including firewalls and intrusion detection systems, should be specifically designed and incorporated in mobile networks to increase the provided level of security.

The rest of the paper is organized as follows. Section 2 provides the background presenting the GSM network architecture, the GSM channels as well as the paging procedure, while Sect. 3 includes the related work. Section 4 elaborates on the performed attacks and evaluates their results and impact. Finally, Sect. 5 contains the conclusions.

2 Background

2.1 Architecture

The technology of GSM is based on Time Division Multiple Access (TDMA) transmission methods, while its radio interface operates in the 900 MHz and 1.8 GHz bands in Europe and in 850 MHz and 1.9 GHz in the US. An outline of the GSM architecture is depicted in Fig. 1(a), focusing only on the network elements relevant to this paper [3]. The Mobile Station (MS) comprises the mobile phone and the subscriber identity module (SIM) card and interacts with the Base Transceiver Station (BTS) over the radio interface. Note that in this paper we will use the words MS and subscriber interchangeably. BTS is responsible for the radio coverage of a given geographical area, while the Base Station Controller (BSC) maintains radio connections towards MSs and terrestrial connections towards the fixed part of the network (core network). Both BTS and BSC constitute the Base Station Subsystem (BSS) that controls the GSM radio path. The GSM service area is divided into Location Areas (LAs), where each LA includes one or more radio cells. Every LA and radio cell has a unique identifier named Location Area Code (LAC) and Cell-ID, respectively.

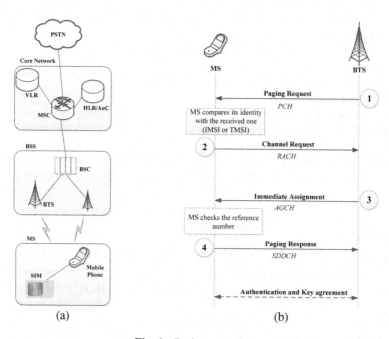

Fig. 1. Paging procedure

The GSM Core Network mainly includes the Home Location Register/Authentication Centre (HLR/AuC), the Visitor Location Register (VLR) and the Mobile Service Switching Centre (MSC). HLR/AuC is a database used for the management of permanent data of mobile users and also maintains security information related to subscribers' identity. VLR is a database of the service area visited by an MS and contains all the related information required for the MS service handling. MSC is a network element responsible for circuit-switched services and provides connectivity to the Public Switched Telephone Network (PSTN).

2.2   GSM Physical and Logical Channels

GSM uses a variety of channels to carry information over the air interface [4], which are broadly divided in two categories: (i) physical and (ii) logical. A physical channel is determined by one or more carrier frequencies, including the hopping sequence and the time slot, while a logical channel is characterized by the information carried within the physical channel. Logical channels are used to carry both data and signaling load and, therefore, can be separated into: (i) traffic and (ii) signaling channels. Traffic channels transmit voice and data packets, while signaling channels carry control information allowing the system to operate correctly. The most important GSM signaling channels that are related to this work are:

- **Broadcast Control Channel (BCCH):** A broadcast downlink channel that repeats system information messages that contain the identity, configuration and available features of the BTS (e.g., Cell-ID, Location Area Identifier that includes the LAC, list of neighboring cells, etc.).
- **Paging Channel (PCH):** A downlink channel used by the BTS to locate and identify an MS.
- **Random Access Channel (RACH):** A shared uplink channel used by MSs to request dedicated channels from the BTS.
- **Access Grant Control Channel (AGCH):** A downlink channel used by the BTS to assign dedicated control channel to MSs in response to the related channel requests received on the RACH.
- **Standalone Dedicated Control Channel (SDCCH):** An uplink and downlink channel employed for call setup, SMS delivery and signaling exchange between BTS and MS.

2.3   Paging

The delivery of GSM services (voice call, SMS, etc.) to a mobile phone, requires from the MSC to discover the exact location of the respective MS, by performing the procedure of paging. First, the core network interrogates the HLR of the target MS to identify which MSC/VLR serves it. Next, the underlying MSC obtains from the employed VLR the LA of the destination MS, and, then it forwards a paging message to all the BSCs of the considered LA. This message includes a list of Cell-IDs and base stations identifiers that constitute the specific LA, where the MS resides [4], as well as the identity of the MS either in the form of International Mobile Subscriber Identity (IMSI) or Temporary Mobile Subscriber Identity (TMSI). TMSI, as its name implies, is a temporary identity (i.e., pseudonym) that provides anonymity.

At this point, the BSC sends a paging command message to all BTSs of the considered LA, which in turn they forward a paging request message to the downlink PCH (see step 1-Fig. 1(b)). Each MS that receives this request compares its own identity with the one that was included in the message. If these match for a specific MS, then the latter sends a channel request that includes a random reference number using the uplink RACH (step 2- Fig. 1(b)). Upon receiving this message, the corresponding BTS allocates radio resources and a dedicated channel, acknowledges the request, and sends the details of the allocated channel to the MS using an immediate assignment message on the AGCH downlink (step 3-Fig. 1(b)). This message also contains the random reference that was included in the respective channel request message of the previous step. Upon receiving this assignment, the MS compares the contained random reference (i.e., with the one sent in the channel request) and if the comparison is true, the MS tunes to the dedicated signaling channel that is assigned by the respective assignment message. At this point, the MS establishes a signaling link over SDCCH and sends a paging response message (step 4-Fig. 1(b)). After this, an authentication and key agreement procedure takes place, but the details of this procedure are omitted, since it is irrelevant to this work.

The GSM specifications [4] specify three types of paging requests (i.e., type 1, 2, and 3) which are related to the number of subscribers that can be addressed with a single procedure. More specifically, type 1 can page one or two subscribers, type 2 two or three subscribers, and type 3 four subscribers at once. Finally, it is important to notice that all of the above messages are transmitted in clear text, which means that an adversary can trivially sniff and eavesdrop on them for malicious purposes, as we analyze below.

3 Related Work

In this section, we present the related work focusing on papers that elaborate on discovered attacks in GSM networks from a practical viewpoint. [12] showed that GSM networks leak enough information that an adversary can exploit to track a mobile user. In particular, the authors proposed several methods to check whether a user is present within a small area, or absent from a large area, simply by listening to the broadcast GSM channels. The necessary information was available simply by dialing the number of the target subscriber and aborting the call, before the cell phone rings to avoid detection. To demonstrate the practicality of this, the authors performed location tracking experiments to specific mobile operators. They were able to track down a cellular device within a 10-block area in Minneapolis, using a T-Mobile G1 smart-phone and a modified OsmocomBB firmware [7], which is a free open-source GSM baseband software implementation. However, it is important to mention that osmo-comBB supports old phones (that don't have an application CPU, but only a modem) and also requires a computer.

Recently, a novel DoS attack was presented in [11]. This attack exploits a race condition where an adversary can attempt to answer to a paging request faster than the intended subscriber. If he/she succeeds to do this, then the BTS ignores the paging response of the intended victim subscriber, which receives a channel release message from the network. In this way, an effective DoS is achieved to the victim subscriber, since he/she cannot answer an incoming call. To demonstrate the feasibility of this attack, the authors modified the osmocomBB firmware [7].

In [13], the authors, quantitatively, characterize a distributed DoS attack to an HLR/AuC, coordinated by a botnet of infected mobile devices. This work provides numerical estimations for various parameters to successfully perform the attack, such as the required number of infected mobile phones, the rate of flooding messages, the service requests and network operations that incur the greatest burden to the HLR/AuC, etc. It identifies that the insert/delete call forwarding requests, which allow a user to redirect incoming phone calls to other devices, are the most suitable, from an attacker perspective, to flood the HLR/AuC. It reveals that the registration procedure is not so effective to flood the HLR/AuC, due to the caching mechanism of authentication vectors in the serving MSC. That is, during an MS registration, the serving MSC may provide to the MS an authentication vector already stored from a previous authentication data request, meaning that the MSC does not have to perform a request to the home HLR/AuC. Finally, the authors have estimated the throughput reduction of an HLR/AuC under DoS attack, using insert call forwarding requests.

The work in [14] presented some design and implementation weaknesses in the TMSI reallocation procedure that allow the identification and/or tracking of mobile subscribers. Using experimental and formal analysis, the authors concluded that the TMSI reallocation procedure is vulnerable to a linkability attack, when the same keys are used to encrypt it. Moreover, they have proposed countermeasures to address the identified security issues.

Finally, in our previous work [8], we have performed practical experiments in which we identified and proved some zero-day vulnerabilities of the 3G network that can be exploited by malicious actors to mount various attacks. Specifically, based on the observations of the conducted experiments, we have revealed an Advanced Persistent Threat (APT) in 3G networks that aims to flood an HLR/AuC of a mobile operator. In this attack, a group of adversaries first collect IMSIs that belong to the same HLR/AuC. Next, residing in roaming networks, they perform successive registrations using the collected IMSIs that trigger the execution of authentication requests to the specific HLR/AuC. The continuous execution of authentication requests, in a very short period of time, incurs the depletion of the computational resources of the HLR/AuC, eventually leading to system saturation. To this end, a mobile application was implemented that performs continuous network registrations using AT commands. The application utilizes the dial command to initiate phone calls using a different IMSI for each call request. This was achieved by employing a device named simtrace [10], which acts as an active man-in-the-middle between the modem and SIM/USIM card changing the IMSI identity, when it is requested by the modem.

4 Practical Attacks in GSM Networks

4.1 Testbed

Our performed attacks were based on a testbed that is exclusively composed of commodity and off-the-shelf hardware and software tools, which are affordable and widely available. The total cost of the equipment was around 100 Euro and the most important components of the testbed are:

- **RTL-SDR/DVB-T TV Tuner 15(€10):** This is a cheap wideband SDR scanner based on a DVB-T TV-Tuner USB dongle. RTL-SDR is broadband (60 MHz to 1700 MHz) and it is capable of sniffing GSM signals as well as Receiving/Decoding GPS signals. RTL-SDR requires the GNU Radio, which is a software development toolkit that provides signal processing blocks to implement software radios and signal processing systems. It is important to notice that RTL-SDR is able to capture only the GSM downlink traffic (BTS to MS), but not the uplink traffic (MS to BTS).

- **Arduino (€20) and GSM Shield 6(€70):** Arduino is an open-source electronics prototyping platform, based on a programmable microcontroller. The functionality of an Arduino board can be easily extended using interchangeable add-on modules, known as shields. One such shield is the GSM shield, which allows an Arduino board to connect to the internet, make/receive voice calls and send/receive SMS messages, using the GSM modem.
- **Open-Source Software Tools:** Our testbed includes various open source and free software tools including: (i) Airprobe for protocol parsing and decoding; (ii) Wireshark for packet analysis, and, (iii) Kalibrate which scans for GSM BTSs in a given frequency band. It is important to mention that all the above tools are available in the Linux operating system.

4.2   Retrieving Security Parameters of Mobile Networks

In this attack, we retrieve sensitive data (identities and keys) from the SIM card with the aim of identifying potential issues regarding the security configuration of the mobile operators. To achieve this, we use the Arduino combined with the GSM shield to simulate a MS. Overall, we have conducted three experiments in total. In the first one, we estimated how often the Kc key is renewed. In the second, we measure how frequently the TMSI identity of a static user (i.e., a MS located in the same LA) is reallocated. And, finally, in the third experiment, we performed a war-driving, in order to estimate how frequently the TMSI of a mobile user (i.e., a MS that changes its LA) is reallocated. All experiments took place at the city of Athens and the three Greek mobile operators: Vodafone, Wind and Cosmote. To carry out the experiments, we have developed custom scripts for Arduino in C ++ programming language, which automate the following procedures: (i) initiate and terminate voice calls repeatedly, (ii) restart periodically the phone, and, (iii) retrieve important parameters from the SIM card including Kc, TMSI, IMSI, LAC and Cell-ID. The custom scripts that we have developed perform the above three procedures by means of AT commands [9], which provide various operations to control a GSM modem. The specific AT commands used in our custom scripts are analyzed in [21].

In the first experiment (see Table 1), we observed that Vodafone updates the Kc key every 16 voice calls, while Wind every 6 voice calls. Cosmote performs Kc updates, arbitrarily, and we didn't identified any specific pattern. For this reason, we computed an average value that is approximately every 10 voice calls. It is evident that a mobile network should update the Kc key as frequent as possible; otherwise, its subscribers are exposed to several threats including interception of phone calls and impersonation for longer time periods and thus, with higher impacts [16]. Unfortunately, the obtained numerical results show that mobile operators in Greece do not refresh the encryption key for every voice call. In the second experiment (i.e., TMSI reallocations for static users), we observed that both Vodafone and Wind do not change the TMSIs of their static users (see Table 2). On the other hand, Cosmote reallocated the TMSI with a new

Table 1. Rate of Kc keys renewals for each mobile operator

Operator	Kc renewal rate
Vodafone	16 voice calls
Wind	6 voice calls
Cosmote	10 voice calls (on average)

Table 2. TMSI values assigned to static users

Cosmote TMSI	Vodafone TMSI	Wind TMSI
23B9C7A8	701590D9	A8B32A7A
23BA25D0	701590D9	A8B32A7A
23BA82D0	701590D9	A8B32A7A
23BAE940	701590D9	A8B32A7A
23BB46B0	701590D9	A8B32A7A
23BBADE8	701590D9	A8B32A7A
23BC0A98	701590D9	A8B32A7A
23BC7448	701590D9	A8B32A7A
23BCD8B0	701590D9	A8B32A7A
23BD4298	701590D9	A8B32A7A
23BDB418	701590D9	A8B32A7A
23BE15D8	701590D9	A8B32A7A
23BE74B0	701590D9	A8B32A7A
23BED9C8	701590D9	A8B32A7A

incremented value (without any specific pattern). It is alarming that both Vodafone and Wind do not perform periodic TMSI reallocation for static users. This means that as long as the mobile subscribers stay in the same location/routing area (i.e., office building, home, etc.) and use their phones, they will have the same temporary identities. This configuration is very weak, because the same TMSI is used for every call/SMS request, allowing an adversary to easily identify and track a user.

Finally, in the third experiment (i.e., TMSI reallocations for mobile users), we observed as shown in Table 3 that each time a user changes its LA, then Vodafone and Cosmote reallocate the TMSIs with a new value. On the other hand, Wind does not update the TMSI, exposing its subscribers. Thus, if an adversary establishes passive devices that sniff the cellular signaling (e.g., like the RTL-SDR/TV-tuner) at the borders of LA, he/she may easily track the movements of almost all the subscribers of Wind.

Table 3. TMSI values assigned to mobile users that change LA

Vodafone		Cosmote		Wind	
LAC	TMSI	LAC	TMSI	LAC	TMSI
004A	4921B2CF	0025	12A83908	3908	58B315A2
0016	18242A12	0020	14A9E4B8	29CC	58B315A2
0025	4823F122	0021	15AF0E08	2744	58B315A2

4.3   Capturing Paging Requests

In this attack we use the RTL-SDR/TV tuner and the Kalibrate tool to sniff, capture and analyze paging requests in a specific LA. In particular, for each one of the Greek mobile operators, we captured paging requests messages from the downlink traffic (i.e., from BTS to MS) and we analyzed them using Wireshark. The latter can correctly decode GSM control packets, allowing us to extract TMSI and IMSI identities from the paging requests.

Figure 2(a) plots the number of paging requests that include either an IMSI or a TMSI during one day in a specific LA. Paging activity varies throughout the time of the day (which is the same for all operators), reflecting human activity. We can point out that during midday the traffic greatly increases reaching its highest point in 14:00 for all mobile operators. Moreover, in Fig. 2(b) we show the percentage of paging requests that include IMSIs or TMSIs versus the total number of paging requests in a specific LA. Ideally, an IMSI should never be transmitted, because a possible attacker can easily read it, as it is conveyed in plaintext. We notice that Cosmote uses IMSIs in a whopping 19 % of paging requests, while Wind and Vodafone in 8.04 % in 3.02 % respectively. On the other hand, Cosmote uses TMSIs 81 % of paging requests, while Wind and Vodafone in 91.96 % in 96.98 % respectively. It is clear that Cosmote follows a poor policy regarding the privacy of MS, since on average one IMSI is exposed in every five paging requests. Due to the loss of mobile subscribers' anonymity, an attacker may achieve to identify and track them. Mobile identities are currently used by market research companies, such as those referred in [17, 18], in order to track the movements of visitors within a specific place (e.g., shopping malls, exhibition centers, etc.). These companies identify and track subscribers to collect information on the shopping habits without their consent, while usually they share the tracking information with third parties to maximize profit [19].

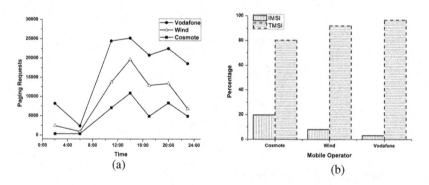

Fig. 2. Paging requests vs. time in a specific LA

An advantageous characteristic of GSM is its international roaming capability, allowing users to seamlessly access the same services when traveling abroad. To this end, we have analyzed the obtained IMSIs to find roaming subscribers as well their foreign mobile operators. Based on this analysis, we can get informed about the different roaming agreements that the Greek Mobile operators have. This information was obtained using the mobile country code (MCC), which is the first three digits of the IMSI followed by the mobile network code (MNC), which is 2 digits or 3 digits. As shown in Table 4, most roaming subscribers of Cosmote are from Germany with the Telecom/T-Mobile mobile operator. For Vodafone, most roaming subscribers are from Turkey with the Vodafone-Telsim mobile operator. Finally, Wind has roaming subscribers mainly from Philippines with Smart mobile operator (see Table 5). It is interesting to mention that there are foreign operators that have roaming agreements with two different Greek mobile operators at the same time. For example, we have discovered IMSIs of the Vodafone-Telsim operator from both Vodafone and Cosmote.

Table 4. Cosmote and Vodafone roaming subscribers

Cosmote			Vodafone		
Subscribers	Country	Operator	Subscribers	Country	Operator
174	Germany	Telecom/T-Mobile	17	Turkey	Vodafone-Telsim
22	Turkey	AVEA/Aria	5	Turkey	AVEA/Aria
20	Finland	TeliaSonera	5	UK	O2 Ltd.
14	Turkey	Vodafone-Telsim	4	Denmark	Telia
10	Austria	T-Mobile/Telering	3	South Africa	Vodacom
9	Czech Republic	T-Mobile/RadioMobile	3	UK	Vodafone
7	Egypt	Vodafone	2	USA	T-Mobile

Table 5. Wind roaming subscribers

Wind		
Subscribers	Country	Operator
9	Philippines	Smart
2	Brazil	Vivo S.A./Telemig
2	Russia	VimpelCom
2	Netherlands	Vodafone Libertel
1	Venezuela	Movistar/TelCel
1	USA	AT&T Wireless Inc.
1	Albania	Vodafone

4.4   A Stealthy Denial of Service Attack to MS

In this attack, we use the Arduino microcontroller combined with the GSM shield to perform a DoS to a targeted MS where the latter can no longer receive any legitimate phone call. The attack vector is simple yet effective. That is, we continuously call the mobile phone of the targeted MS. As a result, the mobile phone of the targeted MS is always occupied (due to the multiple calls) and legitimate calls to the mobile phone cannot be performed. The key characteristic of this attack is that it is performed in a stealthy manner in the sense that the victim MS cannot identify that he/she is under attack, because the phone does not actually ring.

To better understand how we perform the attack and achieve to keep occupied a phone without ringing, consider the time sequence of Fig. 3, which shows three events that occur successively: (1) phone dialing, (2) paging request and (3) phone ringing. More specifically, at time t0 suppose that we dial the phone number that we want to perform a call (see Fig. 3). At time t1, assume that the related paging request is transmitted from the BTS to the phone. Notice that from time t1 and afterwards, the phone is occupied meaning that all other paging requests initiated from other calls to the phone are rejected. Moreover, as shown in Fig. 3, the phone ringing occurs at time t2. We have experimentally estimated the time differences between the three events shown in Fig. 3. That is, we have estimated that the elapsed time between the dialing of the phone number and the paging request is on average 3 s (t1-t0 = 3 s.), while the elapsed time between the paging request and the actual phone ringing is on average 2.5 s (t2-t1 = 2.5 s.). Thus, the total time from the moment that a phone number is dialed until the phone actually rings is on average 5.5 s (t2-t0 = 5.5 s.).

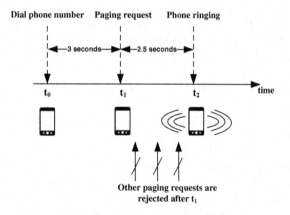

Fig. 3. Time sequence of a call setup

We have exploited the above observations to perform a stealthy DoS attack. That is, we have developed a custom script for Arduino based on AT commands, which repeatedly calls a mobile phone, and after L seconds terminates the call. Evidently, the value of L should be less than 5.5 s (i.e., L < 5.5), in order to avoid phone ringing (see Fig. 3). In this way, we can achieve to occupy a targeted phone by continuously dialing and terminating calls, without however actually ringing the phone. As a result, the victim (i.e., the owner of the phone) cannot become aware of the attack, since no call activity occurs in his/her phone. It is important to mention that the attacker's repetitive calls are not shown in the targeted phone as missed calls.

The focal point of this attack is that an adversary equipped with commodity hardware, like Arduino, can perform a DoS to a MS, simply, by performing continuous phone calls. The simplicity of this attack depicts the alarming fact that no security mechanisms are implemented to block or mitigate this kind of DoS attacks in cellular networks.

4.5   Users Location Area Leakage

Lastly, we demonstrate an attack for user tracking with a granularity of a radio cell coverage area using the Arduino and the GSM shield as well as the RTL-SDR/TV tuner. The only prerequisite for this attack is that the adversary knows the mobile phone number of the targeted MS that wants to geographically track. It is important to mention that the adversary is capable to sniff only the downlink channel of GSM, due to the limitations of the RTL-SDR/TV tuner (see Sect. 4.1). The attack consists of two sequential phases. In the first phase, the adversary locates the LA (i.e., a wide area network segment served by a group of BTSs), where the MS resides. Then, in the second phase the adversary tries to locate the respective MS in the geographic area of a radio cell. More specifically, the attack is performed as follows.

Phase A: Discover the Current LA of the MS. Assume that the adversary wants to discover whether the targeted MS resides in a specific LA that we name it as LA_X. This phase includes 3 steps.

1. The adversary resides in the coverage area of a randomly chosen BTS of the LA_X. Using Arduino and the GSM shield, the adversary performs k consecutive phone calls to the targeted MS (we elaborate below on the exact value of k). To avoid raising suspicions, the adversary may use the same technique as in the previous attack (i.e., stealthy DoS attack to MS) exploiting the delay between the paging and phone ringing. That is, the MS receives paging requests, but the calls are terminated before the phone rings.
2. At the same time, the adversary captures the downlink traffic of the BTS that resides using the RTL-SDL/TV tuner.
3. After steps 1 and 2 of phase A, the adversary analyzes the captured packets of the downlink traffic using Wireshark. If the adversary discovers k paging requests that include the same IMSI or TMSI, he/she may infer that both (i.e., the targeted MS and the adversary) are located in the same LA (i.e., LA_X). This can be justified as follows. First recall from Sect. 2.3, that paging requests are broadcast messages conveyed in plaintext and used as an identifier the IMSI or TMSI of the MS. Recall also that during an incoming call to a MS, the mobile network instructs all BTSs of the LA that MS resides in, to broadcast paging requests. Therefore, if the targeted MS is indeed in the same LA with the adversary (i.e., LA_X), then all the BTSs of LA_X (including the BTS that the adversary captured the downlink traffic) will broadcast k paging requests with the IMSI or TMSI of the targeted MS. This means that if the adversary discovers k paging requests, which were performed during the k calls in step 1, he/she can deduce that a MS resides in LA_X.

Phase B: Discover the Current Radio Cell That MS is Located. The adversary now knows that MS resides in LA_X. Based on this information, in this phase the adversary now wants to identify in which specific cell of LA_X the targeted MS resides.

1. The adversary resides in the coverage area of a randomly chosen BTS of the LA_X. The adversary repeats steps 1 and 2 in a randomly selected radio cell of the identified LA. Similarly to step 1 of phase A, the adversary performs z consecutive calls to the targeted MS.

2. Similar to step 2 of phase A, the adversary captures the downlink traffic using the RTL-SDL/TV tuner.
3. The adversary now investigates the captured packets. If the adversary discovers z immediate assignments messages to the targeted MS (we elaborate below on the exact value of z), then he/she can infer that both (i.e., the adversary and the targeted MS) are located within the same radio cell. This can be justified as follows: Recall that immediate assignment messages are transmitted from BTS to MS, only when the latter is included in the coverage area of the former, and includes the description of the dedicated channel to be used for authentication and cipher negotiation. Therefore, the discovery of z immediate assignment messages to the MS indicates that the MS and the adversary are located in the same cell.
4. If the adversary does not find z immediate assignments, then he/she can repeat step 1 and 2 using another BTS of the LA_X.

To prove the feasibility of this attack and estimate the numerical values of the parameters k and z, we have performed experiments in a mobile operator. The experiments were conducted in low traffic load hours (i.e., nightly hours) in order not to overload the channel and disrupt the normal operation of the network. In order to distinguish our paging requests with legitimate ones, we have experimentally found that the minimum number of consecutive calls for phase A should be 80 (i.e., $k = 80$). Regarding phase B, we have experimentally found that the minimum number of consecutive calls should be 100 (i.e., $z = 100$).

5 Conclusions

This paper elaborated on four different attacks in GSM networks using commodity hardware and open source tools. The described attacks can be performed by script kiddies and include:

1. Retrieve sensitive data (identities and keys) from the SIM card with the aim of identifying potential issues regarding the security configuration of the mobile operators in Greece.
2. Sniff, capture and analyze paging requests and derive useful observations regarding traffic load, security policies and the number of roaming subscribers for the Greek mobile operators.
3. Perform a stealthy Denial of Service (DoS) attack to a targeted MS. The result of this attack is that the victim MS cannot receive legitimate phone calls, without noticing any suspicious activity.
4. Track MS with a granularity of a cell coverage area.

We have experimentally proved the feasibility of each one of these attacks using a common DVB-T TV tuner as well as an Arduino microcontroller combined with its GSM shield. The simplicity yet effectiveness of our attacks depicts that no security mechanisms are implemented to prevent, block or even monitor malicious activities in cellular mobile networks. We believe that security mechanisms, such as firewalls and intrusion detection systems described in [20], should be specifically designed and incorporated in cellular mobile networks to increase the provided level of security.

Acknowledgements. This research has been funded by the European Commission as part of the SMART-NRG project (FP7-PEOPLE-2013-IAPP Grant number 612294).

References

1. Ericsson mobility report, June 2014. http://www.ericsson.com/res/docs/2014/ericsson-mobility-report-june-2014.pdf
2. Xenakis, C.: Malicious actions against the GPRS technology. Comput. Virol. **2**(2), 121–133 (2006)
3. 3GPP TS 03.6 (V7.9.0), GPRS Service Description, Stage 2, September 2002
4. 3GPP TS 04.01 V8.0.0 – Mobile Station - Base Station System (MS - BSS) interface; General aspects and principles, March 2000. http://www.3gpp.org/ftp/Specs/html-info/37801.htm
5. The mobile economy, GSMA (2014)
6. Arduino: The Open Source Electronics Platform. http://arduino.cc
7. The osmocombb project – open source gsm baseband software implementation. http://bb.osmocom.org/
8. Xenakis, C., Ntantogian, C.: An advanced persistent threat in 3G networks: attacking the home network from roaming networks. Comput. Secur. **40**(1), 84–94 (2014)
9. 3GPP TS 27.007 V11.5.0 (2012-12), 3rd Generation Partnership Project, Technical Specification Group Core Network and Terminals, AT command set for User Equipment (UE) (Release 11)
10. Simtrace. http://bb.osmocom.org/trac/wiki/SIMtrace
11. Golde, N., Redon, K., Seifert, J.-P.: Let me answer that for you: exploiting broadcast information in cellular networks. In: 22nd USENIX Conference on Security, Washington DC, USA, August 2013
12. Kune, D.F., Koelndorfer, J., Hopper, N., Kim, Y.: Location leaks on the GSM air interface. In: Network and Distributed System Security Symposium (NDSS), San Diego, California, USA (2012)
13. Traynor, P., Lin, M., Ongtang, M., Rao, V., Jaeger, T., McDaniel, P.D., La Porta, T.F.: On cellular botnets: measuring the impact of malicious devices on a cellular network core. In: ACM Conference on Computer and Communications Security, pp. 223–234 (2009)
14. Arapinis, M., Mancini, L.I., Ritter, E., Ryan, M.: Privacy through pseudonymity in mobile telephony systems. In: 21st Network and Distributed System Security Symposium (NDSS), California, USA (2014)
15. http://www.rtl-sdr.com/
16. Nohl, K.: Attacking Phone Privacy. BlackHat, USA, Las Vegas (2010)
17. http://www.pathintelligence.com
18. http://www.smart-flows.com
19. http://www.theregister.co.uk/2012/01/11/phone_tracking_expert/
20. Lee, P.P.C., Bu, T., Woo, T.Y.C.: On the detection of signaling DoS attacks on 3G/WiMax wireless networks. Comput. Netw. **53**(15), 2601–2616 (2009)
21. Xenakis, C., Ntantogian, C.: Attacking the baseband modem of mobile phones to breach the users' privacy and network security. In: 7th International Conference on Cyber Conflict (CyCon 2015), Tallinn, Estonia, May 2015

On the Efficacy of Static Features to Detect Malicious Applications in Android

Dimitris Geneiatakis[1]([⊠]), Riccardo Satta[2], Igor Nai Fovino[2],
and Riccardo Neisse[2]

[1] Electrical and Computer Engineering Department,
Aristotle University of Thessaloniki, GR541 24 Thessaloniki, Greece
`dgeneiat@auth.gr`
[2] European Commission, Joint Research Centre (JRC),
Institute for the Protection and Security of the Citizen (IPSC),
Via Enrico Fermi 2749, 21027 Ispra, Italy

Abstract. The Android OS environment is today increasingly targeted
by malwares. Traditional signature based detection algorithms are not
able to provide complete protection especially against ad-hoc created malwares. In this paper, we present a feasibility analysis for enhancing the
detection accuracy on Android malware for approaches relying on machine
learning classifiers and Android applications' static features. Specifically,
our study builds on the basis of machine learning classifiers operating over
different fusion rules on Android applications' permissions and APIs. We
analyse the performance of different configurations in terms of false alarms
tradeoff. Results demonstrate that malware detection accuracy could be
enhanced in case that detection approaches introduce additional fusion
rules *e.g.,* squared average score over the examined features.

1 Introduction

Android is the dominant operating system for mobile devices; it currently has
the largest installed base [14] mainly because (a) it supports a huge variety
of different devices such as watches, tablets, TV sets, *etc.*, and (b) it provides
to end-users a large variety of applications for accomplishing their daily needs
through its official market. Its large diffusion and the fact that it is used for
every day end-user digital tasks attracted in recent years the attention of malicious developers/hackers which started to target this operating system. Even
if Google bouncer [1] scrutinises applications before allowing them to be published in Google-Play, there are evidences [2] showing that yet among legitimate
applications one can found malicious software (malware) as well. In most of the
cases, the target of malware for Android is the access to sensitive resources *e.g.,*
personal data, phone billing system, geo-location, home banking info, *etc.*

Android builds a part of its security on a *"permission restricted access model"*
on sensitive sources (*e.g.,* sd card, contacts). This means that applications, to
gain access to such resources, should declare in the manifest the appropriate
permissions, which users should grant during the installation. However, in such

© Springer International Publishing Switzerland 2015
S. Fischer-Hübner et al. (Eds.): TrustBus 2015, LNCS 9264, pp. 87–98, 2015.
DOI: 10.1007/978-3-319-22906-5_7

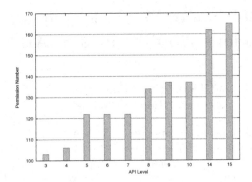

Fig. 1. Android permission evolution.

a model applications might "manipulate" the requested permissions and gain access to private information, without users' consent at all. A typical example is that of those applications that request more permissions than what they actually need, named as over-privileged [9,10]. Such applications can be transformed silently into malware, whenever an operating system or an application update occurs (privilege escalation through updating (pileup) [27]).

Furthermore, Android OS permission number expansion from its first version (100 permissions) to the latest version (170), as Fig. 1 illustrates, is indeed making, in a way, larger the attack surface exposed to an adversary. Thus, we believe that permissions and other related information (*i.e.,* APIs) residing in applications should be considered as an important information source for detecting malicious applications. In this paper, we introduce an analysis approach to enhance the performance of anomaly machine learning based techniques used to assess whether an application is malicious or not, on the basis of applications permission related information, elaborating on previous research works [3,5,26] in the direction of achieving higher accuracy.

To do so, we employ a feature extraction tool based on Dexpler [7] and Soot framework [24], and we study the behavior of different supervised machine learning classifiers *i.e.,* k-NN, SVM and AdaBoost, experimenting under different score-level fusion rules combining applications' APIs and permission features. We assess the capability of our approach to detect malicious applications, and study the trade-off between False Positive Ratio (FPR) and False Negatives (FNR), based on a sample of 300 legitimate applications downloaded from Google market, and 1400 malware applications published in [31]. Results show the effectiveness of our approach and motivate further research in utilizing both permissions and APIs to detect malicious applications.

The main contributions of our work can be summarized as follows:

- We show the effectiveness of combining Android application static features with different fusion rules in order to improve malware detection accuracy.
- We evaluate our approach against a number of well-known legitimate and malicious applications.

– We provide the data set and our code as open source tool[1]. This will facilitate additional experimentation with our approach and the validation of our outcomes.

The rest of the paper is structured as follows. In Sect. 2 we overview the related work focusing on permission based malware detection models while we present Android's security model in Sect. 3. In Sect. 4 we describe our approach for assessing applications' maliciousness, while in Sect. 5 we present the experimental outcomes and briefly report on static features observations both for legitimate and malicious applications. Finally, we conclude our work and give some pointers for future directions in Sect. 6.

2 Related Work

In this section, we provide an overview of the scientific literature linked with the approach proposed in this paper.

RiskMon [29] introduces an automated service to assess the security and privacy risk of a given application taking into account legitimate users normal behavior. RiskMon leverages on (a) machine learning and (b) trusted applications different run-time features to build user's legitimate model. RiskRanker [12] detects zero day related Android malware by analysing whether a particular application exhibits dangerous behavior based on static analysis. Droid Analytics [30] develops a solution to scrutinise Android application at the byte code level, and generates the corresponding signatures that can be used by anti-virus software. In the same direction, Shahzad et al. in [23] rely on bi-grams sequences of op-codes retrofitting in machine learning classifiers to detect malware, while Permlyzer [28] analyses application's permission usage based on both static and dynamic analysis. Barrera et al. [6] accomplish a permission analysis based on Self-Organising Map (SOM), while Xuetao et al. [25] study Android's permissions evolution. Other solutions such as Whyper [17] reason about the necessity of requesting an access to specific permission. To do so, Whyper relies on Natural Language Processing (NLP) by extracting information from the keywords and description defined in the application. Similarly, TatWing et al. [33] build a permission based abnormal model leveraging on application description and its permission.

Yajin et al. [32] introduce a tool for the systematic study of applications that might passively leak private information, due to vulnerabilities stemming from built-in Android components, such as read/write operations to content provider. Applications are statically analysed to identify such data flows. Analogously, Liang et al. [16] propose a malware detection engine that relies on the semantic analysis of an examined application. In [22], Sbirlea et al. develop techniques for statically detecting Android application vulnerabilities to attacks aiming at obtaining unauthorised access to permission-protected information.

Complementary to other researches, DroidAPIMiner [3], DREBIN [5] and DroidMat [26] extract APIs and permissions both from malware and legitimate applications, and classify them using well-known machine learning classifiers.

---

[1] http://code.google.com/p/android-permissions-feature-analysis/.

Analogous techniques are followed by [13, 18–21]. The approach we introduce in this work indeed perform very close to DroidMat [26] and DREBIN [5], however, we experimented with additional machine learning classifiers combining also the extracted features to achieve better accuracy. We believe that our work is complementary to existing ones as we focus on improving the accuracy by eliminating false alarms.

3   Android Framework

Android framework builds on a layered architecture (see Fig. 2). The core OS is built on the basis of Linux kernel. A custom virtual machine to optimise memory and hardware resources in a mobile environment operates over the kernel. Every Android application runs in its own VM, protected from other running applications. Libraries facilitates the invocation of basic kernel functionalities by the applications, either directly or through the application framework provided to the developers.

By default applications are not allowed to invoke methods involving "sensitive" resources, unless it has been declared in the application's manifest. In other words, the application's manifest, as Listing 1.1 shows[2], is a repository that includes all the high level declarations to offer access to mobile phone's "sensitive" resources. For example, to access the `getCellLocation()` method, the ACCESS_COARSE_LOCATION permission should be declared by the application, otherwise when an invocation occurs, a security exception will be thrown.

The relation between permissions and methods is not a one-to-one mapping, instead is a one-to-many, meaning that a single permission gives access to many sensitive resources. For instance, the INTERNET permission provides access on behalf of the application to the following methods `getActiveNetworkInfo()`, and `sendData()`.

Applications might manipulate silently this access since the end users have no means to identify which methods are accessed by a given application, as mentioned previously. For that reason we believe that the information related to the permissions granted to a given application is extremely relevant in the malware identification context.

```
<android.permission.CAMERA/>
<android.permission.ACCESS_COARSE_LOCATION/>
<android.permission.INTERNET/>
<android.permission.ACCESS_NETWORK_STATE />
<android.permission.READ_PHONE_STATE/>
<android.permission.READ_CONTACTS/>
<android.permission.VIBRATE/>
<android.permission.WRITE_CALENDAR/>
```

Listing 1.1. An example of a real Android mobile application manifest records. The application requests access to various resources such as *Camera, Internet, Calendar, etc.*

---

[2] The proper syntax is the following: uses-permission android:name=permission-name.

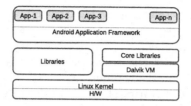

Fig. 2. Android software modular architecture.

4   Machine Learning Malware Identification for Android

In this section we present our approach and the classifiers adopted, while in the following section we will present the experimental results obtained.

4.1   Feature Set

Android applications are distributed and installed through their proprietary Android Application Packages (APKs) containing, among the other things, a manifest file and the application's compiled code. The former includes the permissions requested to access application sensitive resources, while the latter incorporate application's functionality in the form of bytecode. From this set of data, we extract the following features in the direction of exploiting them to detect malicious applications:

– Permissions declared in the manifest.
– Applications APIs.

We model both of these features in one dimension vectors in which we set each vector's element to zero (0) value if the examined application lacks the feature otherwise we set it to one (1). More specifically, for permissions we build a vector which is composed by 197 elements corresponding to the permission' list of Android Software Development Kit (SDK) 17, while APIs vector is composed by 1310 elements considering only the APIs that are related to a permission, on the basis of the permission' map published in [9]. Note that at the current analysis we do not check if the corresponding permission exist in the manifest. As will be showed in Sect. 5, for each application analysed, we extracted the features mentioned and modeled them in the described vectors. These vectors will be then given as input to a set of classifiers, which will be used to discriminate between malicious and licit applications.

4.2   Classifiers

We used three different machine learning algorithms to classify an application as legitimate and malicious based on the Permission and on the API vector separately. We then combined the decisions of the classifiers at score-level, *i.e.,* by merging the two classification scores, using two fusion rules. Classification algorithms and fusion rules are described below.

The first classifier is the well known k-**Nearest Neighbour** (kNN) algorithm [4]. Possibly one of the simplest machine learning algorithms, kNN assigns to an unseen sample the most frequent class among the k nearest training samples in the training set. The parameter k is chosen as to minimise the average leave-one-out classification error in the training set.

The second classifier is a **Support Vector Machine** (SVM) with a linear kernel [8]. Linear SVMs map the data in a higher dimensional space where the classification problem is solved linearly (*i.e.*, by finding an optimal separation hyper-plane between the classes).

The third classifier uses a **boosting algorithm** (AdaBoost) [11] and stump each classifiers associated to one feature, to find the most relevant features for the classification problem at hand. Specifically, the AdaBoost training process attempts to select only those features that increase the predictive power of the learned model.

These three classifiers are applied separately to the permission and API vectors. Then, the classification scores s_{API} and $s_{Permissions}$ are combined into a single score $\hat{s}$ using one of the following two fusion rules:

1. **Average score:**
$$\hat{s} = \frac{s_{API} + s_{Permissions}}{2} \tag{1}$$

2. **Average of squared scores:**
$$\hat{s} = \frac{(s_{API})^2 + (s_{Permissions})^2}{2} \tag{2}$$

Intuitively, the second rule should emphasise the contribution of an high score, and in turn penalise the contribution of a low one.

5 Experimental Evaluation

In this section we report on the effectiveness of our approach to distinguish legitimate and malicious applications. We study the detection accuracy in terms of false alarms under different configurations. Specifically, we apply the kNN, SVM, and AdaBoost classifiers on permission, APIs and their combination using also two fusion rules (*i.e.*, average and square average scores), to demonstrate that such combination helps in attaining a better detection performance.

5.1 Dataset and Protocol

We evaluate the capability of our approach to detect malicious applications with higher accuracy, based on 300 legitimate applications downloaded from Google Play, and a sample of 1400 malware published in [31].

To attain a binary decision *i.e.*, legitimate versus malicious, one has to apply a threshold Th tothe score returned by the classifier, so that if the score for a certain application is higher than Th, the application is deemed as malicious, and vice-versa. Different values of Th will lead to higher or lower False Positives (FP) *i.e.*, applications misleadingly classified malicious, as well as False

Negatives (FN) *i.e.,* infected applications classified as legitimate. Therefore, the threshold Th is an important parameter available to the system designer to tune classification algorithms according to the desired behaviour for instance to accept a higher probability of FP while ensuring all malicious applications will be identified.

Furthermore, to better evaluate the effect of Th, we study also the trade-off between the False Positives Ratio (FPR) and False Negative Ratio (FNR), usually referred to as Receiver Operator Characteristics (ROC) analysis. These metrics are respectively defined as:

$$FPR = \frac{FP}{FP + TN} \tag{3}$$

$$FNR = \frac{FN}{FN + TP} \tag{4}$$

where FP, FN, TP, TN indicate the number of FP, FN, True Positives (TP) and True Negatives (TN) and vary depending on the selection threshold (see below). It is worth pointing out that a study of such a trade-off is almost overlooked in previous work, with the exception of DREBIN [5]. Note that the two metrics are normalised with respect to the number of positive (malicious) and negative (legitimate) applications of the test set, thus providing an unbiased performance estimation even with an unbalanced dataset such as the one we used in the experiments.

Experiments have been carried out using a three-fold cross validation: the data set was split randomly into three folds of equal size, with uniform sampling to preserve the distribution of legitimate and malicious applications. Each fold in turn was used for testing, and the remaining two for training, for a total of three tests. Results were finally averaged. All the proposed classifiers and combination rules do not output a sharp decision, but instead return a score that measures the likelihood of "maliciousness" of a given application, according to the learned model.

5.2   Results

To assess the accuracy of the classifiers presented in the previous section, we perform a comparative analysis between FPR and FNR, as there is not a perfect detection approach. To do so, we vary the threshold (Th), at which the decision is taken, to different values. We show the ROC of FPR versus FNR for all the examined features, classifiers, and score combination rules. For the sake of completeness we report also the Equal Error Rate (EER). Note that the EER is the value at which FPR equals to FNR.

Figure 3 to Fig. 6 overview the performance of kNN, SVM and AdaBoost algorithms between FPR and FNR under different configurations. Specifically:

- Fig. 3 shows the performance attained when the API feature vector is used,
- Fig. 4 shows the performance using the permissions feature vector,
- Figs. 5 and 6 report the performance reached when combining API and permissions, respectively using Eqs. 1 and 2.

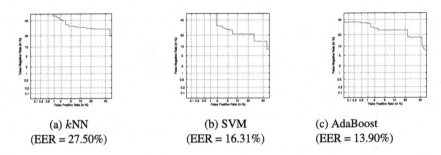

(a) kNN
(EER = 27.50%)

(b) SVM
(EER = 16.31%)

(c) AdaBoost
(EER = 13.90%)

Fig. 3. Trade-off between FNR and FPR for APIs feature vector.

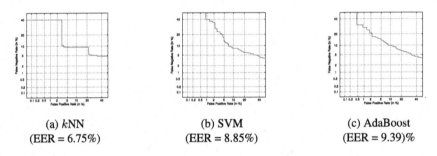

(a) kNN
(EER = 6.75%)

(b) SVM
(EER = 8.85%)

(c) AdaBoost
(EER = 9.39)%

Fig. 4. Trade-off between FNR and FPR for permissions feature vector.

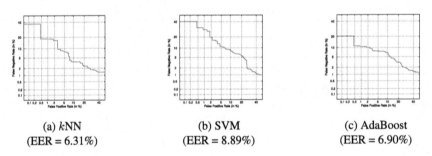

(a) kNN
(EER = 6.31%)

(b) SVM
(EER = 8.89%)

(c) AdaBoost
(EER = 6.90%)

Fig. 5. Trade-off between FNR and FPR for the average score of permissions and APIs feature vectors.

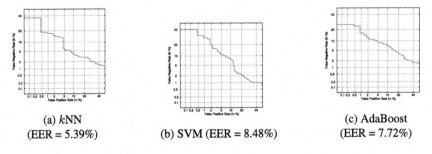

(a) kNN
(EER = 5.39%)

(b) SVM (EER = 8.48%)

(c) AdaBoost
(EER = 7.72%)

Fig. 6. Trade-off between FNR and FPR for the average squared score of permissions and APIs feature vectors.

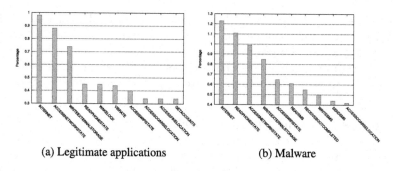

(a) Legitimate applications   (b) Malware

Fig. 7. Android applications permissions distribution on the examined data set.

All classifier achieve the worst performance when they build the corresponding model based solely on API feature vector, with kNN, SVM and AdaBoost result to 27.50 %, 16.31 % and 13.90 % EER values respectively. Using permission features instead increases consistently the performance with kNN to attain an EER value to 6.75 %, while SVM and AdaBoost perform slightly worse on 8.85 % and 9.39 % correspondingly. The combination of API and permissions further decreases the EER, with the exception of SVM with average score combination rule, Eq. 1, which performs slightly worse than the same classifier with the permissions feature vector. The best performing algorithm is kNN using API and permission feature vectors, combined through Eq. 2 resulting an EER as little as EER 5.39 %.

Apart from the EER, it is important to point out that the ROC curves attained when APIs and permissions are combined, lay below the ones attained when APIs or permissions are used alone. This allows the system designer to have more flexibility in the choice of the trade-off between FPR and FNR. Let consider for example the performance of a kNN classifier reported on Fig. 4(a) and Fig. 6(a), which respectively illustrate the best result for a single feature vector, and for the combination of feature vectors. On one hand, in the former case to perform a FNR of, *i.e.,* 2 % a FPR rate of more than 40 % should be accepted. In fact in this example, FNR does not even reach 2 % within the FPR range of Fig. 4(a)). On the other hand, in the latter case a FNR of 2 % can be reached with a far lower level of FPR of 30 %.

Furthermore, interestingly during the analysis of applications we observed that malicious applications permission distribution in some cases exceeds the percentage of 100 % *e.g.,* INTERNET and READ_PHONE_STATE permission as Fig. 7 illustrates, while we did not remark similar distribution for APIs. Thus, we further scrutinised malware applications, and we identified that they have multiple declarations of the same permission on their manifests. This fact explains the reason why permissions could be used (even solely) to identify whether a given application is malicious or not, with high accuracy according to our results.However, this means also that in case malware follows a permission distribution similar to those of legitimate applications permission distribution such an approach would evade such a detection method.

Overall, results indicate that the detection of Android malicious applications benefits from the combination of APIs and permissions information, and suggests that the two sources of information are complementary in defining a fine-tuned discrimination model. Thus, we believe that static features could be used efficiently to detect uncommon Android software prior its execution.

6   Conclusions and Future Work

Android applications security model relies on permission restricted access control on sensitive resources through the corresponding APIs. Users have to trust these built-in features of every applications that they would like to execute. Android malware exploits this trust to gain access to otherwise restricted resources. In this paper we studied the effectiveness of using permissions and APIs to deduce whether a given applications is malicious or not. We analysed the behavior of different supervised machine learning algorithms under different combination, and we demonstrated that higher malware detection accuracy can be achieved when permissions and APIs features are combined over additional fusion rules.

We foresee to extend our work in the direction of achieving higher accuracy by combining other additional rules *e.g.,* by optimising the relative weights of the two feature vectors using a trained statistical classifier, as well as introducing feature criteria on permission and APIs. Furthermore, we are planning to extend the current data set for validating our initial outcomes. On top of that, an interesting point of investigation is to assess the robustness of the proposed approach against an adversary that tries to evade permission and APIs signatures to more closely resemble a legitimate application. In particular, we will focus on the analysis of APIs and permissions minimum change causing a false alarm by the proposed classifiers. The theoretical framework of *adversarial learning* [15] could be used to perform such an analysis.

References

1. Android and security: Google bouncer. http://googlemobile.blogspot.it/2012/02/android-and-security.html
2. Report: malware-infected android apps spike in the google play store. http://www.pcworld.com/article/2099421/report-malwareinfected-android-apps-spike-in-the-google-play-store.html
3. Aafer, Y., Du, W., Yin, H.: Droidapiminer: mining api-level features for robust malware detection in android. In: Zia, T., Zomaya, A., Varadharajan, V., Mao, M. (eds.) Security and Privacy in Communication Networks. LNICST, vol. 127, pp. 86–103. Springer International Publishing, Heidelberg (2013)
4. Altman, N.S.: An introduction to kernel and nearest-neighbor nonparametric regression. Am. Stat. 46(3), 175–185 (1992)
5. Arp, D., Spreitzenbarth, M., Hubner, M., Gascon, H., Rieck, K.: Drebin: effective and explainable detection of android malware in your pocket. In: 21st Annual Network and Distributed System Security Symposium, NDSS 2014, San Diego, California, USA, 23–26 February 2013 (2014)

6. Barrera, D., Kayacik, H.G., van Oorschot, P.C., Somayaji, A.: A methodology for empirical analysis of permission-based security models and its application to android. In: Proceedings of the 17th ACM Conference on Computer and Communications Security, CCS 2010, pp. 73–84. ACM, New York (2010)

7. Bartel, A., Klein, J., Le Traon, Y., Monperrus, M.: Dexpler: converting android dalvik bytecode to jimple for static analysis with soot. In: Proceedings of the ACM SIGPLAN International Workshop on State of the Art in Java Program analysis, SOAP 2012, pp. 27–38. ACM, New York (2012)

8. Burges, C.J.C.: A tutorial on support vector machines for pattern recognition. Data Min. Knowl. Disc. **2**(2), 121–167 (1998)

9. Felt, A.P., Chin, E., Hanna, S., Song, D., Wagner, D.: Android permissions demystified. In: Proceedings of the 18th ACM Conference on Computer and Communications Security, CCS 2011, pp. 627–638. ACM, New York (2011)

10. Felt, A.P., Greenwood, K., Wagner, D.: The effectiveness of application permissions. In: Proceedings of the 2Nd USENIX Conference on Web Application Development, WebApps 2011, p. 7. USENIX Association, Berkeley (2011)

11. Friedman, J., Hastie, T., Tibshirani, R.: Additive logistic regression: a statistical view of boosting. Ann. Stat. **28**, 2000 (1998)

12. Grace, M., Zhou, Y., Zhang, Q., Zou, S., Jiang, X.: Riskranker: scalable and accurate zero-day android malware detection. In: Proceedings of the 10th International Conference on Mobile Systems, Applications, and Services, MobiSys 2012, pp. 281–294. ACM, New York (2012)

13. Huang, C.Y., Tsai, Y.T., Hsu, C.H.: Performance evaluation on permission-based detection for android malware. In: Pan, J.S., Yang, C.N., Lin, C.C. (eds.) Advances in Intelligent Systems and Applications - Volume 2. Smart Innovation, Systems and Technologies, vol. 21, pp. 111–120. Springer, Berlin (2012)

14. IDC: Worldwide smartphone os market in 4q12, May 2013

15. Laskov, P., Lippmann, R.: Machine learning in adversarial environments. Mach. Learn. **81**(2), 115–119 (2010)

16. Liang, S., Might, M., Horn, D.V.: Anadroid: malware analysis of android with user-supplied predicates. CoRR abs/1311.4198 (2013)

17. Pandita, R., Xiao, X., Yang, W., Enck, W., Xie, T.: Whyper: towards automating risk assessment of mobile applications. In: Proceedings of the 22Nd USENIX Conference on Security, SEC 2013, pp. 527–542. USENIX Association, Berkeley (2013)

18. Sanz, B., Santos, I., Laorden, C., Ugarte-Pedrero, X., Bringas, P.: On the automatic categorisation of android applications. In: Consumer Communications and Networking Conference, CCNC 2012, pp. 149–153. IEEE, January 2012

19. Sanz, B., Santos, I., Laorden, C., Ugarte-Pedrero, X., Bringas, P.G., Álvarez, G.: PUMA: permission usage to detect malware in android. In: Herrero, Á., Snášel, V., Abraham, A., Zelinka, I., Baruque, B., Quintián, H., Calvo, J.L., Sedano, J., Corchado, E. (eds.) CISIS 2012-ICEUTE 2012-SOCO 2012. AISC, vol. 189, pp. 289–298. Springer, Heidelberg (2013)

20. Sanz, B., Santos, I., Laorden, C., Ugarte-Pedrero, X., Nieves, J., Bringas, P.G., lvarez Maran, G.: Mama: manifest analysis for malware detection in android. Cybern. Syst. **44**(6–7), 469–488 (2013)

21. Sato, R., Chiba, D., Goto, S.: Detecting android malware by analyzing manifest files. Proc. Asia-Pac. Adv. Netw. **36**, 23–31 (2013)

22. Sbirlea, D., Burke, M., Guarnieri, S., Pistoia, M., Sarkar, V.: Automatic detection of inter-application permission leaks in android applications. IBM J. Res. Develop. **57**(6), 10:1–10:12 (2013)

23. Shahzad, R., Lavesson, N.: Veto-based malware detection. In: ARES 2012 Seventh International Conference on Availability, Reliability and Security, pp. 47–54, August 2012
24. Vallee-Rai, R. Co, P., Gagnon, E., Hendren, L., Lam, P., Sundaresan, V.: Soot - a java bytecode optimization framework. In: Proceedings of CASCON 1999 (1999)
25. Wei, X., Gomez, L., Neamtiu, I., Faloutsos, M.: Permission evolution in the android ecosystem. In: Proceedings of the 28th Annual Computer Security Applications Conference, ACSAC 2012, pp. 31–40. ACM, New York (2012)
26. Wu, D.J., Mao, C.H., Wei, T.E., Lee, H.M., Wu, K.P.: Droidmat: android malware detection through manifest and api calls tracing. In: Proceedings of the 2012 Seventh Asia Joint Conference on Information Security, ASIAJCIS 2012, pp. 62–69. IEEE Computer Society, Washington (2012)
27. Xing, L., Pan, X., Wang, R., Yuan, K., Wang, X.: Upgrading your android, elevating my malware: Privilege escalation through mobile os updating. In: Proceedings of the 2014 IEEE Symposium on Security and Privacy, SP 2014, pp. 393-408 (2014)
28. Xu, W., Zhang, F., Zhu, S.: Permlyzer: Analyzing permission usage in android applications. In: IEEE 24th International Symposium on Software Reliability Engineering, ISSRE 2013, pp. 400–410, November 2013
29. Yiming, J., Ahn, G.J., Ziming, Z., Hongxin, H.: Riskmon: continuous and automated risk assessment of mobile applications. In: Proceeding of the 4th ACM Conference on Data and Application Security and Privacy (CODASPY) (2011)
30. Zheng, M., Sun, M., Lui, J.C.S.: Droid analytics: a signature based analytic system to collect, extract, analyze and associate android malware. In: Proceedings of the 2013 12th IEEE International Conference on Trust, Security and Privacy in Computing and Communications, TRUSTCOM 2013, pp. 163–171. IEEE Computer Society, Washington (2013)
31. Zhou, Y., Jiang, X.: Dissecting android malware: characterization and evolution. In: 2012 IEEE Symposium on Security and Privacy (SP), pp. 95–109, May 2012
32. Zhou, Y., Jiang, X.: Detecting passive content leaks and pollution in android applications. In: Proceedings of the 20th Annual Symposium on Network and Distributed System Security (2013)
33. Zhu, J., Guan, Z., Yang, Y., Yu, L., Sun, H., Chen, Z.: Permission-based abnormal application detection for android. In: Chim, T., Yuen, T. (eds.) Information and Communications Security. LNCS, vol. 7618, pp. 228–239. Springer, Heidelberg (2012)

Protecting Android Apps Against Reverse Engineering by the Use of the Native Code

Mykola Protsenko$^{(\boxtimes)}$ and Tilo Müller

Department of Computer Science, Friedrich-Alexander-Universität
Erlangen-Nürnberg, Erlangen, Germany
{mykola.protsenko,tilo.mueller}@cs.fau.de

Abstract. Having about 80 % of the market share, Android is currently the clearly dominating platform for mobile devices. Application theft and repackaging remains a major threat and a cause of significant losses, affecting as much as 97 % of popular paid apps. The ease of decompilation and reverse engineering of high-level bytecode, in contrast to native binary code, is considered one of the main reasons for the high piracy rate. In this paper, we address this problem by proposing four static obfuscation techniques: *native opaque predicates, native control flow flattening, native function indirection,* and *native field access indirection.* These techniques provide a simple and yet effective way of reducing the task of bytecode reverse engineering to the much harder task of reverse engineering native code. For this purpose, native function calls are injected into an app's bytecode, introducing artificial dependencies between the two execution domains. The adversary is forced to analyze the native code in order to be able to comprehend the overall app's functionality and to successfully launch static and dynamic analyses. Our evaluation results of the proposed protection methods witness an acceptable cost in terms of execution time and application size, while significantly complicating the reverse-engineering process.

1 Introduction

The latest annual mobile market report from Gartner [1] has again demonstrated the clear leadership of Android, which currently possesses an impressive 80 % market share. Android apps are usually programmed in Java language. Certainly, among the reasons of such popularity, is the ease of application development. Such comfort of development and distribution, however, also has a significant drawback because it provides reverse engineers with high-level information of an app, making popular apps an attractive target for pirates. Indeed, a recent security report [2] indicates that among both paid and free apps, 97 % and 80 % respectively have been found victims of unlicensed code (re-)use. According to the Bloomberg Business estimate of 2012 [3], mobile application developers may suffer 20 % to 50 % decrease in sales due to application piracy, an extremely high figure taking into account over 10 billion market size.

One possibility of mounting a defense against application piracy is the detection of illegal code reuse in various markets, for which many valid systems have

© Springer International Publishing Switzerland 2015
S. Fischer-Hübner et al. (Eds.): TrustBus 2015, LNCS 9264, pp. 99–110, 2015.
DOI: 10.1007/978-3-319-22906-5_8

been proposed [4–6]. Such approach, however, is only of practical use if combined with effective response actions, i.e., removal of illegal apps from markets and punishment of responsible individuals. This seems to be not a trivial task, taking into account the global availability of a large number of online application markets and download centers in various countries with different legal and political systems. Therefore, we argue that *software protection* should be considered the main defense strategy to counter forms of piracy such as unlicensed code modification and reuse.

1.1   Contributions

In this paper we propose four static obfuscation techniques capitalizing on the execution domain plurality in Android: the Dalvik Virtual Machine (VM), since recently replaced with the new Android Runtime (ART), and the native code. While the first one provides the ease of development in Java language, it also is vulnerable to reverse engineering, which is facilitated by numerous tools [7–10] providing human-readable high-level view of the app's logic, up to high quality *decompilation* to Java source code [9,10]. At the same time, the tools available for the native code support, e.g. the IDA Pro disassembler [11], can only provide a *disassembly* of the target architecture's machine code. Furthermore, some dynamic analysis frameworks are unable to process the native component with the same precision as Dalvik bytecode [12,13]. Above that, native code can be a subject of such strong obfuscation techniques as self-modifying [14] and self-decrypting [15] code, which are not available within the type-safe Java programming language.

In this context, we can draw the conclusion that forcing an adversary to analyze both domains in order to gain the full understanding of the program's logic can significantly raise the reverse engineering burden. To achieve this goal, we propose four methods of introducing interdependencies between Dalvik and native execution flows:

- *Native opaque predicates*: opaque values generated by the native function and used by the bytecode part.
- *Native control flow flattening*: flattening of the control flow with successor basic block determination performed in the native code.
- *Native method call indirection*: outlining of method invocations to the native code.
- *Native field access indirection*: outlining of field accesses to the native code.

These transformations can easily be applied to existing apps, do not require the resolution of reflective calls, as it is the case for many obfuscating transformations targeting the program's object-oriented design, and are fully compatible with Android's new runtime environment ART.

For the proposed transformations we have performed a practical evaluation, covering such aspects of obfuscation quality as cost, measured by app size increase and performance drawback, and potency, assessed by means of the common software complexity metrics supplemented by additional measure of the native calls complexity. Our results indicate the usefulness of the presented protection, achieved at affordable cost level.

2   Background and Related Work

This section aims to provide basic context information about the Android platform and its execution domains, as well as to overview important publications related to software protection.

Android is a Linux-based system, originally equipped with the Dalvik VM, which executes a high-level bytecode format compiled from the Java programming language. Similarly to the Java VM, Dalvik supports a Java native interface (JNI) for embedding the native code execution into the app's life cycle. Android apps are distributed in form of apk files, which contain the bytecode and additional resources required for the app's execution.

Since Android version 5, the Dalvik VM was superseded by ART, the Android Runtime. The main feature of ART is ahead-of-time compilation of the bytecode to machine code at installation time. Nevertheless, the apk file format has not changed, meaning that the apps are still distributed in form of the Dalvik bytecode, such that the process of reverse engineering is hardly affected by this innovation. For this reason, we refer to "Dalvik execution environment" as an opposite to the truly native part of the app, for which no high-level representation is available to an adversary.

In our work we focus on code obfuscation, as one of major software protection techniques, besides watermarking and tamperproofing [16]. We utilize the notion proposed by Collberg, Thomborson, and Low [17], which describes the process of obfuscation as application of code transformations, aiming to increase reverse engineering effort. For a comprehensive survey of such protection methods we refer to Collberg and Nagra [16].

3   Design and Implementation

In this section we introduce the key design features and implementation details of the obfuscating transformations which utilize the native execution environment to increase the overall complexity of obfuscated apps.

3.1   General Principle: Native Function

In order to implement the native-based protection mechanisms, we integrate a native library into an existing application. This library contains only one function which is used for all four obfuscation techniques presented below in this section. The motivation behind using a single function is the following. With only one function being involved, for an adversary it is generally harder to decide which of the four possible actions is hidden behind this particular native function invocation; it might be a field access, a method call, or just the generation of an opaque value.

The native function receives two parameters. The first one is of type integer and represents the 'operation code', which indicates what action should be triggered by the native code.

The second parameter is an array of objects, used to pass values that might be required by the native function in order to perform its task. Such values may include a base to access instance members, i.e., fields and methods, arguments for a method call, and a new value for the set-field operation. To add some extra confusion, we also insert *'dummy'* values and apply a random permutation to the resulting parameter array. The dummy values are selected from the set of local variables with *live* definitions at the native function callsite. The dummy selection process is performed randomly, guided by the general goal of increasing the number of possible operations (see SubSects. 4.2 and 4.3 for more details on native function call complexity notions). If required parameters are of primitive types, they are wrapped up with the corresponding object types before being inserted into the object array.

The return type of the native function is `Object`, so its invocation is followed by the cast operation to the desired object type, or extraction of the primitive value from the wrapper object.

3.2   Running Example: Recursive Fibonacci

To make the description of proposed obfuscation methods more clear, we demonstrate the impact of each technique on a small example, for which we have selected a simple implementation of the Fibonacci function with recursion and memoization. For code representation we utilize a shortened form of the Soot's Jimple IR, which is close to Dalvik bytecode [18]. The source code and the corresponding Jimple IR of the original unobfuscated version are depicted in Listings 1.1 and 1.2 respectively.

Listing 1.2. Original Fibonacci Jimple IR

```
1   public int fib(int) {
2        $r0 := @this;
3        $i0 := @parameter0: int;
4
5        if $i0 > 1 goto label1;
6        return $i0;
7
8   label1:
9        $r1 = $r0.<table>;
10       $i2 = $r1[$i0];
11       if $i2 != 0 goto label2;
12       $i2 = $i0 + -1;
13       $i2 = $r0.<fib>($i2);
14       $i1 = $i0 + -2;
15       $i1 = $r0.<fib>($i1);
16       $i1 = $i2 + $i1;
17       $r1 = $r0.<table>;
18       $r1[$i0] = $i1;
19
20   label2:
21       $r1 = $r0.<table>;
22       $i2 = $r1[$i0];
23       return $i2;
24  }
```

Listing 1.1. Original Fibonacci Source

```
int[] table //...

int fib(int n){
    if (n <= 1) return n;
    if ( table[n] == 0 ){
        int f = fib(n−1)
            + fib(n−2);
        table[n] = f;
    }
    return table[n];
}
```

3.3   Native Control Flow Flattening

The control flow flattening is one of the well known control flow obfuscation techniques [16]. Its practical implementation for high-level programming languages with exceptions was discussed on example of C++ by László and Kiss [19].

The main idea of this obfuscation transformation is to indirect control flow transitions between basic blocks through a dedicated *dispatcher block*, responsible for the decision on the successor block in accordance to an *index* variable, which is updated in the end of each basic block corresponding to the desired target. Here we enhance this method by outlining the modification of the index variable to the native code.

All possible Dalvik bytecode branching conditions belong to one of the two basic types: an arithmetic comparison of the primitive data types, or equality check of object references. Hence, the evaluation of them can be easily moved to the native code. In this way, we can replace the conditional branching instructions with a native function call, which updates the index value corresponding to the outcome of the condition evaluation, followed by a jump to the dispatcher. Therefore, the dispatcher block and index variable modification are placed within different execution domains, which complicates deobfuscation of this transformation.

Listing 1.3. Fibonacci CF Flattening

```
1  label1:
2    lookupswitch(_i5) {
3      case   870: goto label6;
4      case 25275: goto label4;
5      case 28161: goto label3;
6      case 30136: goto label5;
7      default: goto label2;
8    };
9
10 label2:
11   _j6 = newarray (java.lang.Object)[2];
12   _j7 = <Integer.valueOf>($i0);
13   _j6[0] = _j7;
14   _j8 = <Integer.valueOf>(1);
15   _j6[1] = _j8;
16   _j9 = <nativefunc>(65118, _j6);
17   _j10 = (java.lang.Integer) _j9;
18   _i5 = _j10.<Integer.intValue()>();
19   goto label1;
```

Listing 1.4. Fibonacci Opaque Predicate

```
1  if $i0 > 1 goto label1;
2  _j6 = null;
3  _j7 = <nativefunc>(25461, _j6);
4  _j8 = (java.lang.Integer) _j7;
5  _i5 = _j8.<Integer.intValue()>();
6
7  if 30688 < _i5 goto label1;
8  return $i0;
9
10 label1:
11   // ...
```

The part of the flattened Fibonacci function code is presented in Listing 1.3. Here, the index variable is _i5 and the dispatcher block occupies lines 2 to 8. The following lines correspond to the first conditional jump from the line 5 of the original function. Evaluation of the condition $i0 > 1 is outlined to the native function. The required values, $i0 and 1 are passed in a wrapped form within the object array, and the corresponding opcode is 65118. The return value of the native function is used to update the index variable, then control is passed back to the dispatcher block.

3.4 Native Opaque Predicates

The most simple and intuitive way to introduce an artificial dependency between native- and bytecode is to enhance the latter one with conditional branches relying on values generated by the native part. In our current implementation, the native function returns a constant integer value which is used to also randomly generate a conditional expression inserted in the app's bytecode. In a similar way one can also use more advanced opaque generation techniques, including the ones proposed by Collberg, Thomborson, and Low [20].

The opaque predicates are utilized to enhance existing conditional branches, using the following simple rules:

$$P \Rightarrow P \wedge OP_T, \quad P \Rightarrow P \vee OP_F$$

with P the previously existing predicate, and OP_T and OP_F denoting the inserted true and false opaque predicates respectively.

The result of enhancing the conditional jump from line 5 of the original Fibonacci code with a false opaque predicate is given in Listing 1.4. The new conditional jump has the same target and is inserted after the original one, which corresponds to the OR-conjunction of two predicates.

3.5   Native Method Call Obfuscation

The native function can also be used to hide the actual target of a method invocation by introducing an indirection. The original callsite is replaced with a native call, which performs the desired invocation. This obfuscation is in a way similar to replacing direct method call with a reflective one – a technique adopted by many commercial tools.

Listing 1.5. Fibonacci Call Obfuscation

```
1  _j5 = newarray (java.lang.Object)[2];
2  _j5[0] = $r0;
3  _j6 = <Integer.valueOf>($i2);
4  _j5[1] = _j6;
5  _j7 = <nativefunc>(40357, _j5);
6  _j8 = (java.lang.Integer) _j7;
7  $i2 = _j8.<Integer.intValue>();
```

Listing 1.6. Fibonacci Field Accces Obfuscation

```
1  _j5 = newarray (java.lang.Object)[1];
2  _j5[0] = $r0;
3  j6 = <nativefunc>(45247, _j5);
4  $r1 = (int[]) _j6;
5  $i2 = $r1[$i0];
```

Listing 1.5 shows a part of the Fibonacci function with the first recursive call being obfuscated according to this method. As previously described, the required parameters, namely the `this`-reference and the int value, are passed through the object array.

3.6   Native Field Access Obfuscation

Similar to the method code obfuscation described above, we can outline field accesses into the native function. Again, such approach of the access hiding resembles to the use of reflection. Note, however, that reflection in general leaves more clues to the adversary than the proposed native obfuscation does. Even if reflection is reinforced by string encryption to conceal the target method or field name, it still remains clear whether it is a field access or method invocation, and how many parameters it takes.

The application of this obfuscation technique to the memoization table access in line 9 of the original code is shown in Listing 1.6.

3.7   Application of Obfuscation Transformations

Our implementation is built upon the Soot Java bytecode generation and transformation framework [21], the development version of which since recently also supports direct input/output of Android .apk files [18].

All four transformations are provided with the *application coverage* parameter, which defines the percentage of the potential targets to which the obfuscation technique shall be applied. For instance, a coverage rate of 50 % for the native opaque predicates transformation indicates that about half of all conditional jumps in code will be extended with opaque constructs. The selection of targets is then performed randomly.

4   Evaluation

Evaluation of the protection quality reachable by our obfuscation approach consists of three main parts. First, we consider how many various actions each native function invocation can result in. Second, we utilize software complexity metrics to assess potency of the proposed obfuscation techniques. And third, we measure the cost in terms of the application size increase and runtime penalty.

4.1   Evaluation Setup

We have obfuscated the apps from the testset with various values of the coverage parameter, which defines to how many of the possible targets the obfuscating transformation will be applied. In the current evaluation we have used the coverage values 10 %, 15 %, 25 %, and 50 % for all transformations except native control flow flattening, which was always applied with a 25 % coverage.

As a test set for our evaluation we utilized 749 applications from the F-Droid online repository for open source apps. Unfortunately, the capability of the Soot framework, on which the current implementation is based, to directly input Dalvik bytecode, is currently under development and is not compatible to all apps. For this reason, processing of some apps crashed, such that we had to decrease the test set to 367 apps which survived processing in all of the configurations we considered. For the performance evaluation we have utilized a Nexus 7 tablet with Android version 5.0.2.

4.2   Potency Measure by the Number of Possible Actions

As mentioned above, we use the same native function to perform three types of actions: return of an opaque value, field access, and method call. One of the possible approaches to measure confusion introduced to an application's code by such technique is enumerating the possible actions at each native function callsite. Intuitively, the number of possible actions depends on the set of parameters provided to the function inside the object array and the way the return value is treated. For instance, each parameter of reference type can serve as a parameter for method invocation, as a new value for a field, or it can be a base for instance member access. Therefore, we define the *native call complexity* as the number of methods and fields that could be potentially called and accessed for the given set of values.

To demonstrate this notion, consider the following example. Let the native function at some place in code be called with the parameters `String` and `Integer`, and the return value be treated as a primitive integer. Furthermore, assume the application classes defining three fields: `fS` of type `String`, `fI` of type `Integer`, and `fi` of type `int`. In this case the possible actions by the native function would include `String.codePointAt(int)`, `String.codePointBefore(int)`, `String. .hashCode()`, `String.length()`, `Integer.hashCode()`, `Integer.intValue()`, `Integer.parseInt(String)`, the get-access to `fi`, and set-accesses to `fI` and `fS`. Therefore, the resulting call complexity of this native function invocation would be 10.

Table 1. Native call complexity

Coverage	Flattening	Opaque	Call obfuscation	Field access obfuscation
10 %	2504	2401	894	549
15 %	2506	2445	917	557
25 %	2513	2503	929	563
50 %	2516	2560	1016	581

Table 1 summarizes the mean native call complexities for the four obfuscation techniques and application coverage of 10 %-50 %, measured for all 367 apps we included in our evaluation. These results show that, mostly independent of the coverage parameter, the native function can stand for a large number of operations, from 500 to 2500.

4.3 Potency Measure by Software Complexity Metrics

A conventional approach to potency measurement is the use of the software complexity metrics, as suggested by Collberg, Thomborson, and Low [17]. For this part of the evaluation we have selected the McCabe's Cyclomatic number [22], as the measure of the control-flow complexity, and a part of the suite by Chidamber and Kemerer [23], as a metric of the Object-Oriented Design (OOD) complexity.

Control Flow Complexity. The Cyclomatic complexity is defined as the number of linearly independent paths through a program's code [22]. Note that metric is affected only by the native opaque predicates insertion and the control flow flattening. The outcome of the Cyclomatic complexity measurement is presented in Table 2. Here, for each app we have measured the mean complexity and sum of complexities of all methods. The table includes mean values for those two indicators, computed over all 367 apps. With the application coverage of 50 % we can almost double the Cyclomatic complexity of the obfuscated app.

Table 2. Complexity metrics

Coverage	mean Cyclomatic	sum Cyclomatic	mean CBO	sum CBO	mean RFC	sum RFC
orig	3.438	1419.3	3.794	516.2	14.3	1431.8
10 %	4.058	1691	12.9	1869.9	30.6	3288.3
15 %	4.293	1783.5	14.7	2153.9	34.8	3758
25 %	4.781	1963.6	17.4	2554.7	41.6	4481.8
50 %	5.926	2421.1	21.8	3159.6	53.8	5725.1

OOD Complexity. The Chidamber and Kemerer metrics suite [23], which we use as a measure of the OOD complexity, contains six metrics, of which we adopt only two: the Coupling Between Object classes (CBO) and the Response Set for a Class (RFC). The CBO value for a given class corresponds to the number of classes this one is coupled to. Here the coupling relationship is defined as the use of method or instance variables of other classes. The RFC is computed as a number of methods which can be called in response to the messages received by a class. The other metrics, like the depth of inheritance tree or the number of children, are not affected by the proposed transformations.

The OOD complexity we consider to be *indirectly* affected by the native call and field access obfuscation techniques. In this context, we define the indirect metric modification in the following way. As the metrics values of the Chidamber and Kemerer suite mostly depend on the method invocation targets and the field accesses by the methods of application classes, in our attempt to assess potency of the discussed native obfuscation, we also consider all possible actions of each native function invocation, similarly to the definition of the native call complexity we presented in SubSect. 4.2.

For each of the evaluated apps we have computed the mean and the sum of the metrics for each class. The mean values of all 367 apps are presented in Table 2. The impact of the proposed obfuscation techniques on the OOD complexity is indicated to be much stronger than it was seen for the control flow complexity. Here, the application coverage of 50 % results in about 6 times higher CBO value and about 3,5 times higher RFC value.

Cost. We consider the cost of protection to be a composition of two parts: the apk file size increase and the performance penalty. The evaluation of both cost factors is presented next.

Apk File Size For all 367 apps used in the complexity evaluation described above we have measured the sizes of the original apk, and after the application of the proposed techniques. The results summarized in the second column of Table 3 indicate that even in case of the 50 % coverage the app size increases only slightly.

Performance To measure the performance penalty introduced by the proposed obfuscation methods we utilize the 0xbench app [24], which provides a suite of mathematical benchmarks: the Linpack linear algebra operations and the Scimark2 function set. For each of the considered coverage values, we have generated

Table 3. Cost Evaluation

Coverage	Apk size, Bytes	Linpack, Mflops	Scimark2 composite
orig	1,019,615 (100 %)	6.31 (100 %)	94.01 (100 %)
10 %	1,120,810 (110 %)	1.14 (18 %)	13.11 (14 %)
15 %	1,134,441 (111 %)	0.25 (4 %)	16.52 (18 %)
25 %	1,161,844 (114 %)	0.33 (5 %)	23.66 (25 %)
50 %	1,189,770 (117 %)	0.21 (3 %)	9.16 (10 %)

five obfuscated versions of the benchmark app, each version was run five times on the device. The mean results for each coverage value are presented in the last two columns of Table 3. Although the measured performance decrease by at most factor 10 to factor 30 depending on the benchmark can be considered high, we assume it in general acceptable for most apps. Note that the unsteady character of the performance scores with respect to the coverage can be explained by the random application of our protection techniques.

5   Limitations and Future Work

The prototype implementation of the obfuscation system for Android based on native code, which we presented in this paper, is to be considered one step towards stronger practical software protection mechanisms. In this section we outline the weaknesses and potential improvements of the proposed method.

The main drawback of the current implementation can be seen in relatively high cost and the lack of appropriate protection for the native code part. In our future work we plan to address these limitation by considering, among other possibilities, the following improvements.

– Selective application of obfuscation. One of the reasons for the high performance penalty lies in the broad application of obfuscation techniques to the whole app's code. In the future, our transformations may be limited to the code parts which represent the most important proprietary app logic, if possible omitting performance hot-spots.
– Native code obfuscation. On the other hand, the protection quality needs to be improved by applying strong obfuscation to the generated native code. For the obfuscation of native binaries, a large body of available techniques exists (e.g., see Collberg and Nagra [16]), through which the app's developer should be guided with the freedom of setting the most suitable trade-off between protection and performance.

To be able to fulfill the outlined goals, we plan to perform larger empirical evaluations of the obfuscation techniques, studying their impact on the code complexity and performance.

6   Conclusion

In this paper we have presented, to our best knowledge, the first protection system for high-level bytecode apps based on the use of the native execution environment. Our prototype implementation includes four obfuscation techniques: native control flow flattening, native opaque predicates, native method call obfuscation, and native field access obfuscation. We demonstrate that using these techniques one can significantly increase complexity of the code, therefore, also relying on the hardness of native code analysis and comprehension, raise the burden on the reverse engineering and illegal use of the proprietary code. Furthermore, many dynamic analysis techniques are not capable of processing native code with the same precision and quality as bytecode [12,13].

The proposed approach has a high practical applicability, as it does not rely on expensive analyses or deep knowledge of the app's code functionality, like resolution of reflective call targets, and its cost in terms of the application file increase and performance penalty is acceptable.

Acknowledgments. The research leading to these results was supported by the "Bavarian State Ministry of Education, Science and the Arts" as part of the FORSEC research association.

References

1. Gartner: Smartphone Sales report (2015). http://www.gartner.com/newsroom/id/2996817. Accessed on 12 March 2015
2. Arxan Technologies: State of Mobile App Security: Apps Under Attack. https://www.arxan.com/assets/1/7/State_of_Mobile_App_Security_2014_final.pdf. Accessed on 17 February 2015
3. Business, B.: Piracy cuts into paid app sales (2012). http://www.bloomberg.com/bw/articles/2012-11-01/piracy-cuts-into-paid-app-sales. Accessed on 18 March 2015
4. Shao, Y., Luo, X., Qian, C., Zhu, P., Zhang, L.: Towards a scalable resource-driven approach for detecting repackaged android applications. In: Proceedings of the 30th Annual Computer Security Applications Conference, ACSAC 2014, pp. 56–65. ACM, New York (2014)
5. Crussell, J., Gibler, C., Chen, H.: AnDarwin: scalable detection of semantically similar android applications. In: Crampton, J., Jajodia, S., Mayes, K. (eds.) ESORICS 2013. LNCS, vol. 8134, pp. 182–199. Springer, Heidelberg (2013)
6. Crussell, J., Gibler, C., Chen, H.: Attack of the clones: detecting cloned applications on android markets. In: Foresti, S., Yung, M., Martinelli, F. (eds.) ESORICS 2012. LNCS, vol. 7459, pp. 37–54. Springer, Heidelberg (2012)
7. Octeau, D., Jha, S., McDaniel, P.: Retargeting android applications to java bytecode. In: Proceedings of the ACM SIGSOFT 20th International Symposium on the Foundations of Software Engineering, FSE 2012, pp. 6:1–6:11. ACM, New York (2012)
8. Schulz, P.: Code Protection in Android. Insititute of Computer Science, Rheinische Friedrich-Wilhelms-Universitgt Bonn, Germany (2012)

9. Desnos, A., Gueguen, G.: Android: from reversing to decompilation. In: Proceedings of the Black Hat Conference. ESIEA: Operational Cryptology and Virology Laboratory, Abu Dhabi, July 2011

10. Enck, W., Octeau, D., McDaniel, P., Chaudhuri, S.: A study of android application security. In: Proceedings of the 20th USENIX Conference on Security, SEC 2011, p. 21. USENIX Association Berkeley (2011)

11. Hex-Rays: IDA (2015). https://www.hex-rays.com/products/ida/. Accessed on 18 March 2015

12. Enck, W., Gilbert, P., Han, S., Tendulkar, V., Chun, B.G., Cox, L.P., Jung, J., McDaniel, P., Sheth, A.N.: TaintDroid: an information-flow tracking system for realtime privacy monitoring on smartphones. ACM Trans. Comput. Syst. $32(2)$, 5:1–5:29 (2014)

13. Arzt, S., Rasthofer, S., Fritz, C., Bodden, E., Bartel, A., Klein, J., Le Traon, Y., Octeau, D., McDaniel, P.: Flowdroid: precise context, flow, field, object-sensitive and lifecycle-aware taint analysis for android apps. In: Proceedings of the 35th ACM SIGPLAN Conference on Programming Language Design and Implementation, PLDI 2014, pp. 259–269. ACM, New York (2014)

14. Madou, M., Anckaert, B., Moseley, P., Debray, S., De Sutter, B., De Bosschere, K.: Software protection through dynamic code mutation. In: Song, J.-S., Kwon, T., Yung, M. (eds.) WISA 2005. LNCS, vol. 3786, pp. 194–206. Springer, Heidelberg (2006)

15. Cappaert, J., Preneel, B., Anckaert, B., Madou, M., De Bosschere, K.: Towards tamper resistant code encryption: practice and experience. In: Chen, L., Mu, Y., Susilo, W. (eds.) ISPEC 2008. LNCS, vol. 4991, pp. 86–100. Springer, Heidelberg (2008)

16. Collberg, C., Nagra, J.: Surreptitious Software: Obfuscation, Watermarking, and Tamperproofing for Software Protection, 1st edn. Addison-Wesley Professional, Boston (2009)

17. Collberg, C., Thomborson, C., Low, D.: A taxonomy of obfuscating transformations. Technical report 148, Department of Computer Science, University of Auckland, July 1997

18. Bartel, A., Klein, J., Le Traon, Y., Monperrus, M.: Dexpler: converting android dalvik bytecode to jimple for static analysis with soot. In: Proceedings of the ACM SIGPLAN International Workshop on State of the Art in Java Program Analysis, SOAP 2012, pp. 27–38. ACM, New York (2012)

19. László, T., Kiss, Á.: Obfuscating C++ programs via control flow flattening. In: Proceedings of the 10th Symposium on Programming Languages and Software Tools, SPLST 2007, pp. 15–29, Dobogókő, Hungary (2007)

20. Collberg, C., Thomborson, C., Low, D.: Manufacturing cheap, resilient, and stealthy opaque constructs. In: Proceedings of the 25th ACM SIGPLAN-SIGACT Symposium on Principles of Programming Languages, POPL 1998, pp. 184–196. ACM, New York (1998)

21. Vallée-Rai, R. Co, P., Gagnon, E., Hendren, L., Lam, P., Sundaresan, V.: Soot - a java bytecode optimization framework. In: Proceedings of the Conference of the Centre for Advanced Studies on Collaborative Research, CASCON 1999. IBM Press (1999)

22. McCabe, T.J.: A complexity measure. IEEE Trans. Softw. Eng. SE $2(4)$, 308–320 (1976)

23. Chidamber, S.R., Kemerer, C.F.: A metrics suite for object oriented design. IEEE Trans. Softw. Eng. $20(6)$, 476–493 (1994)

24. 0xlab: 0xbench (2011). https://code.google.com/p/0xbench/. Accessed on 10 March 2015

Security and Privacy in the Cloud

Designing Privacy-Aware Systems in the Cloud

Christos Kalloniatis[✉]

Cultural Informatics Laboratory, Department of Cultural Technology
and Communication, University of the Aegean, Aegean, Greece
chkallon@aegean.gr

Abstract. Nowadays most Internet users use resources and services belonging
to the cloud. Without a doubt elasticity of cloud environments offer a wide range
of advantages to users and IT companies through a wide range of pay-as-you-go
services, platforms and infrastructure facilities. However, Internet users express
great concerns about the sufficient protection of their privacy when accessing
cloud services and more specifically over public clouds. The structure of the
cloud environment hinders new privacy issues that designers and developers
need to consider when realising cloud services in order for the latter to be trusted
by the prospective users. This paper presents a number of privacy-oriented
technical concepts that analysts need to consider when designing and modeling
privacy-aware systems in a cloud environment. Also it extends the PriS method
by presenting a new conceptual model and a respective process for assisting in
cloud services' design and implementation.

Keywords: Cloud computing · Privacy · Requirements · Design · Conceptual
model · Process

1 Introduction

During the last decade privacy has gained great attention especially from online
Internet users participating in incidents regarding unauthorised data exploration, misuse
of information stored in social media websites, data undetectability over the Internet,
disclose of personal information to third parties without users' consent any many more
without their willingness. Based on two researches conducted in 2014 [1, 2] about how
Internet users feel regarding their privacy when they are online 92 % of Internet users
answered that are afraid about the available amount of their personal data existing
online without their consent. In the same research 58 % of users asked are afraid that
their personal data are given to third parties without their approval while 47 % believes
that there actions are monitored while online on order to get targeted advertisements
and web content. Also, 59 % of users asked believe that they cannot be anonymous
online while the same amount of users believe that they should be able to be anonymous in cases where identification is not required for accessing a resource or service.
Finally some 68 % of Internet users believe current laws are not good enough in
protecting people's privacy online and 24 % believe current laws provide reasonable
protections. Thus, it is obvious that privacy needs to be considered when realising
information systems or independent services irrespective of the functional environment
the system or services will be demonstrated.

© Springer International Publishing Switzerland 2015
S. Fischer-Hübner et al. (Eds.): TrustBus 2015, LNCS 9264, pp. 113–123, 2015.
DOI: 10.1007/978-3-319-22906-5_9

Parallel to user concerns the need for addressing privacy as a separate design criterion during the software life cycle has also been identified as a major issue from the respective research community. Recent research [3–6] have identified that privacy should be treated as a separate requirement criterion, since privacy itself is a multi-faceted concept. In order for privacy to be treated properly a number of concepts need to be defined in order to assist in transforming a generic concept into specific technical requirements that will be able to be addressed during elicitation and modeling phases as well as to be implemented by respective Privacy Enhancing Technologies (PETs) accordingly. Pfitzmann and Hansen [7] have identified and described the basic privacy concepts that need to be considered when designing privacy-aware systems.

The new cloud computing environments along with the respective models and services offered brings new privacy concerns on the field of user's privacy protection due to the diversity of the existing delivery and deployment models. Specifically, cloud computing is based on three delivery models: Infrastructure as a Service (SaaS), Platform as a Service (PaaS) and Software as a Service (SaaS). Each model provides virtualised and on demand resources, application development platforms and software services, respectively. Each delivery model is considered as a separate layer that is depended from the others with IaaS being the foundation, PaaS building upon IaaS and SaaS building upon PaaS. As a result, any attack to any cloud service layer can compromise the upper layers [8]. The service model also dictates end users' scope and control over the computational environment. In general, the higher the level of support available from a cloud provider, the narrower the scope and control the cloud user has over the system. IaaS is the model that enables more direct control but also leaves the cloud service user responsible for the implementation of privacy measures. Still the IaaS provider will typically take responsibility for securing the data centers, network and systems, and will take steps to ensure that its employees and operational procedures comply with applicable laws and regulations [9]. Thus, the cloud provider has an important role on managing and implementing security and privacy measures in all three levels of abstraction.

Privacy is also affected by the selected cloud deployment model. The deployment model denotes the management and disposition of computational resources, as well as the differentiation between classes of users. In a private or community cloud for example, the computational resources are exclusive to a single organisation or to a number of 'trusted' organisations that have common privacy considerations, thus reducing perceived privacy risks. In a public or hybrid cloud resources are shared between multiple users. However, in all cases the same threats related to the nature of cloud computing apply and therefore, privacy protection measures still need be considered.

In our previous work [10, 11] the major security and privacy concerns in cloud computing have been identified and presented. The scope of this paper is twofold. Firstly it presents a complete set of privacy-related concepts based on [6, 7, 10, 11] that need to be considered when designing privacy-aware services over the cloud. Secondly it extends PriS method [6] by presenting a novel conceptual model and a process for eliciting, modeling and realising privacy requirements in cloud-based systems.

The rest of the paper is organised as follows. Section 2 presents the set of privacy-related concepts for cloud environments. Section 3 presents the suggested conceptual model along with the respective process. Section 4 addresses related work on the field of privacy requirements engineering and finally Sect. 5 concludes the paper and raises future research objectives.

2 Privacy Issues in Cloud Environments

Although privacy is a common concern in distributed information systems, additional privacy issues arise due to the nature of cloud computing. The main advantages of cloud computing like its ability to scale rapidly, store data remotely and share services in a dynamic environment, have also created a number of vulnerabilities in terms of data protection. These vulnerabilities are reflected in a number of security threats reported in [8, 12, 13]. In [14] we have compiled a comprehensive list of 14 cloud related threats and vulnerabilities indicating the cloud service model, to which they apply. All of the identified threats and vulnerabilities represent potential circumstances that may lead to misuse of information or resources. However, in order to deal with these circumstances, it is important to identify the privacy-related properties that are affected by each threat or vulnerability. The concepts presented here beside the previous works already stated are also identified based on the European Commissions reports [15, 16] as well as the Microsoft report on privacy issues in the cloud era in [17].

2.1 Isolation

The specific concept is referred to the complete seal of user's data inside the cloud computing environment. Isolation is meant to address data disclosure in two ways, firstly, from purpose limitation point of view and secondly from the aspect of the proper technical implementation techniques [15]. Cloud computing resources are shared among a multitenant environment. Thus, excessive cloud employee's access rights, posing the risk of any kind of Personal Identifiable Information disclosure and thus violating user's privacy. The specific concept is matched with the following threats derived from [12], Abuse and Nefarious Use of Cloud Computing, Insecure interfaces and APIs, Malicious Insiders, Shared technology issues, Data Loss or Leakage, Privileged user access and Lack of Data Segregation.

2.2 Provenanceability

The specific concept is referred to the provenance of the data related to the authenticity or identification, the quality of the results of certain procedures, modifications, updates and vulnerabilities, the provenance of certain actions inside the cloud, the detection of origins of security violations of an entity [18], the auditability of client's data and matters that are related to the cloud's subsystem geographical dispersion referred to the legal issues, regulations, policies and each country's rules as far as data processing and protection is concerned. All the above constitute a potential privacy violation if they are not realised properly by implementing the appropriate technical measures.

2.3   Traceabillity

Traceability concept aims to give the user the ability, to trace her data. This property is examined from the proper/improper data erasure aspect, which is a major problem in web-based systems and still continues to exist in clouds. Many cases have been documented for privacy violation due to improper data deletion (documents, photos, etc.). The traceability concept aims to protect privacy, through the ability of tracing them among the data repositories and reassuring that the data have been completely deleted or maintained invisible and anonymised after their deletion. The clients should be able to trace the physical location of their data and to be able to verify that they are processed according to their collection purpose.

2.4   Interveanability

Interveanability concept is referred to the fact that, the users should be able to have access and process their data despite the cloud's service architecture. A cloud provider may rely on other provider's subcontractor services in order to offer her services. That should not be an obstacle for the user to intervene with her data in case she suspects that her privacy is violated by the subcontractors. In fact cloud providers must be able to provide all the technical, organisational and contractual means for accomplishing this functionality for the user including all respective subcontractors that the provider cooperates and interrelates [15]. The same applies for the situation that a cloud provider or the subcontractors are bankrupted and client's data are moved to another provider.

2.5   CSA Accountability

Accountability concept is referred to the fact that cloud providers should be able to provide at any given time information about their data protection policies and procedures or specific cloud incidents related to users' data. The cloud architecture makes a complex form of an information system. In terms of management and audit controls, this fact could result in very difficult manageability of the protections mechanisms and incidents. In case of a privacy violation, a cloud provider should be able in any given time to provide information about what, when and how an entity acted and which procedures followed to tackle it [15].

2.6   Anonymity

The anonymity concept means the state of being anonymous or virtually invisible, and having the ability to operate online without being tracked [19]. Therefore, anonymity is the ability of a user to use a resource or service without disclosing his/her identity [20]. Anonymity serves the great purpose of hiding personal identifiable information when there is no need of revealing them. Browsing the Internet only for collecting information is one of many issues that anonymity plays a significant role and must be attained.

2.7   Pseudonymity

Pseudonymity is the user's ability to use a resource or service by acting under one or many pseudonyms, thus hiding his/her real identity. However, under certain circumstances the possibility of translating pseudonyms to real identities exists. Pseudonyms are aliases for a user's real identity. Users are allowed to operate under different aliases. Nevertheless revelation of user's real identity occurs when acting unlawfully. Pseudonymity has characteristics similar to anonymity in that user is not identifiable but can be tracked through the aliases he/she uses [19]. Pseudonymity is used for protecting user's identity in cases where anonymity cannot be provided (e.g. if the user has to be held accountable for his/her activities [7, 20].

2.8   Unlinkability

The unlinkability concept expresses the inability to link related information [19]. In particular, unlinkability is successfully achieved when an attacker is unable to link specific information with the user that processes that information. Also unlinkability can be successfully achieved between a sender and a recipient. In that case unlinkability means that though the sender and recipient can both be identified as participating in some communication, they cannot be identified as communicating with each other. The ability to link transactions could give a stalker an idea of your daily habits or an insurance company an idea of how much alcohol your family consumes over a month. Ensuring unlinkability is vital for protecting user's privacy.

2.9   Undetectability and Unobservability

The concept of undetectability expresses the inability to detect if a user uses a resource of service. Pfitzmann and Hansen in [7] define undetectabilty as the inability of the attacker to sufficiently distinguish if an item of interest exists or not. In previous works undetectability was absent as a privacy concept and the gap was fulfilled by unobesrvability. However, since 2010 undetectability is used as the concept for defining the inability of data, processes, or user detection from an attacker's perspective. Undetectability is usually used to satisfy steganographic systems where information hiding plays a crucial role.

Undetectability has nothing to do with anonymity – it does not mention any relationship between item of interest and subjects. Even more, for subjects being involved in an item of interest, undetectability of this item of interest is clearly impossible. As Pfitzmann and Hansen in [7] state, *early papers designing new mechanisms for undetectability designed the mechanisms in a way that if a subject necessarily could detect an item of interest, the other subject(s) involved in that item of interest enjoyed anonymity at least.* Thus, unobservability is defined as the undetectability that uninvolved subjects have in a communication together with anonymity even if items of interest can necessarily be detected by the involved subjects.

3 Conceptual Model

In this section the proposed conceptual model for the extension of PriS method is presented. PriS, initially introduced in [5, 21, 22], is a privacy requirements engineering method developed for assisting designers on eliciting, modeling, designing privacy requirements of the system to be and also providing guidance to the developers on selecting the appropriate implementation techniques that best fit the organisation's privacy requirements. PriS is a privacy requirements engineering methodology, which provides a set of concepts for modelling privacy requirements in the organisation domain and a systematic way-of-working for translating these requirements into system models. PriS identifies privacy as a multifaceted concept and defines it in the context of eight technical privacy requirements (such as anonymity and unlinkability) and adopts the use of process patterns as a way to: (a) describe the effect of privacy requirements on business processes; and (b) facilitate the identification of the system architecture that best supports the privacy-related business processes.

PriS was designed for supporting the realisation of privacy-aware information systems on traditional environments and not for the cloud. Cloud environments introduced a number of new privacy related concepts that along with the ones already stated form a new set of concepts that need to be considered when designing privacy-aware services over the cloud.

This paper presents an initial effort on mapping the new privacy-related concepts along with the ones already included in PriS under a new conceptual metamodel. Also through this paper a number of alterations among the relationships of privacy concepts are identified and introduced compared to the previous version of PriS. Specifically, in the previous versions each privacy concept was mentioned independently without providing any interrelations among them. Finally, data protection is redefined compared to the previous versions of PriS based on the new concepts presented before.

The proposed conceptual model uses the concept of goal as the central and most important concept as shown in Fig. 1. Goals are desired state of affairs that need to be attained. Goals concern stakeholders, i.e. anyone that has as interest in the system design and usage. Also goals are generated because of issues. An issue is a statement of a strength, weakness, opportunity or threat that leads to the formation of the goal. Cloud Service Providers (CSPs) constraint the functionality of the developed system or service due to the technologies they use, the policies they follow, the contractual requirements with third parties, etc. Thus, the CSP may provide requirements that designers need to take under consideration during the realisation of the system. Protection of users' privacy is stated in many European and national legislations through the form of laws, policies, directives, best practices etc. All these sources need to be taken under consideration during the identification of functional and non-functional requirements for traditional and cloud-based systems. Thus, goal identification needs to take under consideration all these elements before further analysis is conducted.

As shown in Fig. 1 there are two types of goals namely organisational goals and privacy goals. Organisational goals express the main organisation objectives that need to be satisfied by the system into consideration. Organisational goals will lead to the realiasion of system's functional requirements. In parallel, privacy goals are introduced

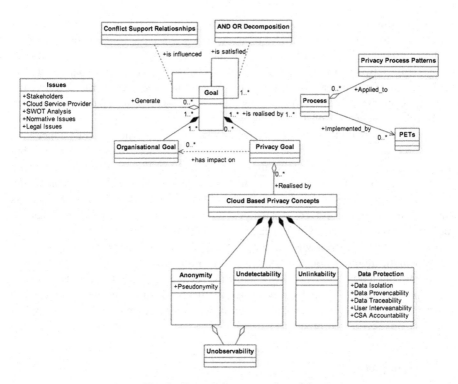

Fig. 1. Proposed conceptual model

because of specific cloud based privacy related concepts namely anonymity, pseudo-nymity, unlinkability, undetectability and data protection. Unobservability is realised if the system sufficiently reliases undetectability among the respective assets and ano-nymity of the user accessing them. Thus it is not accomplished directly but indirectly through the realisation of the respective two concepts. Finally, the concepts of isola-tion, provenanceability, traceability, interveanability and accountability are related to data protection of user's or systems data over the cloud as it was explained previously. Thus, all these concepts are grouped under the data protection class. Privacy goals may have an impact on organisational goals. In general, a privacy goal may cause the improvement/adaptation of organisational goals or the introduction of new ones. In this way, privacy issues are incorporated into the system's design.

Goals are realised by processes. However, goals cannot be mapped directly onto processes. The transition process from goals to processes includes the causal trans-formation of general goals into one or more subgoals that form the means for achieving desired ends. During this process, in every step new goals are introduced and linked to the original one through causal relations thus forming a hierarchy of goals. Every subgoal may contribute to the achievement to more than one goals, thus the resulting structure is a graph rather than a hierarchy. As it can be seen from the figure the satisfaction relationships between original goals and their subgoals, in the goal graph, are of the AND/OR type.

Besides the satisfaction type relationship between a goal and its successor goals another relationship type exists. The influencing relation type, which is based on two subtypes namely goal support relationship and goal conflict relationship. A support relationship between two goals means that the achievement of one goal assists the achievement of the other; however the opposite is not necessarily true. Finally, the conflict relationship between two goals implies that the achievement of one goal hinders the achievement of the second one.

As it was mention before goals are realised by processes. The proposed conceptual model proposed the use of privacy process patterns as a more robust way of bringing the gap between the design and the implementation phase. Privacy process patterns are usually generalised process models, which include activities and flows connecting them, presenting how a business should be run in a specific domain. Privacy process patterns are applied on privacy related processes in order to specify the way that the respective privacy issues will be realised through a specific number of steps. This assists also the developer who can understand in a better and specific way, how to implement the aforementioned privacy concepts. Privacy process patterns are also used for identifying a number of Privacy Enhancing Technologies (PETs) already available for implementing the system's privacy requirements. In this way the developer can choose the most appropriate technology based on the privacy process patterns applied on every privacy-related process.

4   Related Work

Privacy has attracted much attention recently, especially as a design criterion that needs to be considered early during system design phase. Thus, a number of software engineering methods supporting the elicitation and modelling of privacy issues have been proposed. Most of them deal with privacy as a security concept or constraint like Secure Tropos, an extension of Tropos methodology proposed in [23], employs the concepts of security constraint, and secure dependency in order to model and analyse security issues during the requirements engineering phase. Similarly, the SecReq approach introduced in [24] describes a systematic approach to derive security requirements from system security objectives. In [25] misuse cases are used in order to represent security threats and to identify "security use cases", i.e., countermeasures that mitigate the threats.

Privacy patters have also been used as a way to model privacy issues. In [26] privacy patterns are used for web-based activity and especially how to convey privacy policies to end-users during online interactions. In [27] a pattern language is proposed, containing 12 patterns for developing anonymity solutions for various domains including anonymous messaging, anonymous voting and location anonymity.

From the legal compliance perspective of privacy Islam et al. [28] use natural language patterns and make use of the Hohfeld legal taxonomy, to extract security requirements from laws and combine them with the ISO/IEC policies. Finally they trace the identified requirements into secure system design. Work presented in [29] describes an approach for evaluating the legal compliance of existing security and privacy requirements, by establishing traceability links from requirements to legal texts.

Cloud computing have also raised the attention of the research community regarding the analysis and modelling of security and privacy requirements. Some works identify existing cloud technology vulnerabilities where various security incidents may occur. In [30] authors present ways that attackers can exploit data duplication techniques to access customer data through hash-code retrieval of stored files. In [31] authors present ways that the side-channel attacks can instantiate new virtual machines in order to monitor neighbouring's virtual machine cached memory. Information or resource misuse through security and privacy incidents is also a very important area. In [32] authors argue that there is a variety of privacy threats based on the cloud scenario and lack of user control, potential unauthorised secondary usage and data proliferation. Finally, in [33] authors suggest the analysis of security and privacy risks as a decision-making criterion for migrating IT services to the cloud.

5   Conclusions

It is a common sense that privacy gains much attention recently especially in untrusted and complex environments. Cloud computing gains also a lot of attention due to its potential to offer services rapidly and with less cost. However, privacy is one of the critical factors that should be implemented for raising the trustworthiness of the services offered. Although many researchers identify that privacy concerns depend on the application context and differ due to the diversity of potential threats existing that can cause harm to various privacy-identifiable assets, most methods deal with privacy as a single requirement. Failing to realise the multifaceted concept of privacy usually leads to inefficient ways of implementation thus creating unreliable and untrusted systems and services. Adopting cloud computing imposes an unavoidable release of control over valuable assets. As a result trust in the cloud provider is required for a confident adoption of cloud computing and full utilisation of its benefits.

This work extended our previous work in the field of privacy requirements engineering and cloud computing security and privacy concepts identification by proposing a novel conceptual framework for mapping the concepts and their relations that should be considered when designing privacy-aware systems and services over the cloud. It is obvious that this work is on an initial stage. Future work includes the establishment of a process for the elicitation and modeling of the respective concepts as well as the application of this work on a real case study scenario.

References

1. Rainie, L, Kiesler, S., Kang, R, Madden, M: Anonymity, Privacy and Security Online, Carnegie Mellon University. http://www.pewinternet.org/2013/09/05/anonymity-privacy-and-security-online/. Accessed 19 April 2015
2. TRUSTe: US Consumer Confidence Privacy Report. http://www.truste.com/us-consumer-confidence-index-2014/. Accessed 19 April 2015
3. Gritzalis, S.: Enhancing web privacy and anonymity in the digital era. Inf. Manage. Comput. Secur. **12**(3), 255–288 (2004). Emerald Group Publishing Limited

4. Koorn, R., van Gils, H., Hart, J., Overbeek, P., Tellegen, R.: Privacy Enhancing Technologies, White paper for Decision Makers. Ministry of the Interior and Kingdom Relations, The Netherlands (2004)
5. Kalloniatis, C., Kavakli, E., Gritzalis, S.: Addressing privacy requirements in system design: The PriS method. Requirements Eng. J. **13**(3), 241–255 (2008)
6. Mouratidis, H., Kalloniatis, C., Islam, S., Huget, M.P., Gritzalis, S.: Aligning security and privacy to support the development of secure information systems. J. Univ. Comput. Sci. **18** (12), 1608–1627 (2012)
7. Pfitzmann, A., Hansen, M.: A terminology for talking about privacy by data minimization: Anonymity, Unlinkability, Undetectability, Unobservability, Pseudonymity, and Identity Management, white paper, v.0.34. http://dud.inf.tu-dresden.de/Anon_Terminology.shtml. Accessed 19 April 2015
8. Hashizume, K., Rosado, D.G., Fernández-Medina, E., Fernandez, E.B.: An analysis of security issues for cloud computing. J. Internet Serv. Appl. **4**, 1–13 (2013)
9. ITU Technology Watch: Privacy in Cloud Computing. International Telecommuni cations Union, Geneva, Switzerland (2012)
10. Manousakis, V., Kalloniatis, C., Kavakli, E., Gritzalis, S.: Privacy in the cloud: bridging the gap between design and implementation. In: Franch, X., Soffer, P. (eds.) CAiSE Workshops 2013. LNBIP, vol. 148, pp. 455–465. Springer, Heidelberg (2013)
11. Kalloniatis, C., Manousakis, V., Mouratidis, H., Gritzalis, S.: Migrating into the cloud: identifying the major security and privacy concerns. In: Douligeris, C., Polemi, N., Karantjias, A., Lamersdorf, W. (eds.) Collaborative, Trusted and Privacy-Aware e/m-Services. IFIP AICT, vol. 399, pp. 73–87. Springer, Heidelberg (2013)
12. CSA Threats: Top Threats to Cloud Computing Results update 2012, Cloud Se-curity Alliance, Seattle, WA, USA (2012)
13. Pearson, S.: Privacy, security and trust in cloud computing. In: Pearson, S., Yee, G. (eds.) Computer Communications and Networks. Springer-Verlag, London (2013)
14. Kalloniatis, C., Mouratidis, H., Manousakis, V., Islam, S., Gritzalis, S., Kavakli, E.: Towards the design of secure and privacy-oriented information systems in the cloud: identifying the major concepts. Comput. Stan. Interfaces **36**, 759–775 (2014)
15. EU Draft: EU Directive for Security issues in Cloud Computing. European Commission, Brussels, Belgium
16. Article 29 Data Protection Working Party, Opinion 05/2012 on Cloud Computing (2012). Accessed 09 December 2014
17. Microsoft Technical report: Privacy in the cloud computing era, a Microsoft perspective, Microsoft Corp, Redmond, USA, November 2009. Accessed 10 January 2015
18. Wei, J., Zhang, X., Ammons, G., Bala, V., Ning, P.: Managing security of virtual machine images in a cloud environment. In: Proceedings of the 2009 ACM workshop on Cloud computing security (CCSW 2009), pp. 91–96. ACM, New York (2009). doi: 10.1145/ 1655008.1655021 http://doi.acm.org/10.1145/1655008.1655021
19. Cannon, J.C.: Privacy: What Developers and IT Professionals Should Know. Addison-Wesley, Reading (2004)
20. Fischer-Hübner, S.: IT-Security and Privacy: Design and Use of Privacy Enhancing Security Mechanisms. LNCS, vol. 1958. Springer, Heidelberg (2001)
21. Kalloniatis, C., Kavakli, E., Kontellis, E.: PriS tool: a case tool for privacy-oriented RE. In: Doukidis, G., et al. (eds.) Proceedings of the MCIS 2009 4th Mediterranean Conference on Information Systems, Athens, Greece, pp. 913–925 (e-version), September 2009

22. Kalloniatis, C., Kavakli, E., Gritzalis, S.: PriS Methodology: incorporating privacy requirements into the system design process. In: Mylopoulos, J., Spafford, G. (eds.) Proceedings of the 13th IEEE International Requirements Engineering Conference – SREIS 2005 Symposium on Requirements Engineering for Information Security, Paris, France. IEEE CPS Conference Publishing Services, August 2005

23. Mouratidis, H., Giorgini, G.: Secure tropos: a security-oriented extension of the tropos methodology. Int. J. Software Eng. Knowl. Eng. **17**, 285–309 (2007)

24. Houmb, S.H., Islam, S., Knauss, E., Jürjens, J., Schneider, K.: Eliciting security requirements and tracing them to design: an integration of common criteria, heuristics, and UMLsec. Requirements Eng. J. **15**, 63–93 (2010)

25. Sindre, G., Opdahl, A.L.: Eliciting security requirements with misuse cases. Requirements Eng. J. **10**, 34–44 (2005)

26. Romanosky, S., Acquisti, A., Hong, J., Cranor, L.F., Friedman, B.: Privacy patterns for online interactions. In: Proceedings of the 2006 Conference on Pattern Languages of Programs (PloP 2006), Portland, Oregon, pp. 12:1–12:9. ACM, New York, 21–23 October 2006

27. Hafiz, M.: A Pattern Language for Developing Privacy Enhancing Technologies. Software Practice and Experience. **43**, 769–787 (2013)

28. Islam, S., Mouratidis, H., Wagner, S.: Towards a framework to elicit and manage security and privacy requirements from laws and regulations. In: Wieringa, R., Persson, A. (eds.) REFSQ 2010. LNCS, vol. 6182, pp. 255–261. Springer, Heidelberg (2010)

29. Massey, A.K., Otto, P.N., Hayward, L.J., Antón, A.I.: Evaluating existing secu-rity and privacy requirements for legal compliance. Requirements Eng. J. **15**, 119–137 (2010)

30. Mulazzani, M., Schrittwieser, S., Leithner, M., Huber, M., Weippl, E.: Dark clouds on the horizon: using cloud storage as attack vector and online slack space. In: Proceedings of the 20th USENIX Conference on Security, San Fransisco, CA, p. 5. USENIX Association, Berkeley, 8–12 August 2011

31. Gong, C., Liu, J., Zhang, Q., Chen, H., Gong, Z.: The characteristics of cloud computing. In: Proceedings of the 2010 39th International Conference on Parallel Processing Workshop, San Diego, CA, pp. 275–279. IEEE Computer Society, Washington, DC, 13-16 September 2010

32. Pearson, S., Benameur, A.: Privacy, security and trust issues arising from cloud computing. In: Proceedings of the 2nd IEEE International Conference on Cloud Computing Technology and Science, Indianapolis, Indiana, USA, pp. 693 – 702. IEEE Computer Society, UK, 30 November–3 December 2010

33. Islam, S., Mouratidis, H., Weippl, E.: A goal-driven risk management approach to support security and privacy analysis of cloud-based system. In: Security Engineering for Cloud Computing: Approaches and Tools. IGI global publication (2012)

Accountability-Preserving Anonymous Delivery of Cloud Services

F. Buccafurri$^{(\boxtimes)}$, G. Lax, S. Nicolazzo, and A. Nocera

DIIES, University Mediterranea of Reggio Calabria, Via Graziella,
Località Feo di Vito, 89122 Reggio Calabria, Italy
{bucca,lax,s.nicolazzo,a.nocera}@unirc.it

Abstract. Cloud computing is an emerging paradigm whose importance both in large and small business is more and more increasing. As one of the reasons motivating the adoption of cloud computing solutions is to alleviate the load of companies related to the solution of security and disaster recovery issues, security is one of the main features to fulfill in a cloud computing system. Moreover, a number of new security and privacy problems arise, such as threats to user's privacy due to the realistic possibility of having *honest-but-curious* cloud providers. In this scenario, we propose an authentication scheme supporting full anonymity of users and unlinkability of service requests. This is done by combining a multi-party cryptographic protocol with the use of a cooperative P2P-based approach to access services in the cloud. As the solution is thought to be adopted in e-government scenarios, accountability of user accesses is always preserved, to prevent misuse and illegal actions of users.

Keywords: Anonymity · Privacy · Accountability · Cloud

1 Introduction

Cloud computing is recently receiving much attention from both research and industrial worlds. The cloud paradigm allows a user to transparently move his storage and computation to servers distributed over the Internet (i.e., clouds) that implement services on-demand. Clouds provide their customers with reliable, efficient, and low cost computing services such as e-mail, instant messaging, storage systems, etc. However, such an outsourcing paradigm introduces new security and privacy threats, mainly related to the fact that cloud providers become owner of (even sensitive) information regarding their customers. Think for example of application contexts like e-government, e-health, or financial services, which are all fields where cloud computing is emerging. In these cases, especially privacy requirements become crucial, by considering that sensitive information can be drawn just by observing which services a user is accessing, even though we assume that contents are fully obscured. Indeed, it is widely accepted that the adoption of an *honest but curious* adversary assumption can be realistically done, concerning cloud providers. In fact, the information regarding customers may give these parties strong strategic advantages. Thus, we can

© Springer International Publishing Switzerland 2015
S. Fischer-Hübner et al. (Eds.): TrustBus 2015, LNCS 9264, pp. 124–135, 2015.
DOI: 10.1007/978-3-319-22906-5_10

assume that cloud providers execute services correctly, but might look at the information passed between entities.

Whereas the aspect of data confidentiality and the related issue of key management have received a lot of attention in the recent scientific literature [25], the problem of information leakage arising from the observation of user requests (i.e., accesses to cloud services) has been much less investigated. Although a number of proposal basing on anonymous authentication schemes, group signatures, zero knowledge protocols exist [10,19], a number of challenging problems should be completely addressed to make these solutions really applicable. Specifically, once a particular domain is set, detailed issues may arise together with specific opportunities that can make a particular solution realistic.

Consider, for example, the case in which a government party has the role of end-service provider offered to citizens through non-government cloud providers. This is an emergent scenario, due to the general difficulty of governments in adopting national clouds. In this case, customers of a cloud can operate promiscuously, both for e-government and private services. Here, an opportunity arises. A trusted third party exists for free (e.g., some e-government entity), which can play a role in the authentication process (consider that we are assisting to a rapid evolution of EU Countries towards digital identity systems [1]), and we may assume that no collusion with cloud providers exists. At the same time, besides the strong requirement of privacy against cloud providers, a specific issue appears. A full accountability of all user activity appears necessary if we consider both the responsibilities coming from low requirements of the involved parties and the general need of security also against terrorism.

In this reference scenario, we propose a solution providing anonymous access to cloud services yet preserving fully user accountability and presenting nice characteristics of computational cheapness. With no collusion of the involved parties, no information about the identity of the user accessing the cloud is possible. Accountability is obtained, in case of need, by merging information coming from multiple parties. From the point of view of the specific scenario and, thus, of the required features and the concreteness of the solution, our proposal appears new, to the best of our knowledge.

Importantly, anonymity of user activity is reached by guaranteeing both the anonymous authentication and the unlinkability of user requests. To do this, we combine a multi-party cryptographic protocol with a cooperative P2P-based approach. We believe that this new way to integrate P2P and cloud computing, in which the customers of the cloud cooperate with each other to obtain privacy features and increased efficiency, is sustainable also from a business point of view, due to the reciprocal advantage obtained by users. Conversely, a solution based on Tor [14], like [17,18], appears not realistic due to legal problems which the subscription to such anonymization system may result in.

The structure of the paper is the following. In the next section, we overview the related literature. In Sect. 3, the idea underlying our approach is presented through a motivating example. The details of the protocol are provided in Sect. 4 and the analysis of its security is discussed in Sect. 5. Finally, in Sect. 6, we draw our conclusion.

2   Related Work

Nowadays, a great variety of computer applications are decentralized in open distributed systems, such as social networks [5–9]. Although a wide amount of work deals with general security issues in cloud computing, only few papers concern anonymous authentication. For instance, an overview of the different security risks that reduce the growth of cloud computing is presented in [24]. [11] analyzes the cost and the feasibility of the implementation of common cryptographic primitives (e.g., AES, MD5, SHA-1, RSA) for cloud security purposes. The authors of [26] focus on cloud data storage security issues, such as error localization and the identification of misbehaving servers. The problem of ensuring the integrity of data storage is addressed in [27]. The authors consider the task of allowing a third party auditor to check the integrity of the dynamic data stored, on behalf of the cloud client. All the works cited above are inherently different from our approach because they do not focus on the definition of techniques for privacy-preserving access to cloud services.

[18] establishes a set of requirements for a secure and anonymous communication system and tries to fulfill those requirements by using a combination of existing systems, such as Tor [14] and Freenet [13]. A client-based privacy manager that helps reducing the risk of data leakage and loss of privacy is proposed in [20]. However, the authors do not take into account the information derived from the possibility of linking different user sessions that may ultimately result in user profiling attacks.

Several works deal with data privacy concerns. Wang et al. [25] propose a distributed scheme with explicit dynamic data support (including block update, delete, and append) to achieve cloud data integrity and availability. They rely on erasure-correcting code in the file distribution preparation to provide redundancy parity vectors and guarantee the data dependability. [17] leverages the Tor architecture to provide data ownership privacy inside cloud. A system parameter controls both the degree of anonymity and the computational overhead imposed by the system.

The most widely used strategies for the anonymization of data content are differential privacy [15] and k-anonymity for privacy preserving microdata release [4,23]. These techniques are used as a preprocessing step to anonymize private data content before their submission to the cloud [17]. The proposals presented in [2,10,12,16,19] take advantage of group signature scheme as anonymous access method. The first definition of group signatures was proposed by Chaum in [10]. This kind of signatures is defined as a "generalization" of the credential/membership authentication schemes, in which one person proves that he belongs to a certain group. A group signature scheme based on bilinear maps without random oracles is presented in [2]. [16] proposes a solution based on ring and group signatures for anonymous and reliable access control and accountability. The authors of [12] implement SPICE, a digital identity management system applicable to cloud environment, which combines two group signatures to make the same signature look different for multiple uses. The authors of [19] provide non-bilinear group signatures to ensure registered users with anonymous access to cloud services, unlinkability and confidentiality of transmitted data. However, this strategy does not prevent user from behavior-based deanonimization attack. The main drawback of group signature scheme is that the signature size grows with the number of users, thus making these approaches inefficient in many application contexts.

A recent proposal presented in [22] describes a decentralized access control technique with anonymous authentication, which provides user revocation and prevents replay attacks. The limitation of such an approach is that the different requests of a single user in a session could be linked, thus resulting in a behavioral-based attack. In contrast, our technique is able to protect users also against such a type of attack.

3 Overview of the Proposal

In this section, we sketch out the idea underlying our proposal through a motivating example. Consider the case in which a user exploits an e-health services of a cloud provider to interact with an health-care institute of a given country and, then, in the same cloud session, makes a flight reservation for that country. This example is illustrated in Fig. 1.

These cross-domain data can be combined by the cloud service provider, assumed honest but curios, to derive information on the private life of the user, and therefore, to obtain data the user was not meant to reveal. In this case, for instance, it is possible to infer that either the user is an employee of the health-care provider who is reaching his working place or a patient who is requiring hospitalization. Therefore, by analyzing the typology of the health-care provider (e.g., mental hospital, orthopedic center, etc.), it is possible to make assumptions on the user's disease.

Consider that the sole application of anonymous authentication schemes like [10,19] is not sufficient to solve our problem. Indeed, the service provider may still obtain user data from the flight reservation and link them with the information on the health-care provider.

Fig. 1. A user accessing the cloud to have information about an hospital and to make a flight reservation.

In our example, our technique proceeds as follows:

1. The user U sends his identity together with the identity of the cloud provider P to a grantor G, which typically is an e-government institution where the user is registered.
2. G responds by sending some *tokens* and the reference to an entry point for the P2P network [3]. Each token includes a *ticket* (i.e., a credential) and a key. The ticket is spent for the service, the key is maintained secret.
3. The user joins the P2P network and uses this network to send two tickets (one for each request) to P anonymously.
4. P receives the two tokens from two users (different from U) of the P2P network, so that the requests appear anonymous and unlinkable. Each ticket contains information that only G and P can decrypt to establish that the credential is valid and to extract a secret key for the secure communication with the user. The service is thus ciphered by this key and delivered to the user by using again the P2P network.

In summary, our approach leverages three basic features: anonymous authentication, unlinkability of user service requests, and traffic flow anonymity in the communication with the cloud service provider. Specifically, the first one is achieved by relying on a solution like [10,19] that leverages the interaction with a grantor, playing the role of trusted third party, to perform anonymous authentication to cloud services. Concerning the unlinkability of service requests, our solution works by assigning different tokens for each request, thus decoupling cross-domain information. However, since the cloud provider may still associate service requests with the IP address of the user, we adopt a strategy leveraging a P2P network for the IP obfuscation (described in Sect. 4). It is worth noting that only the combination of the two strategies (i.e., multiple anonymous tokens and P2P user interface) achieve the privacy goal.

Finally, we discuss about accountability. The provider P logs all user's activities by associating them with the random number included in the corresponding credential. Thus, no information can be drawn from the analysis of logs even about behavioral patterns of the user. Only in case of need (for example, in case of illegal actions), logs can be linked to the identity of the user by using information kept by G, thus allowing full accountability. In the next section we describe in detail how the protocol is defined.

4   The Service Delivery Protocol

In this section, we describe the design of our protocol for anonymizing the access to cloud services. Preliminarily, we report in Table 1 the notation used throughout the rest of the paper.

The protocol we propose relies on an underlying P2P network, which is used to anonymize communications. In particular, this avoids that the cloud service provider may obtain useful information from the analysis of IP addresses of users accessing the services.

Table 1. Notations.

Symbol	Description
U	A user accessing a service
P	The cloud service provider
G	The grantor
$\mathcal{N_S}$	Nodes of the P2P network
A	An entry point of the P2P network
$\mathcal{H}$	Cryptographic hash function
K	Cryptographic key
$E^K(x)$	The encryption of x with the key K
$D^K(x)$	The decryption of x with the key K
r	Nonce
T	Ticket
τ	Timestamp
$\|$	Concatenation operator

The entities involved in our protocol are:

1. The user U who needs to access cloud services.
2. A trusted third party said *grantor* G, which identifies users and provide them with *tickets* necessary to enjoy cloud services.
3. The *provider* P, which supplies cloud services.
4. The open ended set $\mathcal{N_S}$ of the nodes of the P2P network.

According to our protocol, a public key infrastructure exists so that both grantor and providers have a certificate containing a public key. The protocol is structured as follows.

Initial Registration. The user U is identified and registered by G. All necessary information to establish a secure channel is now exchanged (e.g., Diffie Hellman key exchange).

Identification. In this phase, the user U submits his identity to the grantor G via secure channel established in the initial registration. Moreover, U sends G the public key certificate of the provider supplying the services he wants to access.

G verifies the identity of the user and his authorizations and grants a set $\mathcal{TK_S}$ of n pairs (where n is suitably set system parameter) (*ticket, key*) and the reference to a node $A \in \mathcal{N_S}$. In particular, $\mathcal{TK_S} = \{(T_i, K_i) : T_i = E^{K_P}(\tau_i\|r_i) \wedge K_i = \mathcal{H}(\tau_i\|r_i)\}$, where τ_i is a (long) validity time, r_i is a nonce, K_P denotes the public key of the provider P (obtained from the certificate of P), and $\mathcal{H}$ is a cryptographic hash function. Moreover, each ticket T_i is signed by G to guarantee authenticity and integrity of the ticket. Observe that the value of n actually sets

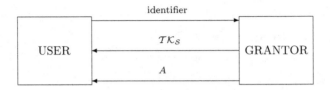

Fig. 2. The identification phase.

the overall number of requests the user can do without re-contacting G. As the size of each pair (T_i, K_i) is small, we can imagine to have a large n to drastically reduce the number of messages exchanged between U and G.

Concerning the node A, it is randomly selected from the last t users who have been authorized by the grantor to access some cloud services, where t is a system parameter set up according to the P2P network dynamics (this approach is aimed at maximizing the probability of finding the entry point alive).

Figure 2 summarizes the messages exchanged between user and grantor in this phase.

Service Request. Once the user has obtained the credentials to anonymously access the cloud, he can require a service to P. First, U joins the P2P network by using A as entry point. Then, U generates a secret S and computes $c_i = E^{f(K_i)}(S)$ encrypting the secret S with a key obtained as function f of the i-th key K_i, where f is a pre-agreed function used to produce a significant change in the key (for example, MD5). Then, he computes $v_i = E^{f(K_i)}(t_i)$, where t_i is the timestamp recording the current time. Now, U creates the service request message m for P having the tuple $\langle T_i, c_i, v_i \rangle$ as authentication credential. This message is sent through the P2P network to reach P with an anonymous IP address. Concerning the use of a P2P network to obtain such an anonymity, we observe that there exist several approaches such as [21,28]. It is worth noting that one of the most simple ways to obtain this goal is as follows. Each node of the P2P network receiving a service request message m for P, with a certain probability delivers the request to P, otherwise forwards the request to another P2P node. Involved nodes maintain the previous hop of the message route, which is used to delivery the reply coming from P.

The use of the P2P network allows for the creation of an anonymous tunnel which varies for different service requests coming from the same user. This way, the provider cannot link the tickets adopted by the same user to access different services from the knowledge of the sender IP address.

Once the provider receives the anonymous message originally generated by U from the P2P network, it verifies authenticity and integrity of the ticket using the public key of the grantor, and then deciphers T_i with its private key, thus obtaining τ_i' and r_i'. Therefore, it verifies the (long term) temporal validity of the ticket checking that τ_i' is less than the current time. Then, it verifies that the nonce r_i' has been never received in the past. If the ticket is expired or already used, the request is denied. Observe that the long term temporal validity is

---

Protocol 1. Authentication and communication

1: **procedure** USER-SIDE
2:     U submits his identity to the grantor G
3:     U sends the public key certificate of P to G
4:     **if** request is rejected **then**
5:         **close**
6:     U generates S and computes $c_i = E^{f(K_i)}(S)$ and $v_i = E^{f(K_i)}(t_i)$
7:     U joins the P2P network by means of A
8:     U sends $m = \langle T_i, c_i, v_i \rangle$ to P via the P2P network
9:     U establishes an encrypted communication channel with P
10:     **close**
11: **procedure** GRANTOR-SIDE
12:     G receives U's request
13:     **if** U has invalid credentials **then**
14:         G rejects the request from U
15:         **close**
16:     G sends the set $TK_S = \{(T_i, K_i) : T_i = E^{K_P}(\tau_i||r_i) \wedge K_i = \mathcal{H}(\tau_i||r_i)\}$ to U
17:     G selects $A \in \mathcal{N}_S$ and sends it to U
18:     **close**
19: **procedure** PROVIDER-SIDE
20:     P computes $D^{K_P}(T_i)$ obtaining τ_i' and r_i'
21:     **if** $\tau_i' <$ current time **or** r_i' has been already received **then**
22:         P returns *false* to U
23:         **close**
24:     P computes $K_i' = \mathcal{H}(\tau_i'||r_i')$
25:     P computes $D^{f(K_i')}(c_i) = S$
26:     P computes $D^{f(K_i')}(v_i) = t_i$
27:     **if** $t_i + \Delta t \geq$ current time **and** $K_i' = K_i$ **then**
28:         P establishes an anonymous encrypted communication channel with U
29:     **else**
30:         P returns *false* to U
31:     **close**

---

used in case of authorizations with validity time that must be reflected in the credentials sent by G to U.

At this point, P computes $K_i' = \mathcal{H}(\tau_i'||r_i')$ and uses $f(K_i')$ as symmetric key to decipher c_i and v_i, thus obtaining the secret S and the timestamp t_i. If $t_i + \Delta t$ is less than the current time (where Δt is a general system parameter set to a small value for security reasons – see Sect. 5), the request is discarded. Otherwise, the protocol proceeds and if $K_i' = K_i$ (i.e., it is the correct key), then this key is valid. At this point, the provider uses this information to establish an encrypted communication (by using S) with the anonymous initial node through the P2P network.

A schematization of the procedures executed by the actors involved in our protocol is reported in Protocol 1.

5   Security Analysis

In this section, we show the robustness of our protocol again the most common types of attacks. This is discussed in the following.

Replay Attacks. This type of attack is done by maliciously re-sending a ticket to access a service. If the ticket has been already spent from the legal owner, then it will be detected as not valid because the nonce r' has been already received. Another possibility is that the attacker intercepts the ticket when it is sent from the user to the provider. The expiration time Δt forces the attacker to use this ticket immediately because otherwise the ticket expires. However, the attacker cannot generate the correct secret S necessary to the communication with the provider because it is sent encrypted by $f(K)$. Moreover, as the messages exchanged between U and P are encrypted by S, the attacker has no advantage from intercepting and replaying them to any party.

Spoofing Attacks. The attacker simulates to be the grantor in order to obtain the login information of the user. The use of a PKI infrastructure for authentication of the grantor avoids this attack.

Password Guessing Attacks. In this case, the attacker tries to obtain the login information of the user by one of the following ways: (i) *on-line*, submitting possible authentication credentials until the grantor does accept the credential. As this attack needs the participation from the grantor, it is contrasted by including a delay in the reply of grantor to limit the number of attempts in the time from the attacker; (ii) *off-line*, in which the adversary guesses a secret without the participation of any other party. The secrets that he could guess are the following. τ and r, because from them he can compute K. Although τ is easy to know as is a timestamp, r is randomly generated and, as a consequence, it is very hard to guess. Also the knowledge of K is hard, because it is a digest computed by a cryptographic hash function. Finally, the secret S is sent encrypted by $f(K)$, so that it is difficult to guess without the knowledge of the ciphering key. Clearly, in these considerations, we assume that the cryptographic functions and keys used are secure, as usual in this context.

Man in the Middle. Here, the attacker monitors, alters or injects messages into the communication between the provider and the user who accesses the service. However, the secret S used to encrypt the communication channel between P and U cannot be known by the attacker. Moreover, he cannot alter the secret S sent to P in the *service request phase* because K (which ciphers S) is known by U and calculated by P. Thus, the attacker is not able to make them believe they are communicating directly to each other (condition necessary for the success of the attack).

Denial-of-Service Attack. This typology of attack is very wide and is carried out from the attacker by sending false requests to interrupt the service provided by P. However, as the service request messages are signed by the grantor, fake requests are easily detected. Moreover, in case a correctly signed message is sent to P more and more times, only the first requests will be accepted, and the others will be discarded. Thus, only one service will be provided with no possibility to overload the provider. Also the attack based on a prior man-in-the-middle attack by blocking and collecting a huge number of tickets and resend it as a burst to overload the service provider fails, because all tickets have a very short expiration time.

Behavior-Based Deanonymization Attack. This type of attack is carried out by identifying recurrent patterns in the usage of services during an authenticated session. The knowledge derived from the analysis of service logs can be used to guess user identity on the basis of his attended behavior inside the cloud. This kind of attacks are contrasted by using different tickets for each service required. Moreover, because the attacker could associate requests coming from the same IP address, all messages to the cloud service provider are sent through a P2P network which adopts a routing protocol guaranteing anonymity.

6 Discussion and Conclusion

In this paper, we have presented a new protocol for accessing cloud services in such a way that no information about users can be drawn from log analysis by a honest but curious cloud provider. The solution combines a multi-party protocol with a P2P approach to obtain anonymity at the granularity of the single user's request and unlinkability between different requests. Accountability is preserved, provided that the trusted third party cooperates. This assumption is coherent with the setting where this solution is thought, where the role of third trusted party can be naturally played by a government entity. Among the strengths of the proposal, besides its scalability and efficiency, we include the consideration that our solution has a realistic business model, as many e-government situations can be recognized where the public sector and the cloud provider market may have reciprocal advantages. The former has the advantage of outsourcing services towards the cloud, the latter has the possibility to exploit the (even attribute-based) digital identity management provided by e-government services. Concerning efficiency and scalability, at the stage of this research, we can argue that the solution appears good only on the basis of quantitative considerations (a few exchanged messages, simple cryptographic operations). Moreover, a possible extension of the P2P role can be done, by enabling multiplexing of the service delivery over multiple virtual (anonymous) channels. Both this extension and an accurate efficiency analysis are planned as the next step of this research. From this point of view, this paper can be viewed as a preliminary paper, where we present an idea appearing interesting and promising that we are implementing within project activities.

Acknowledgment. This work has been partially supported by the TENACE PRIN Project (n. 20103P34XC) funded by the Italian Ministry of Education, University and Research and by the Program "Programma Operativo Nazionale Ricerca e Competitività" 2007–2013, Distretto Tecnologico CyberSecurity funded by the Italian Ministry of Education, University and Research.

References

1. Electronic identification and trust services (eIDAS): regulatory environment and beyond (2015). http://ec.europa.eu/dgs/connect/en/content/electronic-identification-and-trust-services-eidas-regulatory-environment-and-beyond
2. Boyen, X., Waters, B.: Compact group signatures without random oracles. In: Vaudenay, S. (ed.) EUROCRYPT 2006. LNCS, vol. 4004, pp. 427–444. Springer, Heidelberg (2006)
3. Buccafurri, F., Lax, G.: TLS: a tree-based DHT lookup service for highly dynamic networks. In: Meersman, R. (ed.) OTM 2004. LNCS, vol. 3290, pp. 563–580. Springer, Heidelberg (2004)
4. Buccafurri, F., Lax, G., Nicolazzo, S., Nocera, A.: A privacy-preserving solution for tracking people in critical environments. In: Proceedings of the International Workshop on Computers, Software and Applications (COMPSAC 2014), pp. 146–151. IEEE Computer Society, Västerås (2014)
5. Buccafurri, F., Lax, G., Nicolazzo, S., Nocera, A.: A model to support multi-social-network applications. In: Meersman, R., Panetto, H., Dillon, T., Missikoff, M., Liu, L., Pastor, O., Cuzzocrea, A., Sellis, T. (eds.) OTM 2014. LNCS, vol. 8841, pp. 639–656. Springer, Heidelberg (2014)
6. Buccafurri, F., Lax, G., Nicolazzo, S., Nocera, A.: Comparing twitter and facebook user behavior: privacy and other aspects. Comput. Hum. Behav. **52**, 87–95 (2015)
7. Buccafurri, F., Lax, G., Nicolazzo, S., Nocera, A., Ursino, D.: Driving global team formation in social networks to obtain diversity. In: Casteleyn, S., Rossi, G., Winckler, M. (eds.) ICWE 2014. LNCS, vol. 8541, pp. 410–419. Springer, Heidelberg (2014)
8. Buccafurri, F., Lax, G., Nocera, A., Ursino, D.: Moving from social networks to social internetworking scenarios: the crawling perspective. Inf. Sci. **256**, 126–137 (2014)
9. Buccafurri, F., Lax, G., Nocera, A., Ursino, D.: Discovering missing me edges across social networks. Inf. Sci. **319**, 18–37 (2015)
10. Chaum, D., van Heyst, E.: Group signatures. In: Davies, D.W. (ed.) EUROCRYPT 1991. LNCS, vol. 547, pp. 257–265. Springer, Heidelberg (1991)
11. Chen, Y., Sion, R.: On securing untrusted clouds with cryptography. In: Proceedings of the 9th Annual ACM Workshop on Privacy in the Electronic Society, pp. 109–114. ACM (2010)
12. Chow, S.S.M., He, Y.-J., Hui, L.C.K., Yiu, S.M.: SPICE – simple privacy-preserving identity-management for cloud environment. In: Bao, F., Samarati, P., Zhou, J. (eds.) ACNS 2012. LNCS, vol. 7341, pp. 526–543. Springer, Heidelberg (2012)
13. Clarke, I., Sandberg, O., Wiley, B., Hong, T.W.: Freenet: a distributed anonymous information storage and retrieval system. In: Federrath, H. (ed.) Designing Privacy Enhancing Technologies. LNCS, vol. 2009, pp. 46–66. Springer, Heidelberg (2001)
14. Dingledine, R., Mathewson, N., Syverson, P.: Tor: the second-generation onion router. Technical report, DTIC Document (2004)
15. Dwork, C.: Differential privacy: a survey of results. In: Agrawal, M., Du, D.-Z., Duan, Z., Li, A. (eds.) TAMC 2008. LNCS, vol. 4978, pp. 1–19. Springer, Heidelberg (2008)
16. Jensen, M., Schäge, S., Schwenk, J.: Towards an anonymous access control and accountability scheme for cloud computing (2010)

17. Khan, S.M., Hamlen, K.W.: Anonymouscloud: a data ownership privacy provider framework in cloud computing. In: 2012 IEEE 11th International Conference on Trust, Security and Privacy in Computing and Communications (TrustCom), pp. 170–176. IEEE (2012)
18. Laurikainen, R.: Secure and anonymous communication in the cloud. Aalto University School of Science and Technology, Department of Computer Science and Engineering, Technical report TKK-CSE-B10 (2010)
19. Malina, L., Hajny, J.: Efficient security solution for privacy-preserving cloud services. In: 2013 36th International Conference on Telecommunications and Signal Processing (TSP), pp. 23–27. IEEE (2013)
20. Mowbray, M., Pearson, S.: A client-based privacy manager for cloud computing. In: Proceedings of the Fourth International ICST Conference on Communication System Software and Middleware, p. 5. ACM (2009)
21. Riahla, M.A., Tamine, K., Gaborit, P.: A protocol for file sharing, anonymous and confidential, adapted to p2p networks. In: 2012 6th International Conference on Sciences of Electronics, Technologies of Information and Telecommunications (SETIT), pp. 549–557. IEEE (2012)
22. Ruj, S., Stojmenovic, M., Nayak, A.: Decentralized access control with anonymous authentication of data stored in clouds. IEEE Trans. Parallel Distrib. Syst. **25**(2), 384–394 (2014)
23. Samarati, P.: Protecting respondents identities in microdata release. IEEE Trans. Knowl. Data Eng. **13**(6), 1010–1027 (2001)
24. Singh, L.V., Bole, A.V., Yadav, S.K.: Security issues of cloud computing-a survey. Int. J. Adv. Res. Comput. Sci. Manag. Stud. **3**(1), 43–49 (2015)
25. Wang, C., Wang, Q., Ren, K., Cao, N., Lou, W.: Toward secure and dependable storage services in cloud computing. IEEE Trans. Serv. Comput. **5**(2), 220–232 (2012)
26. Wang, C., Wang, Q., Ren, K., Lou, W.: Privacy-preserving public auditing for data storage security in cloud computing. In: 2010 Proceedings IEEE INFOCOM, pp. 1–9. IEEE (2010)
27. Wang, Q., Wang, C., Ren, K., Lou, W., Li, J.: Enabling public auditability and data dynamics for storage security in cloud computing. IEEE Trans. Parallel Distrib. Syst. **22**(5), 847–859 (2011)
28. Xu, Z., Min, R., Hu, Y.: Hieras: a dht based hierarchical p2p routing algorithm. In: Proceedings. 2003 International Conference on Parallel Processing, pp. 187–194. IEEE (2003)

Till All Are One: Towards a Unified Cloud IDS

Nikolaos Pitropakis[1]([✉]), Costas Lambrinoudakis[1],
and Dimitris Geneiatakis[2]

[1] Department of Digital Systems, University of Piraeus, 18534 Piraeus, Greece
{npitrop, clam}@unipi.gr
[2] Electrical and Computer Engineering Department,
Aristotle University of Thessaloniki, 541 24 Thessaloniki, Greece
dgeneiat@auth.gr

Abstract. Recently there is a trend to use cloud computing on service deployment, enjoying various advantages that it offers with emphasis on the economy which is achieved in the era of the financial crisis. However, along with the transformation of technology, several security issues are raised and especially the threat of malicious insiders. For instance, insiders can use their privileged position to accomplish an attack against the cloud infrastructure. In this paper we introduce a practical and efficient intrusion detection system solution for cloud based on the advantages of CUDA technology. The proposed solution audits the deployed virtual machines operation, and correlates the collected information to detect uncommon behavior based on Smith-Waterman algorithm. To do so, we collect the system calls of cloud virtual machines and compare them with pre-defined attack signatures. We implement the core of the detection module both sequentially and in parallel on CUDA technology. We evaluate our solution on experimental CUDA enabled cloud system in terms of performance using well known attack patterns. Results indicate that our approach improve highly the efficiency of detection in terms of processing time compared to a sequential implementation.

Keywords: Cloud computing · Security · Malicious insider · IDS · System calls · Smith Waterman · CUDA

1 Introduction

Cloud Computing cannot offer physical isolation among virtual machines (VMs), since its resources are shared by design. Various attack vectors have been developed to identify shared resources and gain unauthorized access to them. Shared memory vulnerabilities [9], privilege escalation [5], and co-residency [9] are only a few examples of attack vectors that could harm cloud's confidentiality, integrity and availability. Compared to the traditional IT services, cloud attack surface has been expanded not only because of the shared resources, but also due to the additional attacking points that an adversary may utilise in order to exploit a vulnerability, e.g., a VM, a cloud management platform, or any other component of the cloud infrastructure. Current approaches inherit methods from conventional information systems to reduce the effects of malicious actions performed through the VMs. Spreading the information

© Springer International Publishing Switzerland 2015
S. Fischer-Hübner et al. (Eds.): TrustBus 2015, LNCS 9264, pp. 136–149, 2015.
DOI: 10.1007/978-3-319-22906-5_11

into multiple parts in the cloud [3], creating multiple Intrusion Detection Systems (IDS) [25] or audit mechanisms [11], are a few of the solutions currently being proposed n literature. In other approaches a network or data isolation is employed for securing the cloud infrastructure [23]. Others monitor the system calls for detecting malicious activities [32, 34, 35]. The aforementioned approaches can be effective in detecting attacks launched on conventional information systems, but they are not appropriate to detect attacks launched against cloud infrastructures from privileged users; the reason being that the majority of them may be executed from separate VMs and do not appear as a threat to conventional IDS systems.

Thus, we introduce the Cloud Realtime Observation Wards (CROW) solution for detecting malicious activities both against the VMs and the cloud infrastructure itself. The principle of the proposed approach is to monitor the system calls of each VM independently, in a way similar to a host based IDS, and then to combine the gathered information to detect attacks targeting not only a VM itself, but also against the cloud infrastructure. Our approach operates on the cloud infrastructure as a service layer, in a transparent manner – meaning that no modifications to the underlying layers are required.

Specifically, we make use of the *'strace'* command [2] to monitor the system calls of each VM, and then we process them in order to generate the attack patterns and detect possible abnormal behaviors. In contrast to other cloud IDSs [31] that use machine learning classifiers as black-box, the proposed system generates attack patterns using the Smith-Waterman algorithm [52] and performs similarity tests between the attack patterns and the data (system calls) collected to decide whether the cloud infrastructure is under an attack or not, with certain level confidence.

We implement the core of detection module both in sequential and parallel mode in a cloud platform running a XEN OS supported by NVIDIA CUDA technology [8], and evaluate its performance in terms of processing time relying on well-known attack patterns. Results show that we can highly improve the detection efficiency in terms of processing times up to 6x, in case of using the parallel instead of the sequential deployment. This way, we transfer IDS processing overhead to the Graphic Processor Unit (GPU) in contrast of relying on cloud infrastructure main resources (CPU and memory). Overall, the contribution of this paper could be summarized to the followings:

- We introduce a CUDA based solution IDS system for cloud infrastructure. The core of IDS relies on a parallel implementation of the Smith Waterman algorithm.
- Our approach enhance the performance of cloud IDS up to 6x, compared to sequential implementation.
- We provide our solution as open source [45]. We believe this can facilitate additional experimentation based on our approach, and replicate our outcomes.

The rest of the paper is organised as follows. Section 2 overviews the related works and compares them with our approach. Section 3 introduces the threat model deal with the scope of this work. Section 4 presents our approach to detect malicious activities in cloud infrastructure. Section 5 evaluates our solution in terms of performance. Finally, Sect. 6 draws the conclusion giving some pointers for future work as well.

2 Related Work

Over the last years there have been several attempts to track, disable or counter the malicious insider threat. The majority of these solutions achieve their goal by focusing on a very specific aspect of the cloud, such as the employees or the network, while only a minority of them aim to provide a general purpose solution.

Spring suggests that a firewall at the cloud border that blocks troublesome packets can reduce, but not eliminate, the risk of known malicious entities to gain access [1]. Alzain et al. [3] suggest that moving from "single-clouds" to "multi-clouds" will greatly reduce the malicious insider's threat as the information is spread among the interclouds and cannot be retrieved from a single cloud infrastructure. Another approach focuses on employing logistic regression models to estimate false positive/negatives on intrusion detection and identification of malicious insiders is proposed in [6]. Furthermore, it insists on developing new protocols that cope with denial of service and insider attacks and ensure predictable delivery of mission critical data.

Magklaras et al. [11] propose an audit engine for logging user actions in relational mode, named LUARM, which attempts to solve two fundamental problems of the insider's IT misuse domain. The first one is the lack of data repositories for insider misuse cases that could be utilized by post-case forensic examiners to aid incident investigations. The second area highlighted is how information security researchers can enhance their ability to accurately specify insider threats at system level.

Tripathi and Mishra [12] insist that cloud providers should provide tools to the customers that can detect and defend against the malicious insiders threats. They also mention that malicious insider threats can be mitigated by specifying human resources requirements as part of legal contracts, conducting a comprehensive supplier assessment. This procedure would lead to reporting and determining security breach notification processes.

"Fog computing" [13] suggests an approach totally different from the others. Each user's data access log is monitored in the cloud and a sort of profiling is maintained. This type of monitoring facilitates the detection of abnormal behaviour. An alternative approach is that of Hoang C. [14], which achieves security in a Xen based hypervisor [15] by trapping hypercalls since they are fewer than system calls. The hypercalls are checked before their execution and thus malicious ones can be detected and countered. Combining the last two approaches, [16] takes advantage of the system calls and classifies them into 'normal' and 'abnormal' through binary weighted cosine metric and k-nearest neighbor (knn) machine learning algorithm.

Paying special attention to access control mechanisms, Kollam and Sunnyvale [17] present a mechanism that generates immutable security policies for a client, and then propagates and enforces them at the provider's infrastructure. This mechanism is one of the very few methods that aim directly at malicious insiders and especially system administrators.

The term "co-residency" (or "co-tenancy") means that multiple independent customers share the same physical infrastructure [18]. It is therefore possible to have VMs owned by different customers being placed on the same physical machine. Since there are several methods to discover neighbouring VMs on a Cloud infrastructure, it is necessary to employ countermeasures for this specific attack. In that direction Adam Bates [19], through his approach reveals that "co-residency" detection is also possible through network flow. This is a type of network converting timing channel, capable of breaking anonymity by tracing the path of the network flow. It can also perform a variety of traffic analysis tasks. However, many drawbacks exist in this method, with the most important one being the introduction of a considerable network delay.

Ristenpart [9] presents the "co-residency" attack on Amazon EC2, one of the largest cloud infrastructures. His methodology employs network tools such as nmap [20], hping [21] and wget [22], which are utilized in order to create network probes that will acquire the addresses of the potential targets. Additionally, the addresses are used to make a hypothetic map of the cloud network. In the manifestation of the method he explores whether two instances are "co-resident" or not through a series of checks, which depend on (a) matching Dom0 (host OS of a cloud infrastructure) IP address, (b) small packet round trip times, or (c) numerically close internal IP address. Project "Silverline" [23], aims to achieve both data and network isolation. "Pseudo" randomly-allocated IP address are used for each VM, hiding the actual IP addresses provided by the cloud provider. There are numerous attempts to protect cloud infrastructures not only from the "co-residency" attack but also from various other network stressing threats, by employing Intrusion Detection Systems (IDS). Most of them make use of multiple agents installed on different Virtual Machines and collect the data into a central point. The disadvantage is that most of these approaches introduce considerable overhead to the cloud infrastructure since they consume significant amount of resources [25–30]. An interesting approach is that of Bakshi and Yogesh [31], who transfer the targeted applications to VMs hosted in another data center when they pick up grossly abnormal spike in inbound traffic.

Alarifi and Wolthusen [32] propose to monitor the system calls in every VM host of an IaaS environment based on KVM hypervisor [33], and then to invoke statistical analysis for classifying the system calls after having collected a large amount of data that includes both normal operation and malicious actions. Rawat et al. [34] and Sharma et al. [35] in their work utilize the kNN machine learning algorithm and the binary weighted cosine metric in order to achieve a similar goal, and classify the processes into normal or malicious using DARPA-1998 data set. The ancestor of the latter techniques is the work of Fofmeyr et al. [36] who suggested the separation of system calls into normal and malicious using the profiling of the operation of a system. A further extension of their methodology came from Eskin, et al. [39] who implemented dynamic windows sizes as the length of the subsequence of a system call trace which is used as the basic unit for modelling program or process behaviour.

Kang, et al. [37] further improve the above suggestions by introducing machine learning techniques using the "bag of system calls" representation in system call sequences. Machine learning techniques are also used by Azmandian et al. [40] and Fatemeh et al. [38].

Although recent research efforts have significant contribution in the area of intrusion detection mechanisms, a decade ago Coull and his team [56] inspired what we have adopted in CROW. They used the system calls as a series of genes and made use of the Smith Waterman algorithm. However they did not use whole patterns something that has resulted in many false positives and false negatives. Furthermore, their idea has been implemented in an isolated system and has nothing to do with distributed systems or cloud computing.

Sotiris Ioannidis et al., [57] made use of the CUDA architecture for executing Snort [58], a modern network intrusion detection system (NIDS), calling their system Gnort. They managed to transfer large portion of the overhead to the GPU, thus speeding up the efficiency of the NIDS, reducing at the same time the overhead on the CPU. During the past few years the continuous evolution of the CUDA technology and the power enhancement of GPUs, have attracted the attention of researchers who have done numerous attempts to parallelize and implement genetic algorithms into CUDA versions. A well-known effort is the CUDASW ++ [59], a project which accelerates the Smith Waterman algorithm through the GPU. However, this implementation focuses on protein database searches and does not take into consideration system calls sequences or other intrusion detection models.

3   Threat Model

According to [48], the term "insider", for an information system, applies to anyone with approved access, privilege, or knowledge of the information system and its services and missions. On the other hand, a "malicious insider" is someone motivated to adversely impact an organization's mission through a range of actions that compromise information confidentiality, integrity, and/or availability taking the advantage of his/her privileges. Similarly, in the case of cloud computing we define an insider as an entity who: (a) Works for the cloud host, (b) Has privileged access to the cloud resources and (c) Uses the cloud services. Consequently, cloud insiders are mostly privileged users, who may be motivated to compromise the cloud infrastructure's security. Their actions may result in a temporary break, permanent interruption of the provided services, or in legitimate users' privacy violation, depending on their privileges. Note that there is VM related information that can be extracted only by privileged users, such as the structure of the virtual network build up for the internal communication, and exploited during attack's next steps. In this direction, a malicious user may try to map all the available virtual machines and extract other VM related information [18] in order to achieve his aim that is to violate cloud security or users' privacy.

For instance, malicious users may combine various utilities such as "nslookup", ping commands and the nmap tool, to identify publicly accessible information for a specific domain of VMs. These actions will result in launching an attack named "co-residence" or "co-tenancy" [9]. Even though these "scans" are harmless, the extraction of such information can be used for future attacks (e.g. exploiting a vulnerability in a specific operating system). Alternatively, an internal malicious user may try to affect directly the availability of a virtual network by congesting the corresponding public and private interfaces with numerous ping requests. Network stressing can also be launched through smurf attacks [49].

Furthermore, the fact that cloud infrastructures lack physical isolation can lead to memory leakages among different VMs. For instance, a malicious VM might try to get access to the shared memory (cache or main memory) and retrieve personal information for the users of the co-resident VMs. In this context, Ristenpart et al. [9] perform cross VM side channel attack on Amazon EC2 and measure the cache activity of other users, while Rochsa and Correia [53] prove that any malicious privileged user can use the memory dumps of a VM to acquire information about its users, such as passwords, social security number and other personal information.

4 Cloud Realtime Observation Wards

4.1 Overview

Our scheme, namely CROW aims at detecting malicious privileged users in the cloud and also provides IDS functionality for the entire infrastructure by individually monitoring the health of each employed VM. To the best of our knowledge CROW is the first of its kind. Its high level architecture is depicted in Fig. 1.

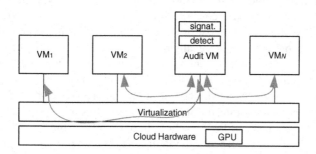

Fig. 1. The CROW architecture

Each VM has a monitoring mechanism, which contains signature for the operations relevant to the work orders of each VM. This mechanism constantly detects the system calls through the kernel of the VM, using the GPU acceleration instead of CPU usage. Whenever an attack signature is detected the information is immediately transferred to the Audit VM, in order to alert the security officers for the necessary actions to be taken.

The audit sub-system monitors the health of each of the provided VMs and is responsible for generating new attack signatures, based on the system call patterns of the attacks. The attack signatures have been generated through the system call analysis of well-known attacks. The detection module monitors each VM and utilizes the attack signatures for computing their similarity with the system calls issued by the VM. The calculation of the similarity score is procedure that requires a lot of effort as matters CPU and RAM.

Our approach focus on transferring the majority of this overhead to the GPU, making the ordinary computational resources constantly available to the cloud infrastructure so as to keep it fully operational, exploiting the advantages of Compute Unified Device Architecture (CUDA). Briefly, CUDA is a parallel computing platform giving access to developers to the virtual instruction set and memory of the GPU.

4.2   Attack Signature Generation

The attack signature generation process consists of two steps. During the first step, the strace [2] command is used for recording the system calls produced during the execution of the attack. Having collected a significant number of system call patterns, following multiple executions of the same attack, they are processed with the Smith-Waterman algorithm [52]. The choice of this specific algorithm has been based on the fact that the data set (system call patterns) that we need to process consists of symbols drawn from a finite discrete alphabet. Furthermore, Smith-Waterman algorithm is the most efficient descendant of the algorithms used to solve the Longest Common Subsequence (LCS) problem [62] of finding the longest subsequence common to all sequences in a set of sequences. It differs from problems of finding common substrings because sequences are required to occupy consecutive positions within the original sequences.

More specifically, the Smith-Waterman algorithm is a dynamic programming algorithm which relies on the construction of a similarity grid between two data sequences that are aligned. The goal of the algorithm is to extract a part of grid nodes which reveal the optimal sequence alignment. To achieve this goal, the algorithm processes the grid iteratively and accumulates a similarity score at each node. During this mode of operation, a node is examined with respect to a possible set of predecessors and the best predecessor is selected. The transition from a predecessor to the target node has the effect of increasing or decreasing the accumulated similarity on the target node, depending on the geometry of the transition. In our work we run the Smith-Waterman algorithm in pairs of two sequences of system calls for the same attack and in each run we reduce the number of our sequences to half, taking the best similarity match. Continuing this iteration for a number of times, we end up with the best similarity match for system calls after having processed all of our results, creating a pattern of the attack. The generated attack signature is the sequence of the system calls invoked during the execution of the attack commands. Note that similar to malware analysis we are aware of the attack, so we execute the corresponding malware and collect the generated system calls to generate the corresponding signatures. For instance, considering that "nslookup" command is a part of an attack we monitor it, and record the system calls that are produced. Afterwards, we analyze the collected system calls through the Smith-Waterman algorithm to generate the appropriate signature as illustrated in Fig. 2.

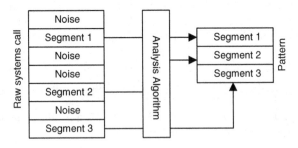

Fig. 2. The segments of the attack pattern are found through the system call sequence using as analysis the Smith-Waterman algorithm.

Specifically, let's assume that we need to create a signature for "co-residency" attack [9], which consists of three distinct phases. The attacker after obtaining the ip address of his virtual machine, is working on finding the Domain Name System (DNS) address. This can be easily retrieved through the command "nslookup" followed by the ip address of the Virtual Machine (VM). This command, executed in a Linux based OS, will return the DNS address. After obtaining the DNS address, the attacker can use the "nmap" command to acquire the ip addresses of all virtual machines (including host) utilising the specific DNS. Specifically the command executed is "nmap –sP DNS_Adress/24". Having the ip addresses of all virtual machines that use the same DNS, the attacker can identify the Operating System of either the Host or of the other Virtual Machines, by executing the command "nmap –v –O Ip_address". Through the aforementioned three distinct steps, all co-residents can be identified along with additional information about their operating systems, something that can allow the attacker to launch further attacks harming the cloud infrastructure. In order to create the signatures, we should first load a test OS on the test VM and then proceed with the execution of the attack in three distinct steps.

During the first step the "nslookup" command is executed and the systems calls invoked are recorded with the help of the "strace" command. The command should be executed several times (let's assume x times) in order to be statistically correct, storing every time the generated system calls. After the x sequences of system calls have been collected, the Smith-Waterman algorithm will be invoked x/2 times, as it is necessary to compare sequence 1 with sequence 2, sequence 3 with sequence 4, etc. In this way x/2 sequences of system calls will be generated by the similarity of the x initial ones. Then we shall be able to produce x/4 sequences of system calls etc, until we reach the final sequence which has no other to be compared with. This sequence will form the signature for the first part of the attack, which is the "nslookup" command. A sample of the "nslookup" signature is illustrated in Table 1.

Table 1. nslookup command's sample signature. Numbers illustrate the id-s of the corresponding system calls.

11	45	33	91	33	5	28	91	6	33		5	3	28

Then the same procedure will be followed for the remaining two steps of the attack (commands "nmap –sP DNS_address/24" and "nmap –v –O target_ip_address"). When the signatures for the three distinct attack steps have been generated, they can be combined to form the signature of the "co-residency" attack.

4.3   Detection Module

The attack signatures can now be utilised for the detection of potential malicious acts. Specifically, the generated signatures are stored in the corresponding database of the audit VM. To detect an attack against the VM and cloud infrastructure itself we monitor the system calls of VMs and send them to the detection module.

The detection module aims to identify the attack segments into the entire sequence of system calls, avoiding the possible noise that has been created by various other irrelevant system calls, following the same approach of attack signature generation. If all the attack segments are identified, then an alert is sent to the audit VM. Then the operators of the audit station will take action contacting the Host VM, which has the authority to do whatever necessary for protecting the entire infrastructure, based on the employed policy.

As already mentioned, the "co-residency" attack consists of three distinct steps, the "nslookup" command and two different executions of the "nmap" command. These three commands when executed in sequence implement the "co-residency" attack. Having the signature of the "nslookup" command, which is harmless in solo execution, will not cause a false alarm consuming unnecessarily time and useful resources. The alarm will be triggered only when all three steps of the attack have been detected in sequence. As the network of a cloud infrastructure is continuously redefined, the solo execution of the "nslookup" or even the "nmap" commands will not bring great results to potential attackers as they have to be performed in sequence and soon enough to earn the pieces of information needed.

To avoid any potential actions that will lead in hiding an attack from the audit station every two seconds the audit station initiates a handshake with each of the VMs to clarify that the communication is good between them.

4.4   Implementation

Aiming not only to improve the security level of a cloud infrastructure but also minimize the overhead of the detection mechanism, we have capitalized on [57] for transferring the computational overhead to the GPU. Thus, we should mention that in terms of cloud computing systems, GPUs are rarely used autonomously by the VMs although this function can be supported by hypervisors such as XEN [15]. We have implemented the detection mechanism both in sequential and parallel modes to show the different overhead impacts on performance. Both, implementations are freely available as mentioned previously.

5   Evaluation

We evaluate the detection core of our approach in terms of performance in an experimental cloud test bed infrastructure consisted of: Intel Xeon E5607 as Central Processing Unit, 8 GB of memory running at 1333 MHz, 300 GB SAS HDD @10000 rpms and GPU NVidia GTX 760, while the platform was running a XEN hypervisor. We should mention that in this work we focus only on evaluating the performance of the proposed solution in terms of introduced overhead, thus we assess the sequential versus the parallel implementations of the detection module. Though one could consider this comparison unbalanced, we would like to show the improvement trend in terms of performance that we can reach. To do so, we relied on co-residency attack splitting it on different segments (i.e. number of signatures) to assess our implementation throughput as the number of signature increased.

Our experimental outcomes are summarized in Table 2 and Fig. 3. Specifically, the sequential implementation time processing overhead growth exponentially as the number of system calls increased. For instance, in the case of processing 100 system calls the overhead is as little as 0,156 s, however, when the system calls increased to one million records the overhead is increased almost 2500x. On the contrary, the parallel implementation under the same testing conditions results increases the overhead up to 350x accordingly. So, using the parallel implementation we can gain in computational resources up to 6x. This way, we transfer cloud IDS computational resource to GPU leaving cloud main resources to its users.

Table 2. Time spent for sequential and parallel execution of the Smith Waterman algorithm

Number of system calls per data set		Time in seconds	
Attack signature	VM system calls	Sequential execution	CUDA parallel
10	10	0,156	0,091
20	30	0,357	0,099
80	150	4,268	0,117
334	334	46,919	0,445
500	600	120,365	0,812
1000	1000	401,937	3,209

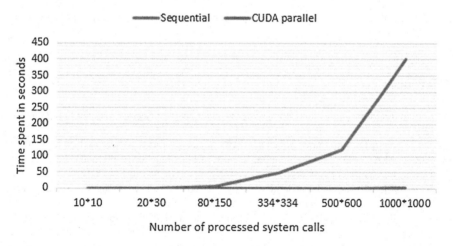

Fig. 3. Time comparison between sequential and cuda parallel execution of the detection module.

As far as the detection accuracy of our approach is concerned it has been analyzed in our previous research works [60, 61]. Mainly it focusses on the accuracy of the Smith Waterman algorithm and its utilization as matters the similarity match between series of system calls in a cloud computing environment. To be specific we created separate test bed environments based either on XEN or KVM hypervisors.

Our collected sets of data proved that similarity between attacks was far greater than similarity between attacks and normal operation of a system. Furthermore, a heavy load of the system, which would result in the creation of large number of system calls did not shrink the similarity significantly, thus not creating any false alarms. In addition to that, the alternation of gap penalty parameter greater increased the similarity between attacks while it was not significantly increased between attacks and normal operation of the systems' used.

6   Conclusion and Future Work

Driven by the lack of focus on malicious privileged user attacks in modern IDS systems for cloud infrastructures, we have proposed CROW, a novel detection method of malicious acts by Cloud insiders and a novel implementation of Smith Waterman algorithm based on CUDA technology. This new parallel implementation results into significant reduction of the overhead as compared to its sequential sibling. Furthermore, a sample creation of insider attacks has been presented as a guide for the creation of the attack signatures databases.

Currently we are experimenting with different cloud infrastructure setups and algorithm tweaks in order to achieve stability and maximum efficiency of the proposed method. Also we test the behaviour and results of alternative pattern recognition algorithms that may support real time detection of attacks.

Acknowledgements. This work has been partially supported by the Research Center of the University of Piraeus.

References

1. Spring, J.: Monitoring cloud computing by layer, part 1. Secur. Priv. IEEE **9**(2), 66–68 (2011)
2. Strace command. http://unixhelp.ed.ac.uk/CGI/man-cgi?strace+1. Accessed 24 May 2015
3. AlZain, M.A., et al.: Cloud computing security: from single to multi-clouds. In: 2012 45th Hawaii International Conference on System Science (HICSS). IEEE (2012)
4. Krutz, R.L., Vines, R.D.: Cloud Security: A Comprehensive Guide to Secure Cloud Computing. Wiley, Indianapolis (2010)
5. Enisa: Cloud Computing – Benefits, Risks and Recommendations for Information Security (2009)
6. Sandhu, R., et al.: Towards a discipline of mission-aware cloud computing. In: Proceedings of the 2010 ACM Workshop on Cloud Computing Security Workshop. ACM (2010)
7. Kandias, M., Virvilis, N., Gritzalis, D.: The insider threat in cloud computing. In: Bologna, S., Hämmerli, B., Gritzalis, D., Wolthusen, S. (eds.) CRITIS 2011. LNCS, vol. 6983, pp. 93–103. Springer, Heidelberg (2013)
8. CUDA technology. http://www.nvidia.com/object/cuda_home_new.html. Accessed 24 May 2015

9. Ristenpart, T., Tromer, E., Shacham, H., Savage, S.: Hey, you, get off of my cloud: exploring information leakage in third-party compute clouds. In: ACM CCS, Chicago (2009)

10. Roschke, S., Cheng, F., Meinel, C.: An advanced IDS management architecture. J. Inf. Assur. Secur. **5**, 246–255 (2010)

11. Magklaras, G., Furnell, S., Papadaki, M.: LUARM: an audit engine for insider misuse detection. Int. J. Digit. Crime Forensics **3**(3), 37–49 (2011)

12. Tripathi, A., Mishra, A.: Cloud computing security considerations. In: 2011 IEEE International Conference on Signal Processing, Communications and Computing (ICSPCC). IEEE (2011)

13. Stolfo, S.J., Salem, M.B., Keromytis, A.D.: Fog computing: mitigating insider data theft attacks in the cloud. In: 2012 IEEE Symposium on Security and Privacy Workshops (SPW). IEEE (2012)

14. Hoang, C.: Protecting Xen hypercalls. MSC thesis, University of British Columbia, July 2009

15. XEN Hypervisor. http://www.xenproject.org/developers/teams/hypervisor.html. Accessed 24 May 2015

16. Rawat, S., Gulati, V.P., Pujari, A.K., Vemuri, V.R.: Intrusion detection using text processing techniques with a binary-weighted cosine metric. J. Inf. Assur. Secur. **1**(1), 43–50 (2006)

17. Sundararajan, S., Narayanan, H., Pavithran, V., Vorungati, K., Achuthan, K.: Preventing insider attacks in the cloud. In: Abraham, A., Lloret Mauri, J., Buford, J.F., Suzuki, J., Thampi, S.M. (eds.) ACC 2011, Part I. CCIS, vol. 190, pp. 488–500. Springer, Heidelberg (2011)

18. Xiao, Z., Xiao, Y.: Security and privacy in cloud computing. IEEE Commun. Surv. Tutorials **PP**(99), 1–17 (2012)

19. Bates, A.: Dtecting cloud co-residency with network flow watermarking techniques. MSC thesis, University of Oregon, September 2012

20. Nmap command. http://nmap.org/. Accessed 24 May 2015

21. Hping command. http://www.hping.org/. Accessed 24 May 2015

22. Wget command. http://www.gnu.org/software/wget/. Accessed 24 May 2015

23. Mundada, Y., Ramachndran, A., Feamster, N.: SilverLine: data and network isolation for cloud services. In: Proceedings of the USENIX Workshop on Hot Topics in Cloud Computing (HotCloud) (2011)

24. Zhang, Y., Juels, A., Oprea, A., Reiter, A.: HomeAlone: Co-Residency Detection in the Cloud via Side-Channel Analysis. In: IEEE Symposium on Security and Privacy (2011)

25. Mazzariello, C., Bifulco, R., Canonico, R.: Integrating a network IDS into an open source cloud computing environment. In: Sixth International Conference on Information Assurance and Security (2010)

26. Schulter, A., Vieira, K., Westphal, C., Westaphal, C., Abderrrahim, S.: Intrusion detection for computational grids. In: Proceedings of the 2nd Int'l Conference New Technologies Mobility, and Security. IEEE Press (2008)

27. Cheng, F., Roschke, S., Meinel, C.: Implementing IDS management on lock-keeper. In: Bao, F., Li, H., Wang, G. (eds.) ISPEC 2009. LNCS, vol. 5451, pp. 360–371. Springer, Heidelberg (2009)

28. Cheng, F., Roschke, S., Meinel, C.: An advanced IDS management architecture. J. Inf. Assu. Secur. **51**, 246–255 (2010)

29. Cheng, F., Roschke, S., Meinel, C.: Intrusion detection in the cloud. In: Eighth IEEE International Conference on Dependable, Autonomic and Secure Computing, China (2009)

30. Bharadwaja, S., Sun, W., Niamat, M., Shen, F.: Collabra: axen hypervisor based collaborative intrusion detection system. In: Proceedings of the 8th International Conference on Information Technology: New Generations (ITNG 2011), Las Vegas, Nev, USA, pp. 695–700 (2011)
31. Bakshi, A., Yogesh, B.: Securing cloud from ddos attacks using intrusion detection system in virtual machine. In: Second International Conference on Communication Software and Networks, ICCSN 2010. IEEE (2010)
32. Alarifi, S.S., Wolthusen, S.D.: Detecting anomalies in IaaS environments through virtual machine host system call analysis. In: 2012 International Conferece for Internet Technology And Secured Transactions. IEEE (2012)
33. KVM Hypervisor. http://www.linux-kvm.org/. Accessed 24 May 2015
34. Rawat, S., et al.: Intrusion detection using text processing techniques with a binary-weighted cosine metric. J. Inf. Assur. Secur. 1(1), 43–50 (2006)
35. Sharma, A., Pujari, A.K., Paliwal, K.K.: Intrusion detection using text processing techniques with a kernel based similarity measure. Comput. Secur. 26(7), 488–495 (2007)
36. Hofmeyr, S.A., Forrest, S., Somayaji, A.: Intrusion detection using sequences of system calls. J. Comput. Secur. 6(3), 151–180 (1998)
37. Kang, D.-K., Fuller, D., Honavar, V.: Learning classifiers for misuse and anomaly detection using a bag of system calls representation. In: Proceedings from the Sixth Annual IEEE SMC Information Assurance Workshop, IAW 2005. IEEE (2005)
38. Azmandian, F., et al.: Securing cloud storage systems through a virtual machine monitor. In: Proceedings of the First International Workshop on Secure and Resilient Architectures and Systems. ACM (2012)
39. Eskin, E., Lee, W., Stolfo, S.J.: Modeling system calls for intrusion detection with dynamic window sizes. In: Proceedings of the DARPA Information Survivability Conference and Exposition II, DISCEX 2001, vol. 1. IEEE (2001)
40. Azmandian, F., et al.: Virtual machine monitor-based lightweight intrusion detection. ACM SIGOPS Operating Syst. Rev. 45(2), 38–53 (2011)
41. Nslookup command. http://www.computerhope.com/unix/unslooku.htm. Accessed 24 May 2015
42. Backtrack Linux. http://www.backtrack-linux.org/. Accessed 24 May 2015
43. Kali Linux. http://www.kali.org/. Accessed 24 May 2015
44. Backbox Linux. http://www.backbox.org/. Accessed 24 May 2015
45. Our CUDA parallel implementation. https://code.google.com/p/smith-waterman-cuda-syscall/. Accessed 24 May 2015
46. GNU Operating System. http://www.gnu.org/software/wget/. Accessed 24 May 2015
47. Hping command. http://www.hping.org/. Accessed 24 May 2015
48. Maybury, M., et al.: Analysis and Detection of Malicious Insiders. MITRE Corp., Bedford (2005)
49. Smurf attack. http://www.ciscopress.com/articles/article.asp?p=1312796. Accessed 24 May 2015
50. Ping6 attack. http://www.tldp.org/HOWTO/Linux%2BIPv6-HOWTO/x811.html. Accessed 24 May 2015
51. Agarwal, A., Agarwal, A.: The security risks associated with cloud computing. Int. J. Comput. Appl. Eng. Sci. 1 (2011)
52. Smith, T., Waterman, M.: Identification of common molecular subsequences. J. Mol. Biol. 147, 195–197 (1981)
53. Krutz, R.L., Vines, R.D.: Cloud Security: A Comprehensive Guide to Secure Cloud Computing. Wiley, Indianapolis (2010)

54. Jose, G., Arul, J., Sanjeev, C., Suyambulingom, C.: Implementation of data security in cloud computing. Int. J. P2P Netw. Trends Technol. **1**(1) (2011)

55. Labib, K., Vemuri, V.R.: An application of principal component analysis to the detection and visualization of computer network attacks. Annales des Télécommunications **61**(1–2), 218–234 (2006)

56. Coull, S., Branch, J., Szymanski, B., Breimer, E.: Intrusion detection: a bioinformatics approach. In: Proceedings of the 19th Annual Computer Security Applications Conference, pp. 24–33. IEEE, December 2003

57. Vasiliadis, G., Antonatos, S., Polychronakis, M., Markatos, E.P., Ioannidis, S.: Gnort: high performance network intrusion detection using graphics processors. In: Lippmann, R., Kirda, E., Trachtenberg, A. (eds.) RAID 2008. LNCS, vol. 5230, pp. 116–134. Springer, Heidelberg (2008)

58. Snort IDS. https://www.snort.org/. Accessed 24 May 2015

59. Cudasw parallel SW CUDA implementation. http://cudasw.sourceforge.net/homepage. htm#latest. Accessed 24 May 2015

60. Pitropakis, N., Pikrakis, A., Lambrinoudakis, C.: Behaviour reflects personality: detecting co-residence attacks on Xen-based cloud environments. Int. J. Inf. Secur. 1–7 (2014)

61. Pitropakis, N., et al.: If you want to know about a hunter, study his prey: detection of network based attacks on KVM based cloud environments. J. Cloud Comput. Adv. Syst. Appl. **3**(1), 20 (2014)

62. Maier, D.: The complexity of some problems on subsequences and supersequences. J. ACM (JACM) **25**(2), 322–336 (1978)

Security Policies / Usability Issues

Security, Privacy and Usability – A Survey of Users' Perceptions and Attitudes

Abdulwahid Al Abdulwahid[1,2(✉)], Nathan Clarke[1,3], Ingo Stengel[1],
Steven Furnell[1,3,4], and Christoph Reich[5]

[1] Centre for Security, Communications and Network Research,
Plymouth University, Plymouth, UK
Abdulwahid.Alabdulwahid@plymouth.ac.uk
[2] Computer Science and Engineering Department,
Jubail University College, Jubail, Saudi Arabia
[3] Security Research Institute, Edith Cowan University, Perth, WA, Australia
[4] Centre for Research in Information and Cyber Security,
Nelson Mandela Metropolitan University, Port Elizabeth, South Africa
[5] Cloud Research Lab, Furtwangen University, Furtwangen, Germany

Abstract. Users are now in possession of an ever-growing number of advance digital devices with a wide range of capabilities which are used for accessing, storing and processing enormous information. A significant proportion of it is often considered sensitive and confidential. Accordingly, each device has its own associated security requirements and configurations. This paper presents the survey results of 302 digital device users, which aimed at exploring their technology usage and security practices, and at investigating their perceptions and satisfaction of associated current and alternative authentication approaches alongside their usability. Furthermore, it sought to analyse users' awareness and attitudes towards related privacy issues. It is revealed that an inconsistency between users' perceptions and real practices exists. Despite the widespread interest in more security, there is a quite low number of respondents using or maintaining the available security measures. However, it is apparent that users do not avoid applying the concept of authentication security but avoid the inconvenience of its current common techniques (biometrics are having growing practical interest). The respondents' perceptions towards Trusted Third-Party (TTP) enable utilising biometrics for a novel authentication solution managed by a TTP working on multi devices to access multi services. However, it must be developed and implemented considerately.

Keywords: Cyber security · Usability · Privacy · User survey · Biometrics · Authentication · Users' perceptions · Users' security practices

1 Introduction

Users are now in possession of an ever-growing number of advance digital devices (i.e. PCs, servers, laptops, tablets, phablets and smartphones) with a wide range of capabilities which are used for accessing, storing and processing personal, financial, medical and business information (some of which are often considered sensitive and

© Springer International Publishing Switzerland 2015
S. Fischer-Hübner et al. (Eds.): TrustBus 2015, LNCS 9264, pp. 153–168, 2015.
DOI: 10.1007/978-3-319-22906-5_12

confidential). This can be realised from the enormous growth in number of Internet users around the world, 2.4 billion, along with the accelerated rise of 150 % per year in mobile data traffic [1]. Moreover, [2] states that the worldwide market share of smartphones and phablets is 70 % of the total smart connected device market and is forecasted to grow to 75.6 % by 2018.

However, these devices, activities, services and information are becoming targets of cybercriminals. For example, 35 % of [3] survey respondents' accounts or personal information were compromised or stolen by imposters. In [4], it was revealed that there was a 42 % increase in targeted attacks. In addition, another report showed that the use of stolen credentials was at the top of the data breach threats [5]. Furthermore, three quarters of financial and travel organisations encountered customer impersonation and identity fraud [6], highlighting that even those organisations running and holding critical information suffer from cyber attacks.

Protecting these assets has thus become evidently paramount. A number of studies have been conducted revolving conventional authentications approaches; however, they fall short of a variety of pitfalls – e.g. cognitive burden of passwords, missing of tokens, and intrusiveness of biometrics [7, 8]. Above these, they are typically used at the beginning of the usage session not throughout exposing the system/device/service to misuse. Therefore, it is apparent that a more innovative, convenient and secure solution for ongoing user authentication is essential. Accordingly, it must be designed and implemented considerately as each of the user devices has typically its own associated security requirements. However, most of the undertaken studies and proposed solutions thus far endure one or more shortcomings; for instance, an inability to balance the trade-off between security and usability, confinement to specific device, lack or negligence of evaluating user acceptance and privacy measures, and insufficiency or absence of real tested datasets [9, 10].

In prior work, the authors have proposed a federated continuous authentication that can be managed by a Trusted Third-Party (TTP) to work over user's devices to enable access to services seamlessly in a location, technology, and service independent manner [11]. Related to this, it is considered desirable to explore and address related aspects to the proposal prior to implementing it or any alternative solution; for instance, the extent of using the technologies including devices, operating systems, and Internet services. To this end, the current paper presents details of a survey that was conducted to investigate the current security measures employed and compares these with the desired and appropriate protection together with the associated experience. The discussion also considers the acceptability of such proposals from the end user perspective, as this is essential if measures are to see sufficiently widespread adoption amongst them.

2 Design and Methodology

The survey was designed to explore and assess users' technology usage and security practices, and to investigate their perception and satisfaction regarding current and alternative authentication approaches. Furthermore, it sought to understand the usability of these practices and to analyse users' awareness and attitudes towards privacy. This was to answer the following research-related aspects:

- whether users utilise multiple Internet-enabled devices;
- whether these devices are of diverse types and operating systems;
- whether users have access to various network technologies and their extent use;
- whether users employ security tools and maintain them properly;
- users perception of several authentication techniques and associated login failures;
- and finally their real practices of privacy-related topics along with their acceptance of aspects related to the proposed authentication model (i.e. storing biometrics with, being monitored by, and passing management of authentication to a TTP).

A set of questions were drafted taking into account the target of achieving these purposes, being understandable by public IT users, and being objective. These were piloted with a number of local participants, and their feedback was used to refine and enhance the survey until it reached the final version.

The survey was conducted over the Internet via an online questionnaire hosted within the Centre for Security, Communications and Network Research at Plymouth University. It was structured to contain twenty seven questions comprising a variety of closed-ended questions including drop down list, multiple choice, and Likert scale with an option for the respondents to comment in some questions where the answer is not listed. The questions were divided into four sections, organised as follows:

1. Demographic: Exploring the participants' demographic characteristics, including questions related to gender, age, education and location.
2. Technology Usage (Services and Devices): Establishing an understanding of persons' technology usage.
3. Security Practices and Convenience: Investigating the role and usability of security related to the aforementioned respondents' technology usage.
4. Privacy: Analysing respondents' experience and acceptance level of privacy-related topics.

The targeted participants were public users who are 18 years or above and, given that it is an online survey, obviously use technology services and/or devices. They were recruited via e-mail, besides other advertisement means, such as the university website and portal. Prior to disseminating the survey, ethical approval was granted to ensure all data is anonymous during the collection, storage and publication phases.

Due to the resultant ordinal data from the responses of the 5-point Likert scale questions, the following arithmetic mean equation is performed to calculate the central tendency of the responses in order to better interpret them.

$$\text{Arithmetic Mean} = \frac{\sum_{i=1}^{5} R_i C_i}{\sum_{i=1}^{5} C_i}$$

Where R = Response rate, and C = Count of responses/R.

3   Results Analysis

In total, 302 completed responses were received during a period of 8 weeks that the survey was active. An analysis of the survey shows that three quarters of the respondents are males. Being within an academic institution, 79 % of the participants are within the age range between 18 and 39, in addition to the fact that the vast majority are either students or employed. Moreover, 74 % reside in Europe or Northern America, as Table 1 illustrates. Even though it is likely to skew the results with regard to the group and gender, the survey sample shows a proportionate representation of the general population – it is in line with the findings of the UK's Office of National Statistics where the age group (16 to 34) were the top users of the majority of the Internet activities with no significant penetration differences between males and females [12]. It can, also, be implied that the majority of respondents are somewhat highly IT literate that entitles them to better understand the surveyed issues.

The survey proceeded by analysing the extent of users' technology usage. Unsurprisingly, as shown in Fig. 1, users currently possess an increasing number of

Table 1. Summary of respondents' demographic characteristics

Demographic Factor	Characteristic	Count	Percentage
Gender	Female	66	21.85 %
	Male	236	78.15 %
Age (in years)	18-29	113	37.42 %
	30-39	125	41.39 %
	40-49	48	15.89 %
	50-59	14	4.64 %
	60+	2	0.66 %
Employment Status	Employed	131	43.38 %
	Self-employed	14	4.64 %
	Student	151	50.00 %
	Other	6	1.99 %
Country of Residence	Europe	192	63.57 %
	North America	30	9.93 %
	Other	80	26.49 %

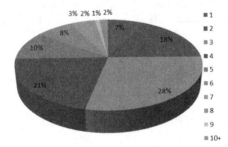

Fig. 1. The Number of Internet-enabled devices in use

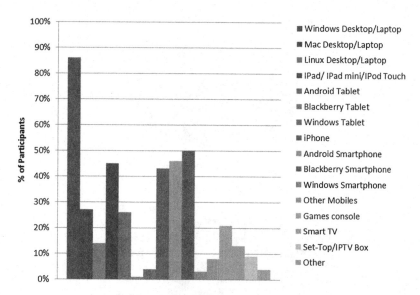

Fig. 2. The Digital devices in use

digital devices – about 75 % of respondents have 3 Internet-enabled devices or more of which 62 % have 4 or more.

These devices represent a variety of models from various manufacturers, thus running a range of differing operating systems (OS) (as illustrated in Fig. 2). From the same perspective, in terms of desktop/laptop computers, Windows OS outweighed its counterparts (Mac and Linux) by 86 %. On the other hand, Apple's tablets prevail over those of its rivals as 45 %, preceded by 26 % for Android-based tablets. However, the iOS and Android smartphones had similar share of users' usages by 43 % and 46 % of respondents respectively, in addition to the use of other devices with distinct OSs such as game consoles which are used by almost 21 %. The results of these two figures draw attention to the fact that a typical today's user most probably owns/uses many digital devices with differing OSs. This, in turn, emphasises the need to consider universal applicability a crucial aspect in any proposed authentication mechanism.

When it comes to cloud services, Fig. 3 reveals that only a small proportion of participants, less than 13 %, do not use any cloud service. Having this ubiquitous employment of cloud computing, supported by the [6] survey results (four fifths of their surveyed participants store confidential data on them), it is likely that sensitive information would be involved, leading to an indication that privacy concerns about it are diminished. Accordingly, this makes the cloud a plausible environment for any solution aiming at broad spectrum of universality and acceptability so users are familiar with and able to access it whenever and wherever they need. The high connectivity can be perceived as most of respondents have access to a wide range of network technologies, such as home WiFi (97 %), public WiFi (61 %), and 3G/4G (81 %). As a result, 53 % spend more than half of the day online while nearly 19 % are always connected, as depicted in Fig. 4. During their online presence, they use diverse services (e.g.

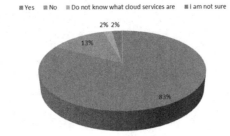

Fig. 3. Cloud services usage

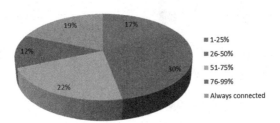

Fig. 4. The percentage of a day spent online

messaging, email, and online banking) in varying frequencies (e.g. hourly, daily, weekly). It can be assumed, therefore, that customers' perceptions towards a cloud-based solution along with its accessibility are likely to be positive.

Moving forward to exploring the users' security practices and the ease of use incurred, Fig. 5 illustrates that nearly two thirds of users are required to authenticate to 51–100 % of the services and devices they use. Additionally, 37 % of the participants need to enter their login credentials several times in a typical day, ranging from frequently (11 times) to too many to remember (above 20 times). As a consequence, this added authentication burden experienced by the users would lead them to either avoid using it when they have the choice whether to enable the authentication feature, or they do not deploy it appropriately.

The former is reiterated by the finding that merely 49 % of the respondents use the authentication tool on their digital devices. Furthermore, an example of the latter, i.e. not complying with authentication's good practices, can be seen from Fig. 6; only 9 % of participants change their password of the most important account on a regular basis (weekly or monthly) whilst 27 % never changed it. Therefore, it is evident that principally relying upon users to secure their IT assets by practising security policies is impractical.

Despite the fact revealed by Fig. 7 that PIN/password/pattern authentication methods are either the preferable (4) or most preferable (5) to 72 % of participants, there are some issues related to complying to their good practice measures (security) as seen previously, alongside with the inconvenience accompanying using them (usability) which can be seen in the succeeding figures. Interestingly, a high percentage of

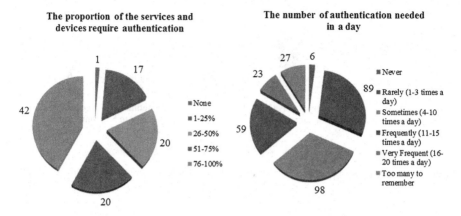

Fig. 5. The extent of authentication repetition

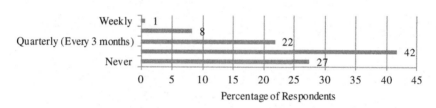

Fig. 6. Respondents changing the password of their most important account

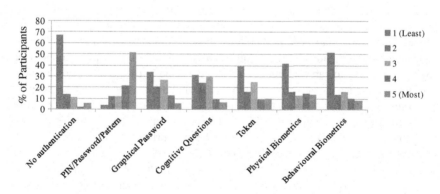

Fig. 7. Participants preferences of authentication methods

respondents (82 %) preferred not to be without authentication. Thus, it can be perceived that users recognise the importance of security. Further noteworthy point in this Figure is the comparable perception of both physical and behavioural biometrics. When combining the responses of ranking 4 and 5 of each category and excluding the PIN/password/pattern, the result shows that participants favoured physical biometrics the most (29 %), followed by behavioural biometrics, graphical password, and token (19 % each), and then the least cognitive questions (16 %).

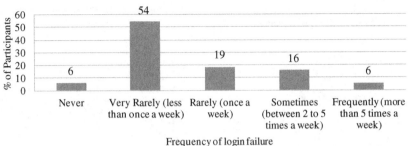

Fig. 8. Percentage of participants experienced login failure vs. Frequency of login Failure

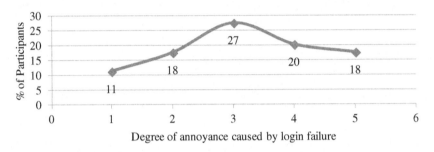

Fig. 9. Degree of annoyance caused by login failure to the participants

Figure 8 demonstrates that about 94 % of respondents experienced authentication failure of which 22 % experienced it several times a week. Accordingly, two thirds of them stated that they had been bothered by those failures as shown in Fig. 9.

Furthermore, authentication techniques that rely mainly on people to remember or recognise secrets or to carry additional devices continue to be the prime contributors to users' inconvenience because most authentication failures are related to them. The results illustrated in Fig. 10 show that the prevalent causes of those experienced failures are forgetting (67 %) or mistyping (55 %) the secret code, followed by the absence of token/mobile (11 %). This, however, could be proportional with the authentication approaches the participants use. The more the users utilise biometrics, the more associated login errors perhaps occur. Even so, users might not be the chief responsible cause of them – biometric errors can be as a result of sensors, environment, and/or classification issues, which can be alleviated in many ways. As a consequence, it can be implied that biometric approaches have the potential to obtain users' acceptance if they offer a less users cumbersome solution than what other authentication approaches cause.

When considering participants concerns about technology-related key aspects, according to the arithmetic mean of the responses ranking, respondents expressed that they were most concerned about privacy (4.06), followed by security (3.93), abuse (3.66), and then convenience (3.62), as demonstrated in Fig. 11. The overall insight of this Figure conveys clearly that respondents are somehow highly concerned about all

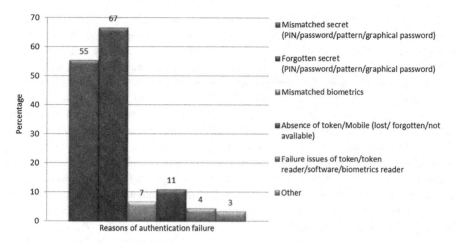

Fig. 10. Percentage of the reasons of authentication failure

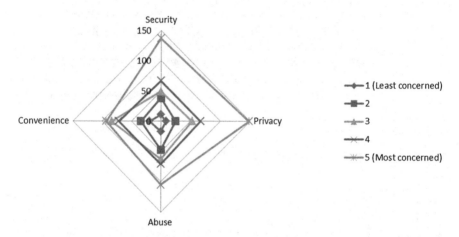

Fig. 11. Ranking of participants concerns about technology-related key aspects

these issues closely, indicating that an effective authentication solution should vigilantly guarantee all of them. Given privacy at the top of respondents concerns implies a reasonable level of privacy awareness they have but their according practices compliance are questionable. Hence, further exploration about privacy-related issues is needed. These results also suggest that a significant proportion of users' data are considered sensitive to them, thus providing a stronger authentication without compromising the ease of use is fundamental. For instance, employing intrusive multi-factor authentication mechanism (e.g. password and hardware token) would promote the protection but lower the usability alike.

Specific questions were asked to investigate users' usability perspectives regarding the use of some authentication mechanisms offered with current devices and services. It seems that there was an inclination from the respondents to the notion that those biometrics-based authentication mechanisms are more usable and easier to use. Figure 12 shows that iOS Touch ID, which employs fingerprint login on the home button, was rated the second highest usable of the alternative mechanisms by achieving 55 % of surveyed respondents rated it somewhat usable ('3'), usable ('4'), or most usable ('5'), preceded by Android pattern unlock (63 %) and followed by Amazon 1-Click (52 %). Although Android face unlock attained only 39 % of the same rate, it can be considered significant because this relatively low percentage might be attributed to the fact that 34 % of respondents were not aware about or had not used it so they responded by N/A. Furthermore, Fig. 13 presents interesting normalised results of the relatively high ratings of the approaches once the N/A responses are taken out. iOS Touch ID became the joint first most usable with Google Authenticator (78 %) followed closely by Android pattern unlock (77 %). It can also be inferred that users tend to prefer using an authentication method that involves minimal effort, with the HSBC Secure Key being considered the least usable.

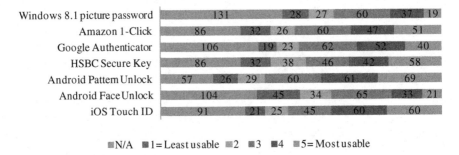

Fig. 12. Respondents' perspectives of the usability of current authentication mechanisms

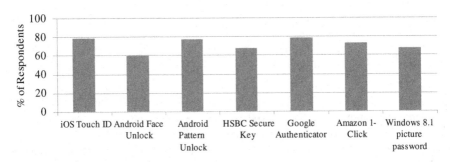

Fig. 13. The percentage of respondents rated some authentication mechanisms by 'somewhat usable', 'usable', or 'most usable' after excluding n/a responses

In relation to participants' practices and attitudes towards privacy-related aspects, one of the countermeasures that users can scrutinise to safeguard their sensitive data against leakage is the End-User License/agreement/App permissions (EULAs). Even though privacy issues gained the highest concerns of the participants as shown in

Fig. 11 the findings in Fig. 14 are perhaps contradictory to that result. 77 % of respondents have never or rarely read the EULAs. Likewise, 68 % of them have never or rarely decided not to use/install or uninstalled a service or application due their EULAs despite the fact that some of them, for instance, access user location unnecessarily. This contradiction between the respondents' perceptions and real practices can be attributed to various possibilities. It perhaps pinpoints the so-called herd behaviour; for instance, there have been a number of privacy awareness campaigns and media attention probably as a reaction to some data breaches and leakages, making users alerted about the buzzword privacy; however, in practice they do not take reasonable care for their privacy or they do not know how to protect it. Another possibility could be the fact that users get used to trust specific service providers historically leading them to tend to accept any further service or update they may offer. Furthermore, other issues may play a role in this negligence, such as cultural tendency towards avoiding reading and the annoying design of such licenses and agreements (e.g. very lengthy, full of jargons).

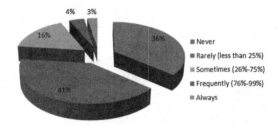

Fig. 14. Frequency of reading the EULAs

A subsequent question in this domain was about the respondents' confidence in storing their biometrics with a TTP, highlighting that this would enable utilising them to perform authentication anywhere to use different devices and services. As appears in Fig. 15, an accumulated 41 % of participants stated that they are confident or very confident storing their biometrics with a TTP, against only 30 % who are unconfident or very unconfident. Given that 29 % had neutral confidence in this issue, the compound result gives an arithmetic mean of 3.1 which indicates that there is a slight tendency towards adopting the concept.

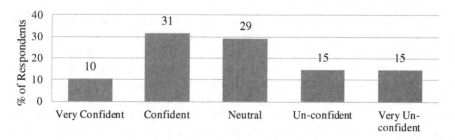

Fig. 15. The confidence in storing biometrics with a TTP

However, Fig. 16 depicts that 57 % of the surveyed users would prefer storing their biometric templates on their own devices only or together with other locations, i.e. 11 % prefer storing them with network operators (e.g. ISP, mobile operator) whereas 26 % with a TTP. On the other hand, there is a low proportion of them (13 %) reject the idea of storing the biometrics anywhere, meaning that they do not favour the use of biometrics at all. Nevertheless, users already trust service providers with their authentication credentials. Additionally, it is likely that recognising the benefits of such a method would shift the preference towards keeping the biometric templates with TTP or both on the device and network operator or TTP as proposed by [13]. For example, biometric templates stored off-board/remotely would remove the processing overhead away from the device, hence saving memory and energy, and allowing better universality and applicability. In the contrary, storing the templates on-board would eliminate the probable time lag introduced through the network traffic. Therefore, having a hybrid approach storing templates between the own device and operator or TTP is reinforced by the variety of responses and by some of current deployments – as already many apps on mobile devices do this (often transparently to the user) such as Siri, iCloud, Dropbox.

Fig. 16. Respondents' preferences of the location(s) of storing biometric templates

From a similar perspective, Fig. 17 reveals an interesting result where the respondents expressed greater acceptance (58 % accepted, leading to an arithmetic mean of 3.6) of their device/service usage being monitored, given that no private data is collected. This supports the previous assumption that whenever the benefits of adopting any proposed solution are clearly elaborated and justified, it would gain higher level of acceptability. It is even supported by the results of two credible surveys [14, 15], where three quarters of respondents were willing to share some personal information in return to the benefits they will receive.

Lastly, Fig. 18 shows that when exploring the extent of participants' willingness to pass the responsibility of managing authentication to TTP, there was a decline compared with the outcome of Figs. 15, 16 and 17 above (where participants were more towards accepting the notion of storing biometrics with and being monitored by a TTP). Only 23 % rated their inclination to the idea by responding by (willing '4' or very willing '5') whereas the majority (40 %) were in the middle of the scale between the willingness and unwillingness. Even though these results are not in line with those represented earlier, the preparedness rate is not that low given that the arithmetic mean is 2.7. In addition, the way of asking this question without any further explanation

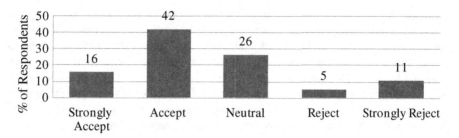

Fig. 17. Acceptance level of participants' usage behaviour being monitored

regarding the potential advantages of doing so may had an adverse effect. Again, having users to better understand a mechanism and the implications involved will most likely lead them to have a more informative decision about it. Moreover, in the reality, users have been delegating the responsibility of managing their login credentials to service providers who run Identity Access Management (IAM) systems in many examples either while using SSO or federated identity (where in one way or another, one of the participating parties in the federation or of the communication standards acts as third party) [16, 17].

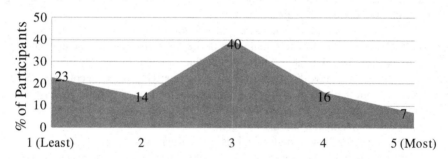

Fig. 18. Willingness to pass the responsibility of managing authentication to a TTP

4   Discussion

The results of the survey are derived from a fair range of participants' with a variety of backgrounds in terms of gender, age, employment, and countries. It is evident the respondents profoundly interact with digital devices, especially those providing Internet access which is being utilised for many online services a significant proportion of the day. Some of these services are categorised sensitive and confidential. As a large number of those questioned are online most of the day, securing the used devices and services throughout these long periods of time against misuse arises as an issue. Prompting users to re-verify periodically is very disruptive and thus apparently inconvenient. It is also found the respondents' devices operate various operating systems and have a broad set of communication technologies. Therefore, the requirements to protect users' information have come to the utmost importance.

Although participants state that they use one or more of the security tools on their devices (e.g. antivirus), they fall foul in using authentication as less than half of them enable it. Even so, they are prompted to authenticate to access their devices as well as services many times a day with which the majority of them encounter frequent login errors and have bothered by that. These errors are caused mainly by secret-knowledge approaches (mismatched and/or forgotten secrets) followed by token-based approaches (absence of token/mobile). Furthermore, non-compliance with password policies by respondents (e.g. 69 % of them have never or rarely changed their passwords despite being for the most important account) can be attributed to users attempts to avoid the above-mentioned nuisance. There is an apparent contradiction between the widespread interest in more security and the quite low number of respondents using or maintaining the available security measures.

It is also perceived that albeit of the high percentage of login failure occurrences, the relatively amplified level of frustration caused by these failures, and being the dominant reasons of them, secret knowledge-based authentication approaches are still preferred by the respondents. This might be due to the fact that most of the users have not been exposed to other techniques, such as biometrics, they have used other alternatives but in a very intrusive manner, or they have associated them with their leading and historical use in criminology and forensics. However, physical biometrics is the second preferred authentication approach by 29 % of the participants outweighing graphical password, cognitive questions and tokens.

These results along with the significant proportion having the information security on top of their concerns show that there is a desire for added but convenient security, which is lacking on the most utilised existing authentication technique – the secret-knowledge. It seems that users do not avoid applying the concept of authentication security but the current available common authentication technique. As such, a move towards continuous and transparent authentication may provide the trade-off between users' convenience and higher security.

The plethora of users with many devices and services which each may has its own security configurations and requirements, together with the widespread access to a wide range of communication technologies and cloud services, yielding to a high success possibility of a prospect cloud-based authentication solution. Such solution that centralise the task of authentication to a TTP would enable providing it in a device and service independent fashion, relieving users of the burden of enrolling and authenticating to each device and service separately and the devices of a significant volume of data processing and storage. This is also supported by and would even improve the comparatively positive responses regarding storing biometric templates with a TTP as well as having usage behaviour being monitored.

5   Conclusions

The survey findings reinforce the observation that users utilise a variety of Internet-enabled devices to carry out a wide range of activities, many of which are considered sensitive. Whilst the most adopted authentication approach is still the secret knowledge-based, it is (followed by tokens) the chief reason of login errors;

consequently high proportion of users either inactivate it or misconduct its use. For instance, two third of participants never or rarely changed the password of their most important account. On the contrary, respondents are overwhelmingly concerned about protecting their information, devices and accounts, revealing that a disjoint between users' perceptions towards security and real practices is in existent. Therefore, it is evident that users do not avoid applying the concept of authentication security but the drawbacks of current available common authentication technique.

Thus, alternative security measures are apparently required given that they do not heavily rely upon users to secure them. Biometrics may have the merit of providing this as physical biometrics is the second preferred authentication approach by 29 %. The revolutionary growth of personal digital devices' capabilities may open the horizon to leverage them for biometrics capturing.

The survey also demonstrates that users are online most of the day performing a wide range of sensitive tasks that are required to be secured throughout the usage session. The respondents incline towards storing biometric templates with a TTP as well as having their usage behaviour being monitored. Advanced connectivity technologies and cloud services are capable to be deployed for a novel authentication security solution managed by a TTP to offer a federated, transparent and continuous authentication in order to be used on multi devices and services. Nevertheless, such mechanism must be designed attentively ensuring various related aspects, such as the security of biometric templates on and during the transmission to the cloud.

References

1. Meeker, M., Wu, L.: Internet Trends (2013). http://www.kpcb.com/insights/2013-internet-trends
2. IDC: A Future Fueled by Phablets. http://www.idc.com/
3. CSID: Consumer Survey: Password Habits. A study among American consumers. http://www.csid.com/
4. Symantec Corporation: Internet Security Threat Report 2013 (2013)
5. Verizon: 2014 Data Breach Investigations Report (2014)
6. PwC: Information Security Breaches Survey (2013)
7. O'Gorman, L.: Comparing passwords, tokens, and biometrics for user authentication. Proc. IEEE **91**, 2021–2040 (2003)
8. Furnell, S.M., Katsikas, S., Lopez, J., Patel, A.: Securing Information and Communications Systems: Principles, Technologies, and Applications. Artech House, Norwood (2008)
9. Li, F., Clarke, N., Papadaki, M., Dowland, P.: Behaviour profiling for transparent authentication for mobile devices. In: The 10th European Conference on Information Warfare and Security (ECIW 2011), pp. 307–314, Tallinn, Estonia (2011)
10. Crawford, H., Renaud, K., Storer, T.: A framework for continuous, transparent mobile device authentication. Comput. Secur. **39**, 127–136 (2013)
11. Al Abdulwahid, A., Clarke, N., Furnell, S., Stengel, I.: A conceptual model for federated authentication in the cloud. In: Proceedings of the 11th Australian Information Security Management Conference (AISM 2013), pp. 1–11. Edith Cowan University, Perth, Western Australia (2013)

12. Office of National Statistics: Internet Access - Households and Individuals, 2013. Stat. Bull. (2013)
13. Karatzouni, S., Clarke, N.L., Furnell, S.M.: Device- versus network-centric authentication paradigms for mobile devices: operational and perceptual trade-offs. In: 5th Australian Information Security Management Conference. pp. 1–13, Mount Lawley, Australia (2007)
14. PwC: Consumer privacy: What are consumers willing to share?. http://www.pwc.ru/
15. Salesforce: 2014 Mobile Behavior Report
16. Madsen, P., Koga, Y., Takahashi, K.: Federated identity management for protecting users from ID theft. In: Proceedings of the 2005 workshop on Digital identity management - DIM 2005, pp. 77–83. ACM Press, New York (2005)
17. Stihler, M., Santin, A.O., Marcon Jr., A.L., Fraga, J.D.S.: Integral federated identity management for cloud computing. In: 2012 5th International Conference on New Technologies, Mobility and Security (NTMS), pp. 1–5. IEEE (2012)

Identifying Factors that Influence Employees' Security Behavior for Enhancing ISP Compliance

Ioanna Topa[(✉)] and Maria Karyda

University of the Aegean, Mytilene, Greece
{itopa,mka}@aegean.gr

Abstract. Organizations apply information security policies to foster secure use of information systems but very often employees fail to comply with them. Employees' security behavior has been the unit of analysis of research from different theoretical approaches, in an effort to identify the factors that influence security policy compliance. Through a systematic analysis of extant literature this paper identifies and categorizes critical factors that shape employee security behavior and proposes security management practices that can enhance security compliance. Research findings inform theory by identifying research gaps and support security management.

Keywords: Security behavior · Information security policy compliance

1   Introduction

Organizations implement security measures to secure their information infrastructure, business processes and services. In order to be resilient in a rapidly changing environment, enterprises invest not only on technical countermeasures, but also employ socio-organizational practices such as security policies to foster security behavior. An Information Security Policy (ISP) is generally "the statement of the roles and responsibilities of the employees to safeguard the information and technology resources of their organizations" [5]. However, having an information security policy doesn't necessarily lead to user conformity. Employees often fail to comply with security policies while pursuing to perform their duties in the most effective and timely manner [9], as following ISPs may entail additional effort and time. Furthermore, in many cases employees are not aware of the importance of following ISPs and show little interest in complying [18].

Relative research has identified numerous factors that influence users to comply with ISPs or fail to do so; however, information security management lacks an overall view of what shapes security behavior so as to improve security compliance.

This paper provides an in-depth review of relevant research and a classification of factors that have been identified as influencing security behavior. The analysis provided can be used as a roadmap for security managers who want to create ISPs that gain the approval of users and also it can serve as the basis for implementing effective security management, by considering the impact of specific factors on users' security behavior and intention to comply with the information security policy [24].

© Springer International Publishing Switzerland 2015
S. Fischer-Hübner et al. (Eds.): TrustBus 2015, LNCS 9264, pp. 169–179, 2015.
DOI: 10.1007/978-3-319-22906-5_13

Section 2 analyzes relevant literature and identifies different factors that influence ISP compliance. Section 3 provides a classification of the factors identified so far, which inform security management and provide suggestions for improving compliance. Finally, research findings and indications for future research are presented.

2 Identifying Factors that Influence Security Behavior

Several relevant studies focus on the individual to identify factors that motivate security behavior in association with users' intentions and attitudes. Lebek et al. [20] through a literature review, found that the constructs of Theory of Reasoned Action (TRA)/ Theory of Planned Behavior (TPB) *(attitude, subjective norms and perceived behavioral control, which consists of self efficacy and controllability)*, are good predictors of the intention to comply with the ISP. They also found that *organizational commitment, perceived effectiveness* of the employee's actions and *technology awareness* can also influence users' intention to comply. Authors argue that actual behavior can't be accurately assessed, for reasons such as that intentions do not necessarily lead to expected behavior [20] and that new methods need to be developed in order to measure actual behavior [21]. In the same direction, Zhang et al. [4] show that *perceived behavioral control* and *attitude* have a significant impact on intention towards complying with ISPs. *Perceived security protection mechanisms* (a term similar to *response efficacy*) were found to have a negative impact on the intention towards complying [4]; this implies that if employees estimate that there is strong technical protection to secure organizational assets, their intention to comply might weaken.

Sommestad et al. [11] focus on the individual to identify that *beliefs* (perceived behavioral control, threat appraisal, descriptive norm, response efficacy) and *values* (perceived value congruence, perceived legitimacy, information security awareness), play a critical role for user compliance with security policies. They also suggest that *rewards and punishments* are poor predictors of compliance. Son [25] found that *perceived value congruence* and *perceived legitimacy* influence the behavior of employees significantly and yield better results compared to factors based on extrinsic motivation such as perceived deterrent severity and perceived deterrent certainty.

Ifinedo [24] draws on Protection Motivation Theory and the Theory of Planned Behavior to show that *perceived vulnerability, response efficacy, self-efficacy, attitude towards compliance with the ISPs* and *subjective norms* influence the intention to comply with the ISPs. This study illustrates how employees are influenced by their colleagues, by their superiors and by other people in the organization's environment in terms of security compliance.

Siponen et al. [16], drawing also on Protection Motivation Theory, show that *visibility* (meaning the degree to which individuals have access to security related material both inside and outside the organization), and *normative beliefs* influence *threat appraisal*, which has an impact on the intention of an individual to comply with ISPs. Siponen et al. [15] study the two constructs of threat appraisal separately and show that *perceived vulnerability* and *perceived severity* have a significant effect on intention. Their study also identifies that *self-efficacy, attitude and normative beliefs* influence the intention towards complying that strongly predicts actual compliance.

Pahnilla et al. [13] also identified the role of *threat appraisal* and *coping appraisal* in user attitude. They found that *information quality* (meaning how useful, clearly stated and informative an ISP is), has a significant effect on actual compliance, and that *normative beliefs*, *attitude* and *habits* influence users' intention to comply. An interesting point following from this research is that security managers should encourage employees to comply with the ISPs, through habit. This study also suggests that *sanctions* have an insignificant impact on employee's intention to comply with the ISPs. Pahnilla et al. [12] also studied the impact of threat and coping appraisal on the employees' intention to comply and found that employees' intention who have high knowledge of the ISPs was influenced by *perceived vulnerability, perceived severity, response efficacy,* whereas employees' intention with low knowledge of the ISPs was only influenced by *perceived severity and response efficacy*. In both cases intention had high impact on actual compliance.

Herath and Rao [9], combining Protection Motivation Theory with Deterrence Theory and the Decomposed Theory of Planned Behaviour, found that *perceived severity* has a significant effect on user attitude and that social influence (*subjective and descriptive norms*) are good predictors of the intention to comply. Furthermore, this study shows that when employees believe that complying with a security policy entails costs such as time, effort, etc., they are likely to form negative feelings towards security policies. Therefore, *response costs* have a negative influence on the attitude to compliance. On the other hand, when employees feel that their compliance will benefit the organization, they may develop positive feelings towards this behavior and adopt it. As a result, employees' *response efficacy (effectiveness of a person's action)* has a significant impact on the attitude towards compliance. The same thing applies to *self-efficacy*, which influences attitude and intention towards complying with security policies. Another interesting finding is that *resource availability* has a significant effect on self-efficacy, which in turn influences intention. This indicates that security trained employees who have direct access to security policies, feel that they have the ability to comply with the ISPs and are more likely to comply with them. Furthermore *organizational commitment* has significant impact on intention to comply. Finally, according to this study *detection certainty* has a significant impact on the intention to comply, whereas the severity of punishment influences employees' intention in a negative way. In a following study, Herath and Rao [10] confirm that employees are more likely to conform to ISPs if they know that they will be caught, whereas the more severe the punishment is, the less willing they are to comply. They also show [10] that both *social influence* and *perceived effectiveness* (describing it similarly to response efficacy) have an impact on the intention to comply.

The role of automatic behaviors, such as habits, is further studied by Vance et al. [17] who show that habits influence *perceived vulnerability, perceived severity, response efficacy* and *self-efficacy* and that perceived vulnerability, rewards, response-efficacy and response cost have a negative impact on users' intention to comply with the ISPs. They also identify that *perceived severity* and *self-efficacy* have a significant effect on the intention to comply.

Bulgurcu et al. [5] studied the impact of the antecedents of attitude on intention to comply with the ISPs using the principles of Rational Choice theory [1]. Their study is based on the idea that individuals predict the possible outcomes of an event and depending on the perceived cost or benefit of the outcome they either adopt or refrain from a specific action [5]. They also found that *attitude*, *normative beliefs* and *self-efficacy to comply* have a significant impact on the intention to comply with the ISPs. Finally, they identified that *Information Security Awareness* influences employees' attitude towards compliance with the ISPs.

Other studies approach security behavior through the lens of technology oriented theories such as the Technology Acceptance Model (TAM) [7]. Dinev and Hu [8] explored the factors that influence users' intention towards the use of protective technologies and found that *technology awareness has* a significant impact on the intention to use a protective technology.

One study conducted by D'Arcy et al. [6] shows that if users are aware of the ISPs of their organization, the existing SETA programs and the computer mechanisms that are in place, they are less likely to engage in misuse of the ISPs. Similarly, in the case of ISP compliance, Al-Omari et al. [2] employ TAM to show that user awareness of information security policies, information security, security awareness and training programs, computer monitoring, along with self-efficacy and controllability have a significant effect on the *perceived usefulness* of *protection* and *perceived ease of use*, which in turn guide users' intention to comply with security policies.

Summarizing, relevant literature has identified several factors that influence users' security behavior. However, different terms are often used to describe similar concepts, while different theoretical approaches show emphasis on different factors, making it extremely hard for security management to navigate through relative research and take advantage of important findings. Though taxonomies have been proposed, e.g. Padayachee's [22] classification of security compliant behavior, security management needs a higher level framework that can enhance security policy implementation. Table 1 summarizes our analysis of relevant literature.

3 Enhancing Security Policy Compliance

Literature analysis shows that a wide variety of factors influence users' security behavior and ISP compliance. Depending on the theoretical background followed, different studies stress the importance of specific factors, while ignoring others. Security management needs the complete picture in order to develop a security-oriented culture, where security practices become part of the organizational routine [19].

Different factors that have been identified can be grouped into three courses of action that security management needs to pursue in order to foster security policy compliance and influence users' security behavior: (i) address individual issues that hinder compliance (e.g. habits), (ii) create a suitable organization setting (e.g. rewards and sanctions) and (iii) take into consideration technology aspects (e.g. usability of security controls), as shown in Fig. 1.

3.1 Addressing Individual Factors

Individual beliefs and perceptions play a critical role in security behavior. Thus, security managers need to provide users with information with regard to information

Table 1. Critical factors that influence security behavior

Factors	Description	Relevant studies
Threat appraisal (or Security breach Concern level)	Users' evaluation of possible threats and their severity.	[9, 13, 16]
Perceived Severity (or Perceived Severity of Security Breach)	Users' perceptions on the severity of the impact of security threats.	[9, 12, 15, 17]
Perceived Vulnerability (or Perceived Probability of Security Breach)	Users' estimation on how possible the occurrence of a security threat is.	[12, 15, 17, 24]
Self-efficacy	Users' evaluation of how capable they are in following ISPs.	[2, 5, 9, 15, 16, 17, 24]
Response efficacy (or Perceived Effectiveness or Perceived Security Protection mechanisms)	Users' perception of the effectiveness of security controls and ISP compliance.	[4, 9, 10, 12, 16, 17, 24]
Response cost (or Cost of compliance)	User's perception of the possible negative consequences, such as inconvenience, additional effort and time, that derive from ISP compliance.	[5, 9, 17]
Perceived Behavioral Control, (Self efficacy and Controllability)	Users' estimation on how easy compliance is and how much control they have on carrying out security tasks.	[4, 8]
Information Security Awareness	Knowledge of information security and of the specific ISP of the organization.	[5]
General Information Security Awareness	Knowledge of information security.	[2, 5, 6]
ISP Awareness	Knowledge of the content of specific ISPs.	[2, 6]
Awareness of SETA programs	Knowledge of Security Awareness and Training Programs.	[2, 6]
Awareness of monitoring mechanisms	Knowledge of the monitoring mechanisms in place.	[2, 6]
Technology Awareness	Knowledge and consciousness of a technological issue that leads the individual to search for possible solutions.	[8]
Habits	Actions conducted unconsciously.	[13, 18]
Perceived Ease of Use	Users' belief of how easy a particular technology is.	[2]
Perceived Usefulness	Users' belief of whether a particular technology will be more efficient.	[2, 8]

(*Continued*)

Table 1. (*Continued*)

Factors	Description	Relevant studies
Rewards	Possible rewards include pay raises, personal mention, promotions, etc.	[5, 18]
Sanctions	Penalties, such as fines, following non compliance.	[5]
Punishment Severity (or Perceived Punishment Severity)	Users' perceptions on the level of punishment for non compliance.	[9, 10]
Punishment Certainty (or Perceived Punishment Certainty)	Users' estimation of the possibility to be detected for non compliance.	[9, 10]
Perceived Cost of Noncompliance	Sanctions, negative feelings and vulnerability of resources connected to failure to comply with the ISPs.	[5]
Perceived Benefit of Compliance	Positive feelings, rewards and decreased vulnerability in resources that result from compliance with the ISPs.	[5]
Perceived Legitimacy	The extent to which users consider the ISPs as appropriate, desirable and just.	[25]
Perceived Value Congruence	The extent to which users share the same values with employers.	[25]
Information Quality	Users' perceived quality and usefulness of the information included in the ISPs.	[12, 13]
Facilitating conditions (or Resource Availability or Controllability or Visibility)	Resources provided to facilitate compliance, including encouragement, time, help from experts, access to ISPs, etc.	[2, 8, 9, 13, 16]
Organizational commitment	The degree to which users share organizational goals.	[9]
Subjective norms (or Normative beliefs)	Perceived expectations of colleagues and superiors.	[2, 5, 9, 10, 13, 15, 16, 24]
Descriptive norms (or Peer behavior)	Users' belief that they should follow their colleagues' behavior.	[9, 10]

security threats and their severity [9, 12, 15, 17], through seminars, email notifications and other security awareness practices. However, as literature suggests, communicating security information, needs to be combined with security training so as to enhance user's confidence on their ability to use security controls and comply with the ISPs

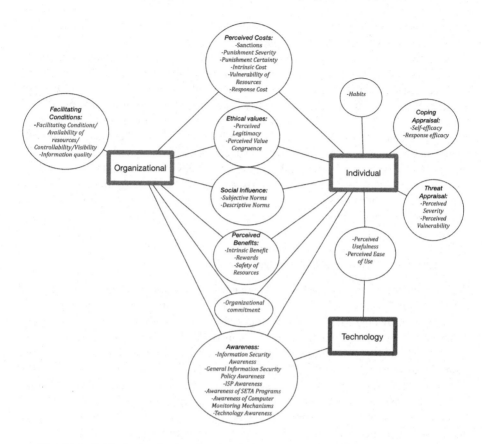

Fig. 1. Individual, organizational, and technical factors influencing security behavior

(self-efficacy) [2, 8, 9, 12, 15, 16, 17]. It is also important to illustrate, possibly through case studies or simulations, the effectiveness of security policies and controls for mitigating security threats and the benefits for the organization and its members *(response efficacy)* [9, 10, 12, 15, 16, 17].

Security awareness is important for security behavior. Furthermore, users' knowledge of the ISPs is also critical [5]. Overall, security education and training awareness programs, enhance individuals' skills to carry out security tasks and foster security compliance [2, 6]. In order to develop a security-oriented culture, security management has to ensure that employees are well informed about the security policies, through awareness and training programs [3] and by employing different communication channels and methods [26].

Security managers should embed security practices and tools into work practices, so as to encourage users to develop security habits [13, 17]. Moreover, these practices and tools need to be seamlessly incorporated into work practices so as to minimize the cost of compliance in terms of effort or time and possible work impediment that negatively influence compliance [5]. It is also important to take into consideration users' ethical values and beliefs so that employees are convinced that security policies and controls are appropriate, ethical and just [11, 25].

Security management should also emphasize on the positive outcomes that derive from ISP compliance, both for users as well as for organizations [5] and illustrate the negative consequences of non compliance. Rewards, such as pay raises, personal mention, promotions may stimulate security behavior and are worth considering [5, 13, 15, 17]. Sanctions, on the other hand, have not been found to promote compliance. However, the possibility that non compliance is monitored, has been connected with increased compliance [2, 6]. Security management needs to encourage users' daily actions that follow security rules and prohibit employees from habits that may result to security violations (e.g. sharing passwords among colleagues). Additional time and effort for complying with security policies (if required) should be properly explained emphasizing on the benefits of effective security.

3.2   Creating a Facilitating Organizational Setting

Besides individual traits and beliefs, the organizational setting also influences strongly users' security behavior. Thus, security management should create a facilitating environment, by providing users with encouragement, time and the appropriate resources in order to follow ISPs and use security controls [9, 13]. This can be achieved by developing and sharing with users security related material, in the form of campaigns, posters and advertisements through different media [16]. Good quality of this material, as well as clarity and comprehensiveness of the ISP can also promote user compliance [12, 13, 15]. ISPs have to be easily accessible, comprehensible and available in many forms, either printed or in electronic form. Employees should also be aware of computer mechanisms that are implemented, in order to detect security violations [2].

Another important issue for compliance is strong management support, as both organizational commitment [9] and social influence [10] play a critical role in shaping employees' security behavior. Expectations of others, such as colleagues and superiors, have been found to influence users' behavior, towards complying with the ISP [2, 5, 8–10, 13, 16]. At the same time, users tend to replicate the behavior of others [9, 10], which is something that security management should take advantage of. Hu et al. [24] illustrate the importance of the involvement of top management for security compliance. The participation of top management influences organizational culture which in turn influences the employees' attitude towards complying with the ISP. In this way, management influences employees by promoting security compliant behavior, which has been identified as more effective than imposing sanctions and other deterrent mechanisms.

Chipperfield and Furnell [26], report that knowledge about security issues to the employees can be conveyed via "pull" or "push" methods. According to Sommestad et al. [11], organizations should enhance the security compliance of their employees by using "pull" methods, by focusing on the values and emotions of the employees, rather than "push" methods (such as sanctions and rewards). Consequently, security managers should encourage the involvement of the employees in the making of ISPs process and in the creation of a common vision for the organization. As a result employees will be more likely to comply with the ISPs, which will be part of the organizational culture.

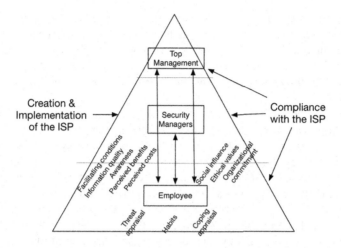

Fig. 2. The influence of organization context on ISP compliance

As depicted in Fig. 2, security managers need to take into consideration different factors that influence employees' security. By applying "pull" methods, that take into consideration the values of the employees and encouraging their involvement in the process of creating ISPs, security managers promote employee compliance and facilitate the development of a security-oriented organizational culture.

3.3 Considering the Technological Aspect

Technological artifacts influence security behavior, as users form expectations with regard to how easy or useful security policies and controls are for them [2, 8]. According to Herath et al. [27], for instance, individuals' intention to use an email authentication service was influenced by the response time of the system (perceived responsiveness). When the service needed long time to check the authenticity of the emails, individuals formed a negative attitude towards its use. Finally, the estimation of the employees' capabilities to identify the malicious emails without using the service was found to influence the intention to use the email authentication service negatively. Payne and Edwards [14], identify usability as an important characteristic of security mechanisms. They report that in many cases authentication and email encryption tools are not used properly or do not gain the approval of users, because of limited user friendliness. Thus, characteristics, such as Revocability, Visibility, Expressiveness, Identifiability etc. should be taken into account when designing security tools and practices.

4 Conclusions and Further Research

This paper analyzes and categorizes factors that influence security behavior as they have been studied in relevant literature. We have identified a large set of factors that are related to individuals (e.g. threat appraisal, coping appraisal, habits), organizational setting and technology. These factors shape (directly or indirectly) users' intention to comply with a security policy as well as their overall security behavior. The paper provides a complete picture of how security behavior is shaped and gives directions to security managers for identifying and tackling critical issues when creating and implementing security policies so as to foster compliance and promote security behavior.

Furthermore, the analysis of relevant research provides interesting findings with regard to what has not been studied up to now. Though security behavior is found to be influenced by a multitude of organizational factors, the outer context of the environment, e.g. technology, type of business, legal environment have not been examined. The role of technology, in particular, needs further investigation. Research in [8] indicates that individuals tend to adopt a certain protective technology irrespective of how easy it is in use, if they know that there will be severe consequences on their system, in case this technology is not used. It is thus important to enhance our understanding of how technology-related factors influence security behavior so as to employ technical countermeasures that are more appropriate for the organization's function and security protection. This stream of research might also lead to the development of user-friendly security tools.

References

1. Akers, R.: Rational choice, deterrence, and social learning theory in criminology: the path not taken. J. Crim. Law Criminol. **81**, 653 (1990)
2. Al-Omari, A., El-Gayar, O., Deokar, A.: Security policy compliance: user acceptance perspective. In: System Science (HICSS), 45th Hawaii International Conference on System Sciences, IEEE (2012)
3. Albrechtsen, E., Hovden, J.: Improving information security awareness and behavior through dialogue, participation and collective reflection. An invention study. Comput. Secur. **29**(4), 432–445 (2010)
4. Zhang, J., Reithel, B.J., Li, H.: Impact of perceived technical protection on security behaviors. Inf. Manag. Comput. Secur. **17**(4), 330–340 (2009)
5. Bulgurcu, B., Cavusoglu, H., Benbasat, I.: Information security policy compliance: an empirical study of rationality-based beliefs and information security awareness. MIS Q. **34**(3), 523–548 (2010)
6. D'Arcy, J., Hovav, A., Galletta, D.: User awareness of security countermeasures and its impact on information systems misuse: a deterrence approach. Inf. Syst. Res. **20**(1), 79–98 (2009)
7. Davis, F.D., Bagozzi, R.P., Warshaw, P.R.: User acceptance of computer technology: a comparison of two theoretical models. Manage. Sci. **35**(8), 982–1003 (1989)
8. Dinev, T., Hu, Q.: The centrality of awareness in the formation of user behavioral intention toward protective information technologies. J. Assoc. Inf. Syst. **8**(7), 23 (2007)
9. Herath, T., Rao, H.R.: Protection motivation and deterrence: a framework for security policy compliance in organisations. Eur. J. Inf. Syst. **18**(2), 106–125 (2009)
10. Herath, T., Rao, H.R.: Encouraging information security behaviors in organizations: role of penalties, pressures and perceived effectiveness. Decis. Support Syst. **47**(2), 154–165 (2009)

11. Sommestad, T., Hallberg, J., Lundholm, K., Bengtsson, J.: Variables influencing information security policy compliance: a systematic review of quantitative studies. Inf. Manage. Comput. Secur. **22**(1), 42–75 (2014)
12. Pahnila, S., Karjalainen, M., Siponen, M.: Information security behavior: towards multi-stage models. In: PACIS (2013)
13. Pahnila, S., Siponen, M., Mahmood, A.: Employees' behavior towards IS security policy compliance. In: System Sciences 40th Annual Hawaii International Conference on System Sciences, pp. 156b–156b. IEEE (2007)
14. Payne, B.D., Edwards, W.K.: A brief introduction to usable security. Internet Comput. IEEE **12**(3), 13–21 (2008)
15. Siponen, M., Mahmood, A., Pahnila, S.: Employees' adherence to information security policies: an exploratory field study. Inf. Manage. **51**(2), 217–224 (2014)
16. Siponen, M., Pahnila, S., Mahmood, A.: Factors influencing protection motivation and IS security policy compliance. In: Innovations in Information Technology, IEEE (2006)
17. Vance, A., Siponen, M., Pahnila, S.: Motivating IS security compliance: insights from habit and protection motivation theory. Inf. Manage. **49**(3), 190–198 (2012)
18. Von Solms, R., Von Solms, B.: From policies to culture. Comput. Secur. **23**(4), 275–279 (2004)
19. Vroom, C., Von Solms, R.: Towards information security behavioral compliance. Comput. Secur. **23**(3), 191–198 (2004)
20. Lebek, B., Uffen, J., Neumann, M., Hohler, B., Breitner, H.M.: Information security awareness and behavior: a theory-based literature review. Manage. Res. Rev. **37**(12), 1049–1092 (2014)
21. Crossler, R.E., Johnston, A.C., Lowry, P.B., Hu, Q., Warkentin, M., Baskerville, R.: Future directions for behavioral information security research. Comput. Secur. **32**, 90–101 (2013)
22. Padayachee, K.: Taxonomy of compliant information security behavior. Comput. Secur. **31**(5), 673–680 (2012)
23. Hu, Q., Dinev, T., Hart, P., Cooke, D.: Managing employee compliance with information security policies: the critical role of top management and organizational culture*. Decis. Sci. **43**(4), 615–660 (2012)
24. Ifinedo, P.: Understanding information systems security policy compliance: an integration of the theory of planned behavior and the protection motivation theory. Comput. Secur. **31**(1), 83–95 (2012)
25. Son, J.Y.: Out of fear or desire? Toward a better understanding of employees' motivation to follow IS security policies. Inf. Manage. **48**(7), 296–302 (2011)
26. Chipperfield, C., Furnell, S.: From security policy to practice: sending the right messages. Comput. Fraud Secur. **2010**(3), 13–19 (2010)
27. Herath, T., Chen, R., Wang, J., Banjara, K., Wilbur, J., Rao, H.R.: Security services as coping mechanisms: an investigation into user intention to adopt an email authentication service. Inf. Syst. J. **24**(1), 61–84 (2014)

Dynamic Deployment and Monitoring
of Security Policies

Jose-Miguel Horcas[1]([⊠]), Mónica Pinto[1], Lidia Fuentes[1], Wissam Mallouli[2],
and Edgardo Montes de Oca[2]

[1] CAOSD Group, Universidad de Málaga, Andalucía Tech, Málaga, Spain
{horcas,pinto,lff}@lcc.uma.es
[2] Montimage, 39 rue Bobillot, 75013 Paris, France
{wissam.mallouli,edgardo.montesdeoca}@montimage.com

Abstract. INTER-TRUST is a framework for the specification, negotiation, deployment and dynamic adaptation of interoperable security policies, in the context of pervasive systems where devices are constantly exchanging critical information through the network. The dynamic adaptation of the security policies at runtime is addressed using Aspect-Oriented Programming (AOP) that allows enforcing security requirements by dynamically weaving security aspects into the applications. However, a mechanism to guarantee the correct adaptation of the functionality that enforces the changing security policies is needed. In this paper, we present an approach with monitoring and detection techniques in order to maintain the correlation between the security policies and the associated functionality deployed using AOP, allowing the INTER-TRUST framework automatically reacts when needed.

Keywords: Aspect-oriented programming · Dynamic deployment · Monitoring · Security policies

1 Introduction

Future Internet (FI) systems encompass a set of pervasive computing devices (e.g., smartphones, vehicles, wearables) always connected to the Internet and continuously exchanging information with remote entities [1]. In order to ensure that the exchange of information is performed securely, the development of such systems requires the creation of a set of security mechanisms that are able to protect the system against different threats that may arise. For instance, let us consider the following case study: an Intelligent Transportation System (ITS) application that dynamically recommends the speed limits for a road according to climate conditions and to unexpected events like accidents or traffic jams, collects the information sent by both the vehicle's sensors (e.g., geolocation, current speed) and the road side sensors (e.g., weather conditions, traffic status). Then, using this information the new recommended speed limit is calculated and notified to the driver on his On Board Unit (OBU). Some of the security

© Springer International Publishing Switzerland 2015
S. Fischer-Hübner et al. (Eds.): TrustBus 2015, LNCS 9264, pp. 180–192, 2015.
DOI: 10.1007/978-3-319-22906-5_14

requirements that could be taken into account in the development of this application are: (1) the *user anonymity* must be assured, otherwise, some users will not agree to send their current speed and location; (2) only *authorized users* subscribed to the service can send information to the ITS server and receive recommendations, and (3) in some contexts (e.g., when a police car is pursuing an offender) all the information sent by the police car should be *cyphered* in order to hide the information from the infractors.

The main problematic of enabling security in FI systems is the heterogeneity and dynamicity of the security policies that determine how the different parties need to interact with each other. On the one hand, the security policies can be heterogeneous because each user can customize his own security policies that answer their security constraints and they can also be different from the security policies expected by the applications. On the other hand, the security policies can be dynamic and can change over time to adapt to new requirements, new regulatory rules or new application contexts, for instance moving from one country to another. In this context, there is a lack of sufficiently rich techniques to tackle the problem of security policy modeling, interoperability, deployment, enforcement and supervision. Moreover, focusing on dynamic security enforcement, there is also a lack of solutions that allow the dynamic adaptation of security to new application requirements and changes in the environment.

In order to solve these issues, the Inter-operable Trust Assurance Infrastructure (INTER-TRUST) framework [2] aims to deal with the problematic of enabling security in heterogeneous and pervasive systems, modeling secure interoperability policies with different constraints, and enabling the dynamic and secure establishment of trusted relationships between systems [3]. The main contributions of the INTER-TRUST framework are the *dynamic specification of security policies*, the *dynamic deployment of security policies*, the *dynamic monitoring of security policies* and the *fuzz and active testing of security policies*. In this paper we focus on the second and third contributions. The dynamic deployment of security policies is performed by using one of the most used enhanced deployment mechanisms to inject dynamic behavior: Aspect Oriented Programming (AOP) [4]. AOP is used to add/implement security aspects (i.e., anonymity, authentication, integrity, encryption, etc.) to application components at runtime so that applications can dynamically adapt their behavior for required/ negotiated security policies. However, the dynamic deployment mechanism can introduce new vulnerabilities and security risks, and thus INTER-TRUST incorporates dynamic monitoring and testing techniques to obtain enriched information of the system's execution, which is used to verify the conformity with the implementations, ensuring a secure interoperability between systems. In this paper, we present an approach to detect changes in the environment and checking that the communicating parties respect the negotiated security policies by maintaining the correlation between the security policies, the security aspects, and the security properties of the monitoring tool. The dynamic monitoring of the security policies allows FI applications to have a global understanding of the changes performed at runtime and can automatically react to new risk or threats that may arise. This approach represents a generic solution that can be applied to many types of pervasive applications.

The rest of the paper is organized as follows. Section 2 explains the correlation between the security policies, the aspects, and the security properties; and briefly overviews the INTER-TRUST framework. In Sect. 3 we present our approach to deploy the security policies and monitor that correlation. Section 4 evaluates the overhead performance of our approach and Sect. 5 discusses related work. Finally, Sect. 6 concludes the paper and presents our future work.

2   Correlation Between Security Policies, Aspects and Security Properties

The correct enforcement and dynamic adaptation of the security policies is based on two cornerstones (see Fig. 1). The first is the correlation defined between the *security policies* that need to be enforced, the *security aspects* that are deployed/undeployed in order to enforce those security policies and the *security properties* that are activated/deactivated in order to check whether or not the system is behaving according to the specified security policies. The second is the monitoring at runtime of this correlation in order to detect any attack that breaks it. These attacks could occur due to different kinds of security vulnerabilities (e.g., an attacker could send a huge number of legitimate requests to a server to monopolize its resources), or due to those vulnerabilities that are introduced by the dynamic deployment mechanism itself (e.g., a malicious aspect). For instance, in order to monitor the correct deployment of the security policy shown in Fig. 1, with three rules that indicate that the system is required to cypher the messages, to ensure the user's anonymity and to allow only the interaction of authorized users, a set of security properties associated with these rules needs to be activated in the monitoring tool. In Fig. 1 we have shown an example of the security property that needs to be verified to ensure that the messages are correctly cyphered. Also, for each rule in the security policy, a set of aspects that fulfill the required functionality are deployed inside the application. For instance, the encryption and decryption aspects are deployed to cypher the messages, the authentication, privacy and pseudonymous certificate aspects are deployed to ensure the user anonymity, and the authorization aspect are deployed to provide user authorization. Finally, the application with the aspects is monitored and the captured traces are sent to the monitoring tool that correlates the deployment of the aspects with the security properties. Note that this correlation must be maintained, both when the user joins the application for the first time (i.e., after the deployment of the initial security policies) and also at runtime, when the security policies are dynamically negotiated and adapted.

The modular architecture of the INTER-TRUST framework that implements the correlation described is shown in Fig. 2. In INTER-TRUST, security policies rely on the OrBAC model [5], and are first specified using a `Security Editor` (e.g. MotOrBac [6]) and then negotiated between the different parties (e.g. a vehicle and an ITS server in the context of a Vehicle-to-Infrastructure communication) using a `Negotiation` module (see the **Dynamic Specification of Security Policies** block in Fig. 2). The negotiated security policies are analyzed

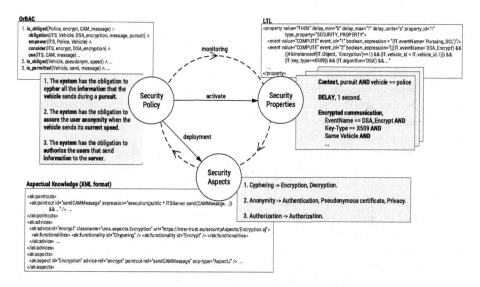

Fig. 1. Correlation of the security policies, the aspects, and the security properties.

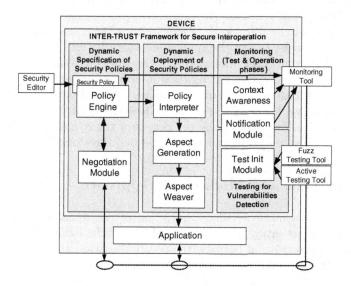

Fig. 2. Architecture of the INTER-TRUST framework.

and interpreted by the `Policy Engine` and the `Policy Interpreter` modules. These modules are responsible for identifying changes in the security policies that require the security concerns deployed inside the application to be adapted. Security policies are dynamically deployed, and/or adapted at runtime using

the `Aspect Generation` and the `Aspect Weaver` modules, which are in charge
of receiving the information generated by the `Policy Interpreter` module and
of incorporating or eliminating the corresponding security aspects in the application (see the **Dynamic Deployment of Security Policies** block in Fig. 2).
Security aspects can be developed in any Java-based AOP language such as
AspectJ, Spring AOP, CaesarJ, or JBoss. The *aspectual knowledge* depicted in
Fig. 1 contains the functionality provided by the aspects for each security policy
and the join points where the aspects can be deployed.

Negotiated security policies are also sent to the `Monitoring Tool` in order to
activate/deactivate the associated security properties that control the fulfillment
of the security policies by the deployed aspects. Security properties are formally
described as conditions in sequences of events [7] based on Linear Temporal
Logic (LTL) to define security rules (i.e., rules that should be respected) or
attacks and misbehaviors [8]. The `Monitoring Tool` relies on an adaptation
of the Montimage Monitoring Tool (MMT) [9] which is an online monitoring
solution that allows a real-time network traffic, application, flow and user level
visibility to be provided. The `Notification` and `Context Awareness` modules
notify the `Monitoring Tool` about application's internal events and changes
in the application context — e.g. network packets, battery of the device, CPU
consumption, etc. (see the **Monitoring (Test and Operation phases)** block
in Fig. 2). Finally, different fuzz [10] and active [11] testing techniques are also
provided as part of the framework (`Fuzz Testing Tool` and `Active Testing
Tool` modules) in order to test the application's security and robustness. During
the testing phase the MMT tool monitors the traces automatically generated
by the fuzz testing and active testing tools in order to simulate the application
behavior (see the **Testing for Vulnerabilities Detection** block in Fig. 2).

In this paper, we focus on the dynamic deployment of the security policies
and on the monitoring phase, while the details of the dynamic specification of
security policies and the testing phases are beyond the scope of this paper.

3   Deployment and Monitoring Approach

Figure 3 provides a more detailed description of the dynamic deployment of
security policies (activities labeled 1, 2, and 3) and the monitoring mechanism
to maintain the correlation between the security policies, the security aspects,
and the security properties (activities labeled 4, 5, and 6).

3.1   Dynamic Deployment of Security Policies

When a security policy needs to be deployed inside the application at runtime (activity labeled 1 in Fig. 3) — e.g., due either to the initial deployment
or to a (re)negotiation of the security policy, the new security policy is sent
to the modules of the framework in charge of: (i) the `Dynamic Deployment of
Security Policies`, which will deploy/undeploy/reconfigure the aspects, and

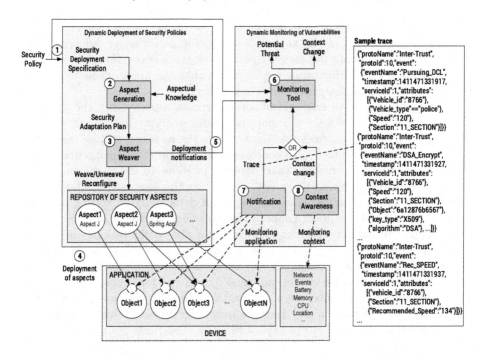

Fig. 3. Our approach for deploying and monitoring security policies.

(ii) the `Dynamic Monitoring of Vulnerabilities`, which will activate/deactivate the corresponding security properties. In order to deploy the security policy, the `Aspect Generation` module receives a *security deployment specification* (activity labeled 2) that is the result of interpreting the security policy and contains the list of security aspects that must be deployed (woven), undeployed (unwoven), and reconfigured (i.e., changing the configuration parameters such as the digital certificate in an authentication aspect) within the application to enforce the new security policy. The `Aspect Generation` module also receives the required *aspectual knowledge* that contains the list of aspects available in the aspect repository of the framework.

The `Aspect Generation` module performs a mapping between the required security functionalities and the aspects that provide these functionalities. The output of this mapping is a new configuration that is analyzed to: (1) obtain the differences between the new and the current configurations of the aspects deployed within the application, and (2) generate a *security adaptation plan* with the list of actions that must be performed over the aspects: weave, unweave, or reconfigure. The security adaptation plan generated by the `Aspect Generation` module is sent to the `Aspect Weaver` module that is in charge of executing the actions by interacting directly with the aspects (activity labeled 3). The `Aspect Weaver` module is a wrapper that translates the list of actions received as input (which is specified independently of a particular AOP language/framework) to the particular syntax of the AOP weaver being used. This means that we provide different instantiations of the **Aspect Weaver** module for using different AOP weavers, since the use of a unique AOP solution does not cover all the dynamicity, expressiveness, and performance requirements that the applications may need (e.g., AspectJ does not support runtime weaving).

Listing 1.1 shows an example of an encryption aspect using the AspectJ language. The aspect defines two main pointcuts: encrypt (line 5) and decrypt (line 6). Each pointcut defines the points where the messages will be encrypted (line 2) or decrypted (line 3). To control the activation of the pointcuts we use the **if()** pointcut constructor that AspectJ provides to define a conditional pointcut expression which will be evaluated at runtime for each candidate join point[1]. This mechanism increases the degree of dynamicity by coding patterns that can dynamically support enabling and disabling advice in aspects [12]. In our example, the **AspectsStatus** class contains the configurations and status (enabled/disabled) of the aspects that are changed at runtime by the **Aspect Weaver** module. The aspect defines two advice associated with the encrypt and decrypt pointcuts: one for encrypting (line 8) and one for decrypting (line 14) CAM messages. The advice use a **CypheringModule** object that provides the functionality for encryption and decryption and is configured with the algorithm and parameters indicated in the **AspectsStatus** class (lines 9 and 15).

Listing 1.1. Encryption aspect in AspectJ language.

```
1 public aspect Encryption {
2    pointcut sendCAMMessage(CAMMessage message): execution(public * ITSServer.
          send(CAMMessage, ..)) && this(Vehicle) && args(message);
3    pointcut receiveCAMMessage(CAMMessage message): execution(public *
          ITSServer.receive(CAMMessage, Vehicle, ..)) && args(message);
4
5    pointcut encrypt(CAMMessage m): if(AspectsStatus.isEnabled("ENCRYPT")) &&
          sendCAMMessage(m);
6    pointcut decrypt(CAMMessage m): if(AspectsStatus.isEnabled("DECRYPT")) &&
          receiveCAMMessage(m);
7
8    Object around(CAMMessage m): encrypt(m) {
9      ChyperingModule chyper = new ChyperingModule(AspectsStatus.getParams("
          ENCRYPT"));
10     CAMMessage chyperedMessage = chyper.encrypt(m);
11     proceed(chyperedMessage);
12   }
13
14   Object around(CAMMessage m): decrypt(m) {
15     ChyperingModule chyper = new ChyperingModule(AspectsStatus.getParams("
          DECRYPT"));
16     CAMMessage clearMessage = chyper.decrypt(m);
17     proceed(clearMessage);
18   }
19 }
```

Once the aspects have been adapted, the **Aspect Weaver** module notifies the **Monitoring Tool** in order to inform about the status of the deployment (activity labeled 5). That is, to notify whether or not the deployment was successfully carried out and which aspects were deployed/deployed/reconfigured.

---

[1] http://eclipse.org/aspectj/doc/released/progguide/index.html.

3.2   Dynamic Monitoring of Security Policies

In order to maintain the correlation between the security policies, the aspects, and the security properties, the application and the aspects are monitored at runtime by the `Notification` module. The `Notification` module reports the application's internal events (e.g., traces with state changes, error conditions, timestamps, method status, etc.) to a monitoring server (the `Monitoring Tool`) (activity labeled 7 in Fig. 3). To operate at runtime, the `Notification` module is introduced into the target application as an aspect in the instantiation phase. The target source code is annotated, using standard Java annotations, to specify the measurement points (or meters) that generate the monitored data. These annotations are also incorporated using AOP without manually modifying the source code of the application. While the target application is operating, the `Notification` module produces a stream of log messages. Measurement points can be attached to classes, methods and attributes, and work on two different levels of scope: local and recursive. Meters operating at the local scope level are always marked by an annotation. Only annotated elements are effected by local scope meters (e.g., calls to nested methods are not tracked). In the next scope level, recursive monitoring, beside the annotated code, all code reachable through control flow is monitored, up to the available call depth. Recursive monitoring may cause a significant performance overhead, so this kind of monitoring should be used by annotating only relevant data for security analysis. Call depth is limited by the available source code, because static aspects operate by modifying accessible source code. The instrumentation therefore does not penetrate precompiled classes, such as .class files or system libraries.

Furthermore, the `Context Awareness` module notifies the `Monitoring Tool` but, in contrast to the `Notification` module, the `Context Awareness` monitors changes in the environment (activity labeled 8) — i.e., contextual changes that are external to the application such as packets over the communication network, battery status of the device, CPU consumption, etc. Both traces and context changes are sent to the `Monitoring Tool` that interprets them (activity labeled 8 in Fig. 3) so it can react to changes or adapt the security rules with the negotiation of a new security policy.

• The right-hand side of Fig. 3 shows an excerpt of a sample trace received by the `Monitoring Tool` with three events generated from the `Notification` module. For instance, the first event (event with name `Pursuing_DCL`) provides the values of the attributes captured by the monitoring annotation. When the first event arrives, the `Monitoring Tool` checks whether it fits one or more of the events defined in the security property (Fig. 1). In the example, the first event received fits the event of the property `event_id="1"` that corresponds with a change in the context. The second event received with the name `DSA_Encrypt` fits the event `event_id="2"` of the property by checking the values of the attributes received in the event with the boolean expression defined in the property. The class object captured is an instance of the `DSAEncryption` aspect that is deployed inside the application of the police vehicle and is using the `DSA` algorithm to encrypt the messages. Other attributes such as the key and the type of the key are also checked against the rule defined in the security property. As the two events received have a delay of less than one second as defined by the security property, the two events consecutively match the rules of the security property. So, in this example the `Monitoring Tool` checks that the CAM messages sent by the police vehicle are being encrypted in the context of a pursuit, and verifies the correct deploying of the encryption aspect required by the security policy, maintainig the correlation between the three parts. A non-match condition in the boolean expression of the rules in the security property, for instance, if the event with the name `DSA_Encrypt` does not occurr, or if the `algorithm` attribute is different to DSA. This means the non-match of the entire security property, and thus the detection of a gap in the correlation between the security policy, the aspects and the security property.

4   Evaluation

We quantitatively evaluate the performance overhead of the dynamic deployment of security policies and the dynamic monitoring of the application. Also, as part of our participation in the INTER-TRUST project, the deployment modules (the `Aspect Generation` and the `Aspect Weaver`)[2], the monitoring modules (the `Notification` and the `Context Awareness`)[3] as well as the Monitoring Tool[4] have been used to implement a demonstrator of the project that provides dynamic adaptation of security policies for two real case studies: the ITS case study presented in this paper and an online electronic voting case study.

4.1   Performance of Deployment

The performance overhead of the deployment process considers the time from the reception of a security deployment specification in the `Aspect Generation` module to the execution of the adaptation plan by the `Aspect Weaver`. We consider the number of aspects that need to be dynamically adapted (i.e., woven, unwoven, or reconfigured) in order to fulfill the required functionality specified in the security policy. The experiments were done on a laptop Intel Core i3 M350, 2.27 GHz, 4 GB of memory, and with 1.7 JVM. Aspects were implemented in AspectJ and Spring AOP. The results are summarized in Fig. 4 where the performance presents a linear increment of the overhead over the number of aspects. For instance, the adaptation process takes 320 ms for deploying 20 aspects specified in the security policy. Reconfiguring aspects takes 20 ms more on average than deploying them, while undeploying aspects takes 15 ms more than deploying them. The results indicate that adapting security policies with AOP at runtime does not suppose a high overhead.

---

[2] https://github.com/Inter-Trust/Aspect_Generation/tree/demonstrator-version.

[3] https://github.com/Inter-Trust/Notification_Module.

[4] https://github.com/Inter-Trust/MMT_Security.

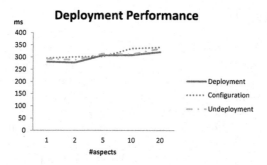

Fig. 4. Performance of deployment security policies.

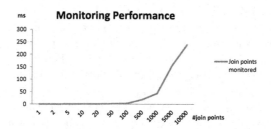

Fig. 5. Performance of monitoring join points at runtime.

4.2   Performance of Monitoring

The performance overhead of the dynamic monitoring considers the time overhead introduced at runtime when the `Notification` and `Context Awareness` modules are integrated as aspects inside the application. We evaluated the time overhead for generating the traces for the most expensive monitor annotation — i.e., the recursive annotation that tracks all methods encountered by the control flow from the annotated method. Figure 5 shows the time overhead based on the number of join points captured. We can observe that the performance presents a linear increment of the overhead over the number of join points while this number is lower than 100. Then, from 100 join points, the increment is higher but still linear. In all cases, the results obtained do not suppose a significative overhead. For instance, monitoring 10,000 join points in the control flow of a method takes 250 ms on average. The analysis of the generated traces is carried out by the `Monitoring Tool` which is independent of the application and can reside in a different computer, and thus, the analysis of the traces does not affect the application's performance.

5   Related Work

The analysis of existing research work and standards in the domain of FI and pervasive systems reveals a common problem: the inexistence of a proper security framework to secure the communications flexibly and efficiently ([13,14]). In [13], the authors propose a framework for specifying, deploying and testing access control policies independently of the security model. The main drawback to this approach is that the generic meta-model only supports access control policies, and thus, it is not possible to specify and deploy other security concerns such as integrity, encryption, or non-repudiation, as the INTER-TRUST framework can. In [14], an Aspect Oriented Permission System (AOPS) for runtime policy enforcement is presented. The policy decisions are based on the execution history-based access control model (HBAC) [15] and implemented in AspectJ following the Java permissions model but applied to AOP. Only security vulnerabilities related to access control permissions are considered (e.g., restricted rights to read and modify attributes of the base system by the aspects). Also, the approach assumes that the weaver as well as the execution environment are trusted, and that the weaver protects against scenarios in which untrusted aspects are incorrectly woven into the application code.

AOP vulnerabilities are well-known and have been identified during the development activity [16–19]. In [16], the authors present bug patterns in AspectJ and illustrate the symptoms of the patterns through examples. The security risks in using AOP to develop secure software are analyzed in [17] from a programming level point of view. An aspect permission system is also proposed to address some of the issues identified (e.g., parameter alteration, invocation hijacking, use of privileged aspects, etc.). In [18], the authors use a combination of static code analysis and protection code generation during the development phase. They focus on security vulnerabilities caused by missing input validation — i.e., the process of validating all the inputs for an application before using it. They analyze the source code and/or binary code without executing it and identify anti-patterns that lead to security bugs. The unexpected vulnerabilities that the dynamic weaving may introduce when the aspects are woven at runtime cannot be covered with the static analysis. In [19], aspect orientation is used to monitor the information flows between objects in a system for the purpose of detecting misuse. That is, identifying behavior that is close to some previously defined pattern signature of a known intrusion. The problem with misuse-based detections is that the anomalies must be known in advance and cannot detect new vulnerabilities at runtime.

Apart from monitoring, there are several techniques to perform dynamic detection of failures in the deployment of security policies such as active testing [11] (to validate the implementation by applying a set of test cases and analyzing its reaction) or fuzz testing [10] (to detect unwanted behaviors or security violation by using random or mutated inputs). However, although these testing techniques are incorporated in the INTER-TRUST framework, these are not suitable to use at runtime as monitoring can be, but are applied at the testing phase.

Finally, the modular architecture of the INTER-TRUST framework allows its integration with different middlewares such as FamiWare [20] in order to provide security and privacy to wireless sensor networks; and with security adaptation services such as a MAPE-K loop approach [21].

6   Conclusions and Future Work

We have defined an approach to maintain the correlation between the security policies that need to be enforced, the security aspects that are deployed/undeployed in order to enforce those security policies and the security properties that are activated/deactivated in order to check whether or not the system is behaving according to the specified security policies. Our approach has been integrated as part of the INTER-TRUST framework, however, it can also be applied to many other types of pervasive systems in other contexts independently of the INTER-TRUST framework, and can also be used to adapt other functionalities implemented as aspects (not only security).

As for future work, we plan to complete our approach by dynamically generating the structure of the aspects and the security properties from the security policies minimizing the aspectual knowledge needed to maintain the correlation.

Acknowledgment. Work funded by the European INTER-TRUST FP7–317731 and the Spanish TIN2012–34840, FamiWare P09-TIC-5231, and MAGIC P12-TIC1814 projects.

References

1. Atzori, L., Iera, A., Morabito, G.: The internet of things: a survey. Comput. Netw. **54**(15), 2787–2805 (2010)
2. FP7 European Project INTER-TRUST: Interoperable Trust Assurance Infrastructure. http://www.inter-trust.eu/
3. Ayed, S., Idrees, M.S., Cuppens-Boulahia, N., Cuppens, F., Pinto, M., Fuentes, L.: Security aspects: a framework for enforcement of security policies using AOP. In: Signal-Image Technology & Internet-Based Systems, SITIS, pp. 301–308 (2013)
4. Kiczales, G., Lamping, J., Mendhekar, A., Maeda, C., Lopes, C., Loingtier, J.M., Irwin, J.: Aspect-oriented programming. In: Akşit, M., Matsuoka, S. (eds.) ECOOP 1997. LNCS, vol. 1241, pp. 220–242. Springer, Heidelberg (1997)
5. Kalam, A., Baida, R., Balbiani, P., Benferhat, S., Cuppens, F., Deswarte, Y., Miege, A., Saurel, C., Trouessin, G.: Organization based access control. In: Policies for Distributed Systems and Networks (2003)
6. Autrel, F., Cuppens, F., Cuppens, N., Coma, C.: MotOrBAC 2: a security policy tool. In: Third Joint Conference on Security in Networks Architectures and Security of Information Systems, SARSSI (2008)
7. Morales, G., Maag, S., Cavalli, A., Mallouli, W., de Oca, E., Wehbi, B.: Timed extended invariants for the passive testing of web services. In: IEEE International Conference on Web Services, pp. 592–599 (2010)
8. Mallouli, W., Wehbi, B., de Oca, E.M., Bourdelles, M.: Online network traffic security inspection using MMT tool. In: System Testing and Validation (2012)

9. Wehbi, B., de Oca, E., Bourdelles, M.: Events-based security monitoring using MMT Tool. In: Software Testing, Verification and Validation (2012)
10. Howard, M., Lipner, S.: Inside the windows security push. IEEE Secur. Priv. **1**(1), 57–61 (2003)
11. Cavalli, A., de Oca, E., Mallouli, W., Lallali, M.: Two complementary tools for the formal testing of distributed systems with time constraints. In: Distributed Simulation and Real-Time Applications(2008)
12. Andrade, R., Rebelo, H., Ribeiro, M., Borba, P.: AspectJ-based idioms for flexible feature binding. In: VII Brazilian Symposium on Software Components, Architectures and Reuse, SBCARS, pp. 59–68 (2013)
13. Mouelhi, T., Fleurey, F., Baudry, B., Le Traon, Y.: A model-based framework for security policy specification, deployment and testing. In: Czarnecki, K., Ober, I., Bruel, J.-M., Uhl, A., Völter, M. (eds.) MODELS 2008. LNCS, vol. 5301, pp. 537–552. Springer, Heidelberg (2008)
14. De Borger, W., De Win, B., Lagaisse, B., Joosen, W.: A permission system for secure AOP. In: Aspect-Oriented Software Development (2010)
15. Abadi, M., Fournet, C.: Access control based on execution history. In: Proceedings of the 10th Annual Network and Distributed System Security Symposium, NDSS, pp. 107–121 (2003)
16. Zhang, S., Zhao, J.: On identifying bug patterns in aspect-oriented programs.In: 31st Annual International Computer Software and Applications Conference, COMPSAC 2007, vol. 1, pp. 431–438 (2007)
17. De Win, B., Piessens, F., Joosen, W.: How secure is AOP and what can we do about it? In: Software Engineering for Secure Systems, pp. 27–34 (2006)
18. Serme, G., De Oliveira, A.S., Guarnieriy, M., El Khoury, P.: Towards assisted remediation of security vulnerabilities. In: 6th International Conference on Emerging Security Information, Systems and Technologies, SECURWARE (2012)
19. Padayachee, K., Eloff, J.: An aspect-oriented model to monitor misuse. In: Sobh, T. (ed.) Innovations and Advanced Techniques in Computer and Information Sciences and Engineering, pp. 273–278. Springer, Netherlands (2007)
20. Pinto, M., Gámez, N., Fuentes, L., Amor, M., Horcas, J.M., Ayala, I.: Dynamic reconfiguration of security policies in wireless sensor networks. Sens. **15**(3), 5251 (2015)
21. Horcas, J.-M., Pinto, M., Fuentes, L.: Runtime enforcement of dynamic security policies. In: Avgeriou, P., Zdun, U. (eds.) ECSA 2014. LNCS, vol. 8627, pp. 340–356. Springer, Heidelberg (2014)

Privacy Requirements
and Privacy Audit

A Taxonomy of Requirements for the Privacy Goal Transparency

Rene Meis[✉], Roman Wirtz, and Maritta Heisel

paluno - The Ruhr Institute for Software Technology,
University of Duisburg-Essen, Essen, Germany
{Rene.Meis,Roman.Wirtz,Maritta.Heisel}@paluno.uni-due.de

Abstract. Privacy is a growing concern during software development. Transparency–in the sense of increasing user's privacy-awareness–is a privacy goal that is not as deeply studied in the literature as the properties anonymity and unlinkability. To be compliant with legislation and standards, requirements engineers have to identify the requirements on transparency that are relevant for the software to be developed. To assist the identification process, we provide a taxonomy of transparency requirements derived from legislation and standards. This taxonomy is validated using related research which was identified using a systematic literature review. Our proposed taxonomy can be used by requirements engineers as basis to systematically identify the relevant transparency requirements leading to a more complete and coherent set of requirements.

1 Introduction

The awareness for privacy concerns is growing in the public. With this awareness comes a call for more transparency on what, why and how software-systems collect, use, and process personal information. Hansen [1] identifies transparency as one of three privacy protection goals ensuring *"that all privacy-relevant data processing including the legal, technical and organizational setting can be understood and reconstructed"* [2]. Hence, it is not sufficient to increase user's privacy awareness, it is also necessary to provide the information needed to users in order to understand how they personal data is processed. Transparency, as all software qualities, is a complex property. It leads to requirements for the representation of static information about the software's intended purpose, but also to requirements on informing users about run-time events, e.g., malfunctions. In addition to the requirements about informing *what* happens, there are also requirements on *how* the information is shown to users to ensure that mechanisms to improve the software's transparency have an impact on the user's privacy-awareness. Especially concerning legal compliance, requirements engineers have to provide an as complete set of requirements as possible to ensure that the software that is built based on these requirements is compliant. I.e., the software requirements have to bridge the gap between the legal requirements and the technical mechanisms to realize them. To empower requirements engineers to identify all transparency requirements relevant for the software to be built, we have to refine the high-level

© Springer International Publishing Switzerland 2015
S. Fischer-Hübner et al. (Eds.): TrustBus 2015, LNCS 9264, pp. 195–209, 2015.
DOI: 10.1007/978-3-319-22906-5_15

privacy goal transparency into more concrete transparency requirements that assist requirements engineers in the elicitation process.

To obtain an as complete taxonomy of transparency requirements as possible, we consider different sources that requirements engineers also should consider. To be compliant with legislation requirements engineers have to consider privacy and data protection laws relevant to them, depending on the application domain of the software to be developed also standards have to be considered, to increase user acceptance, the user's needs have to be considered. We used as sources for the creation of our taxonomy the ISO/IEC 29100:2011 standard [3] and the draft of the EU Data Protection Regulation [4]. We then considered relevant research in the field of privacy, transparency, and awareness including empirical research on user's privacy concerns to validate the completeness of the proposed taxonomy.

The rest of the paper is structured as follows. Our privacy requirements taxonomy is derived and presented in Sect. 2 and validated using related work identified using a systematic literature review in Sect. 3. Section 4 concludes the paper.

2   Deriving and Structuring Requirements on Transparency

In Sect. 2.1, we systematically analyze the privacy principles described by ISO/IEC 29100:2011 [3] and the draft of the EU data protection regulation [4] to derive the transparency requirements they contain. To derive the requirements, we analyzed the description of the privacy principles and the formulations of the regulation. We looked for verbs like *inform, notify, document, present, provide, explain, communicate* and related nouns. We keep the formulation of the identified transparency requirements close to the original documents from which we identified them. In Sect. 2.1, we enumerate these derived requirements using the notation Tn. As the ISO principles and EU articles partly overlap, we identified several refinements of identified requirements. We relate those requirements using a *refines* relation. If a transparency requirements Tn_1 refines a part of another requirement Tn_2, this means that Tn_1 adds further details on how or what information has to be made transparent. The *refines* relation is visualized in form of an initial ontology of transparency requirements in Fig. 1. In Sect. 2.2, we structure the transparency requirements identified in Sect. 2.1 into a taxonomy of transparency requirements. This taxonomy is presented as an extensible metamodel.

ISO/IEC 29100:2011 and the draft of the EU data protection regulation do not use the same terminology. To avoid ambiguities, we will use the following term definitions from the draft of the EU data protection regulation in this paper.

Data subject *"means an identified natural person or a natural person who can be identified, directly or indirectly, by means reasonably likely to be used by the controller or by any other natural or legal person, in particular by reference to an identification number, location data, online identifier or to one or more factors specific to the physical, physiological, genetic, mental, economic, cultural or social identity of that person."* This term is called *PII principal* in ISO/IEC 29100:2011.

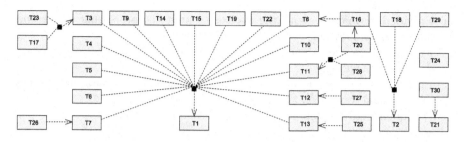

Fig. 1. Initial ontology of transparency requirements

Personal data *"means any information relating to a data subject."* This term is called *personally identifiable information (PII)* in ISO/IEC 29100:2011.

Processing *"means any operation or set of operations which is performed upon personal data or sets of personal data, whether or not by automated means, such as collection, recording, organization, structuring, storage, adaptation or alteration, retrieval, consultation, use, disclosure by transmission, dissemination or otherwise making available, alignment or combination, erasure or destruction."*

Controller *"means the natural or legal person, public authority, agency or any other body which alone or jointly with others determines the purposes, conditions and means of the processing of personal data; where the purposes, conditions and means of processing are determined by Union law or Member State law, the controller or the specific criteria for his nomination may be designated by Union law or by Member State law."* This term is called *PII controller* in ISO/IEC 29100:2011.

2.1 Requirements Identification from Privacy Principles and Legislation

ISO/IEC 29100 Privacy Principles. To derive our taxonomy of transparency requirements, we first consider the international standard ISO/IEC 29100:2011 [3], which defines 11 privacy principles which are a superset of the OECD principles [5] and the US fair information practices (FIPs) [6].

We start our analysis of the privacy principles with the *openness, transparency and notice principle*, which is obviously concerned with transparency. From this principle, we obtain the following transparency requirements.

T1 Inform data subjects about the controller's policies, procedures and practices with respect to the processing of personal data.

T2 The information about the management of personal data has to be clear and easily accessible for data subjects (and the public).

T3 Explain the purpose of data processing to data subjects.

T4 Specify the persons to whom the personal data might be disclosed.

T5 Provide the identity of the controller including contact information to data subjects.

T6 Provide information about the choices to limit the processing of personal data to data subjects.

T7 Provide information about the means to access, correct and remove personal data to data subjects.

T8 Provide information in the case that a decision that a data subject can make has an impact on the data subject.

T9 Document and communicate all contractual obligations that impact personal data processing externally to the extent those obligations are not confidential.

T10 Provide information about the personal data required for the specified purpose to data subjects.

T11 Provide information about how and what personal data is collected to data subjects.

T12 Provide information about how, what and to whom personal data is communicated to data subjects.

T13 Provide information about how and what personal data is stored to data subjects.

T14 Provide information about authorized natural persons who will access personal data to data subjects.

T15 Provide information about data retention and disposal requirements.

T1 and T2 are the most general requirements in our initial ontology. Hence, they form the root elements (cf. Fig. 1). T1 is considered with *what* information has to be presented and is refined by T3-T15 that are all also concerned with about what data subjects have to be informed. In contrast, T2 is concerned with *how* that information has to be presented to data subjects.

The *consent and choice principle* strengthens that data subjects have to give their consent on a *"knowledgeable basis"* and hence, they have to be informed before obtaining consent. This information has also to contain information about *"the implications of granting or withholding consent"*. We identify the following requirement.

T16 Before data subjects are asked to give consent to use their data, provide all information necessary to make this decision to them, including the implications of granting or withholding consent.

This requirement refines T2 in the sense that the point in time when the information has to be provided is specified. Additionally, T16 refines T8 by describing which data has to be provided to data subjects when they make the decision to give consent.

The principle *purpose legitimacy and specification* stresses that data subjects have to be informed about the purpose of data collection and use before it is used for the first time or for a new purpose. This information has to be presented using language *"which is both clear and appropriately adapted to the circumstances."* In the case that sensitive data is processed, sufficient explanations have to be provided to the data subject. Hence, we obtain following requirements.

T17 Inform data subjects about the purpose of data collection and use before it is collected or used for the first time for this purpose.

T18 The language used for providing information to data subjects has to be clear and appropriately adapted to the circumstances.

T19 Provide sufficient explanations whenever sensitive data is used to data subjects.

Requirement T17 complements T3 with the information when data subjects have to be informed. T18 is a refinement of T2 by adding the notice that the presentation has to be adapted to the circumstances in which this information is shown. T19 places emphasis on providing explanations whenever sensitive data is used and hence refines the top-level requirement T1.

The principle *collection limitation* is concerned with limiting the collected personal data to the minimum needed. We obtain the following additional requirement.

T20 Provide information to data subjects about if it is optional to provide personal data.

This requirement complements T11 and T16, because it is important to inform data subjects before data collection and giving consent whether it is optional to provide the questioned personal data.

The principle *accountability* contains the following transparency requirements that are concerned with the occurrence of privacy breaches, which is not yet covered by other transparency requirements, because the other requirements are concerned with the normal behavior of the system under consideration.

T21 Inform data subjects and other relevant stakeholder (as required in some jurisdictions) about privacy breaches that can lead to substantial damage to data subjects as well as the measures taken for resolution.

The principle *information security* implies the following transparency requirement that refines the transparency requirement T1.

T22 Inform data subjects about the (security) mechanisms to protect their personal data.

Draft of the EU Data Protection Regulation. To identify further transparency requirements and to refine the already identified requirements, we analyze the draft of the EU Data Protection Regulation [4] that is currently under review and will be when accepted by all member states be mandatory to be implemented by all EU member states. In contrast to the situation in the US where no privacy regulations covering all industrial branches exist [7], the EU Data Protection will cover all industrial branches.

Article 5 (b) adds the need that the purpose has to be legitimate to requirement T3. Hence, we obtain the following refined requirement.

T23 Explain data subjects why the purpose of data collection is legitimate.

Article 12 prescribes the implementation of procedures and mechanisms for exercising the rights of data subjects and says that *"If the controller refuses to take action on the request of the data subject, the controller shall inform the data subject of the reasons for the refusal and on the possibilities of lodging a complaint to the supervisory authority and seeking a judicial remedy"*. Hence, we identify a transparency requirement that, similar to T21, is not concerned with the normal system behavior.

T24 If requests of data subjects for exercising their rights are rejected, then the reasons for the refusal has to be provided.

From Article 14, we can derive following transparency requirements that refine previously identified requirements.

T25 Provide the period for which the personal data will be stored to data subjects.

T26 Provide information about *"the existence of the right to request from the controller access to and rectification or erasure of the personal data concerning the data subject or to object to the processing of such personal data"*

T27 Provide information about data transfer *"to a third country or international organisation and the level of protection afforded by that third country or international organization"*.

T28 Inform the data subject about the source the personal data used originates from.

T29 Provide information to data subjects *"at the time when the personal data are obtained from the data subject; or where the personal data are not collected from the data subject, at the time of the recording or within a reasonable period after the collection, having regard to the specific circumstances in which the data are collected or otherwise processed, or, if a disclosure to another recipient is envisaged, and at the latest when the data are first disclosed."*

T25 refines T13 by adding the need for specifying the duration of data storage. T26 adds a legal need to T7. T27 refines T12 by requiring special treatment when data is transferred to third countries or international organizations. T28 refines T11 by adding the need to provide information of the source of the personal data used. T29 refines T2 with information about when to provide information to data subjects.

Article 31 is concerned with the notification of personal data breaches and refines T21 by adding a duration after which the supervisory authorities have to be informed.

T30 Notify supervisory authorities (and data subjects) about the occurrence of a personal data breach not later than 24 hours after having become aware of it.

2.2 Setting up a Transparency Requirements Taxonomy

In this section, we structure the identified preliminary transparency requirements into a transparency requirements taxonomy. Figure 2 shows our taxonomy in the

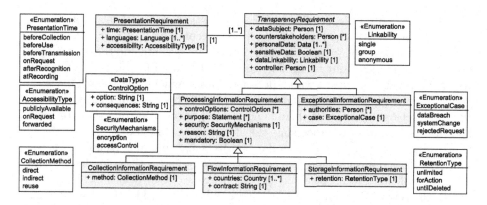

Fig. 2. Our proposed taxonomy of transparency requirements.

Table 1. Mapping of transparency requirements to preliminary requirements

Requirement	Attribute	Tn
TransparencyRequirement	data subject, personal data	T1
	controller	T5
	counterstakeholder	T4, T14
	linkability	T16
	sensitiveData	T19
PresentationRequirement	accessibility	T2
	language	T18
	time	T16, T29, T30
ExceptionalInformationRequirement	case	T17, T21, T24, T30
	authorities	T21
ProcessingInformationRequirement	controlOptions	T6, T7, T8, T26
	mandatory	T10, T20
	purpose, reason	T3, T17, T23
	security	T22
CollectionInformationRequirement	method	T11, T28
StorageInformationRequirement	retention	T13, T15, T25
FlowInformationRequirement	contract, country	T9, T12, T27

form of a metamodel using a UML class diagram. We structured the transparency requirements into a hierarchy, which is derived from the initial ontology shown in Fig. 1. We describe our taxonomy in the following from the top to the bottom. An overview of the mapping between the transparency requirements taxonomy to the initial transparency requirements is given in Table 1.

Transparency Requirement. The top-level element of our hierarchy is the general TransparencyRequirement which corresponds to the initial requirement T1. In our metamodel we declared this requirement as *abstract*, i.e., it is not possible to instantiate it, only its specializations can be instantiated. It has six attributes. First, the dataSubject who has to be informed. Second, a set of counterstakeholders who are involved in the processing of the data subject's data and the data subject has to be informed about them. For example, T4 and T14 prescribe to specify the (authorized) persons to whom personal data might be disclosed. This is the case for many requirements in our taxonomy and hence, we put this attribute to the top-level requirement. If there is no need to specify persons who are somehow involved in the data processing, the attribute counterstakeholder is left empty. Our taxonomy suggests to consider data subjects and counterstakeholders as persons. The data subject should be a natural person, whereas the counterstakeholders can be natural, legal, or artificial persons, e.g., organizations or authorities. Third, the set of personal data of the data subject for which the transparency requirement is relevant. Almost all transparency requirements that we identified previously refer to the data subject and his/her personal data. Hence, all transparency requirements in our taxonomy have the data subject and his/her personal data as attribute. Fourth, we document whether the specified personal data represents senstiveData, because of T19 sensitive data needs special consideration. Fifth, the attribute linkability documents whether the personal data is linkable to a single data subject, a group of possible data subjects, or is anonymous. This attribute is not explicitly motivated from the requirements, but T16 mentions that in the case of giving consent all information necessary to make this decision has to be provided to data subject and we think that the linkability of the personal data to the data subject is such an information. Sixth, in accordance with T5 the data subject has to be informed about who the controller is.

Presentation Requirement. The initial transparency requirements T2, T16, T18, T29, and T30 are in contrast to the other requirements not mainly concerned with *what* information shall be provided to the data subject, but with *how* this information has to be presented. To decouple the *how* from the *what* in our taxonomy, we introduce PresentationRequirements. Every TransparencyRequirement has exactly one PresentationRequirement assigned, which describes how the information has to be provided to the data subject. On the other side, the same PresentationRequirement can be related to multiple TransparencyRequirements. The attribute time reflects T16, T29, and T30 that prescribe the time when information has to be provided. The possible values for this attribute are summarized in the enumeration PresentationTime (cf. Fig. 2). We derived these values from T16, T29 and T30. Nevertheless, we do not consider this enumeration, such as all other enumerations presented in our taxonomy, as complete and whenever necessary they can be extended. The attribute languages is not explicitly mentioned in a transparency requirement, but to provide information clearly and adapted to the circumstances to data subjects (in accordance with T18) one should present this information using at best the first language of each possible data subject. The attribute accessibility serves to document the requirements on how data subject shall be able to access the information, indicated by T2. An information may has to be publiclyAvailable, onRequest of the data subject, or the information is forwarded to the user when needed.

ExceptionalInformationRequirement. Most transparency requirements are concerned with providing information about the normal behavior of the considered system. This information can be considered as rather static. In contrast, T21, T24, and T30 require to inform data subjects in cases where unexpected events occur. For this purpose, we refine the general TransparencyRequirement into the requirement ExceptionalInformationRequirement. The attribute case stores the kind of unintended event the data subject has to be informed about. This can be a dataBreach as mentioned in T21 and T30, a systemChange that e.g., changes the purpose of data processing (cf. T17), or a rejectedRequest of a data subject as described in T24. In addition to the data subject that has to be informed, T21 also states that authorities may have to be informed. The attribute authorities is used to document the natural, legal, or artificial persons that have to be informed if the respective exceptional case occurs.

ProcessingInformationRequirement. The requirement ProcessingInformationRequirement refines TransparencyRequirements and contains the properties that all *static* transparency requirements, which refine the initial requirement T1 (cf. Fig. 1), have in common. The attribute controlOptions summarizes (using the data type ControlOption) the options the data subject has to limit the processing of personal data (T6), means to access, correct and remove personal data (T7 and T26), and the consequences implied by these options (T8). T3, T17, and T23 require that the purpose for data processing is explained to data subjects. The attribute purpose is used to provide a set of Statements that could consist of functional requirements and knowledge about the software environment for which's fulfillment the personal data of the data subject is needed. Furthermore, the attribute reason is used to provides information about why the personal data is needed for the purpose and why it is legitimate to use it. Due to T10 and T20, data subjects have to be clearly informed whether the provision of personal data is optional and whether the information is needed for the specified purpose. The attribute mandatory is used to capture this information. The attribute security is used to represent how the personal data is protected as required by T22. Possible protection mechanisms are e.g., encryption and accessControl.

CollectionInformationRequirement. Requirement T11 prescribes that data subjects have to be informed about how and what data is collected from them. For this purpose, we refined the ProcessingInformationRequirement into the CollectionInformationRequirement. In addition to the information that is already inherited from TransparencyRequirement and ProcessingInformationRequirement, we derived from T28, which is a refinement of T11 (cf. Fig. 1), the attribute method that reflects whether the data collection is direct, indirect, or whether existing data of the subjects is reused.

FlowInformationRequirement. Requirement T12 implies a further refinement of ProcessingInformationRequirement that we call FlowInformationRequirement. This requirement prescribes to inform data subjects about the flow of their data. From T9 and T27, we derived that for each information flow, it is important to inform the data subject about the contractual obligations and policies the data receiver is bound to. This information is represented in the attribute contract. Furthermore, T27 puts an emphasis on taking care of data transfer to *third countries* and international organizations. Hence, we added the attribute countries to capture the geographical destination of the data flow.

StorageInformationRequirement. From T13, we derive the requirement StorageInformationRequirement that is also a refinement of ProcessingInformationRequirement. This requirement is used to represent the information that is needed to inform the data subject about the storage of his/her personal data. In addition to the attributes inherited from TransparencyRequirement and ProcessingInformationRequirement, T15 and T25 require that the data subject is informed about the duration of storage and the data retention and disposal requirements. To reflect this information, we use the attribute retention. The possible values of this attribute can indicate that personal data is stored for an unlimited time, as long as it is needed for the purpose it was collected for (forAction), or until it is deleted (untilDeleted) after there is no reason to keep the data anymore, but not directly.

The complete taxonomy is shown in Fig. 2. Note that the taxonomy is easily extensible by further refinements of requirements, adding further attributes and relations, and adapting the suggested enumerations to the needs implied by the application domain and relevant legislation of the software to be developed. Table 1 provides an overview of how the initial requirements Tn that we derived from ISO 29100 and the draft of the EU Data Protection Regulation are reflected by the proposed taxonomy.

3   Validation of the Taxonomy Using Related Literature

In this section, we give an overview of existing research that also contains considerations about the privacy goal of transparency. To validate our proposed taxonomy, we map the notions and concepts used in the related literature to our taxonomy to check whether it is suitable to reflect the shapes of transparency used in the literature.

To identify the relevant related work, we performed a systematic literature review using backward snowballing [46]. To obtain the starting set of papers for our review, we manually searched the proceedings and issues of the last 10 years of computer science conferences and journals that are mainly concerned with at least one of the topics privacy, requirements, and software engineering and ranked at least as *B-level* in the CORE2014[1] ranking. First, we checked whether title or abstract of a paper indicated that the paper is concerned with privacy (requirements), transparency, or awareness. If this was the case, we analyzed the full text of the paper. Due to the manual search process, we have to deal with the threat of validity that our starting set of papers does not contain all relevant literature, because it was published in a source that we do not consider or was published earlier than in the last 10 years, To mitigate this threat, we applied backward snowballing. I.e., we also considered the papers referenced in

---

[1] http://www.core.edu.au/coreportal.

Table 2. Mapping of transparency notions from the literature to our proposed taxonomy

Source	PR	EIR	PIR	SIR	FIR	CIR	Source	PR	EIR	PIR	SIR	FIR	CIR
Privacy (Requirements) Engineering							**Empirical Research on Privacy Awareness**						
Breaux [8]	X						Reinfelder et al. [9]			X	X		X
Deng et al. [10]		X	X	X	X	X	Sheth et al. [11]	X		X	X	X	X
Rost & Pfitzmann [12], Hansen [1], Bier [13]			X	X	X	X	Zviran [14], Sheehan and Hoy [15]			X			X
Fhom and Bayarou [16]			X	X	X		**Privacy from the Legal Perspective**						
Spiekermann and Cranor [17]	X		X		X	X	Breaux and Gordon [18], Tomaszewski [19]		X				
Hoepmann [20]		X	X	X	X		Jones and Tahri [21]			X			
Kung et al. [22]			X	X	X	X	Mulligan [23], Wright [24]	X			X	X	X
Langheinrich [25]	X					X	Otto et al. [26]	X	X	X	X	X	X
Masiello [27]	X		X	X	X	X	Solove [28]			X	X		X
Wicker and Schrader [29]	X		X	X	X	X	Van der Sype and Seigneur [30]	X	X	X	X	X	X
Mouratidis et al. [31,32]	X		X				Wright and Raab [33]	X					X
Pötzsch [34]	X		X	X			**Privacy Policies and Obligations**						
Feigenbaum [35]	X		X			X	Alcade Bagüés et al. [36]		X	X	X	X	
Hedbom [37]			X	X	X	X	Antón et al. [38,39,40]	X	X	X	X	X	X
Miyazaki et al. [41]		X	X				Casassa Mont [42]	X	X	X	X	X	X
PR: PresentationRequirement							Kelley et al. [43,44]	X		X		X	
EIR: ExceptionalInformationRequirement							Lobato et al. [45]	X	X	X	X	X	X

SIR: StorgeInformationRequirement, **PIR**: ProcessingInformationRequirement,
FIR: FlowInformationRequirement, **CIR**: CollectionInformationRequirement

the papers that we identified as relevant until no new candidates were found. In total, we identified 403 papers that seemed to be relevant after reading title and abstract. After the analysis of the full text, we finally identified 39 papers as related work.

Due to space limitations, we cannot present all details of the literature review in this paper. The details can be found in a technical report[2]. The list of considered conferences and journals can also be found in this technical report. We were able to map each explicitly mentioned transparency related concept in the literature to an element of our taxonomy. This mapping is provided in Table 2. We categorized the identified literature into the four categories *Privacy (Requirements) Engineering*, *Empirical Research on Privacy Awareness*, *Privacy from the Legal Perspective*, and *Privacy Policies and Obligations*.

From Table 2, we can see that almost all papers in the category *Privacy (Requirements) Engineering* have considered *what* information has to be provided to data subjects, but only the halve of these papers mentioned that it is important *how* this information is provided. Only three contained aspects related to notification of data subjects in exceptional cases, e.g., data breaches. Note that none of the papers in this category covered all elements of our taxonomy. The papers in the category *Empirical Research on Privacy Awareness* mainly investigate the users' awareness of data processing. The papers did not give recommendations on how data subjects shall be informed about exceptional

---

[2] https://www.uni-due.de/imperia/md/content/swe/trans-tech.pdf.

cases. In the category *Privacy from the Legal Perspective*, we have papers that consider single laws or aspects that can be reflected by single elements of our taxonomy, and papers that consider a larger legal framework or privacy impact assessments and hence, cover (almost) all elements of our taxonomy. The papers in the category *Privacy Policies and Obligations* provide the most structured, detailed, and complete concepts related to transparency requirements. Nevertheless, we did not find any literature that provides an as structured, detailed, and complete overview of transparency requirements as our proposed taxonomy shown in Fig. 2.

4   Conclusions

In this paper, (1) we systematically derived requirements for the privacy goal transparency from the ISO/IEC 29100:2011 standard [3] and the draft of the EU Data Protection Regulation [4]. These two documents belong to the most relevant sources for privacy requirements that have to be considered by software developers. (2) We then structured these requirements in a metamodel for transparency requirements. This metamodel provides an overview of the identified kinds of transparency requirements and shall help requirements engineers to identify and document the transparency requirements relevant for them and the information needed to address the transparency requirements. (3) We performed a systematic literature review and provide an overview of the relevant research related to transparency requirements. (4) We validated that our taxonomy contains all necessary aspects mentioned in the identified literature. The literature review showed that all aspects of the privacy goal transparency mentioned in the literature are reflected in the proposed taxonomy. Furthermore, we did not find any literature that presents transparency requirements in an as structured, detailed, and complete manner. Our proposed metamodel of the taxonomy can easily be adopted and extended.

As future work, we plan to develop a systematic process that assists requirements engineers to identify the relevant transparency requirements based on a given set of functional requirements. Furthermore, we will develop a tool to generate human-readable representations of the instantiated transparency requirements of our proposed metamodel based on text templates.

References

1. Hansen, M.: Top 10 mistakes in system design from a privacy perspective and privacy protection goals. In: Camenisch, J., Crispo, B., Fischer-Hübner, S., Leenes, R., Russello, G. (eds.) Privacy and Identity Management for Life. IFIP AICT, vol. 375, pp. 14–31. Springer, Heidelberg (2012)
2. Probst, T., Hansen, M.: Privacy protection goals in privacy and data protection evaluations. Working paper, Unabhängiges Landeszentrum für Datenschutz Schleswig-Holstein, July 2013

3. ISO/IEC: ISO/IEC 29100:2011 Information technology - Security techniques - Privacy Framework. Technical report, International Organization for Standardization and International Electrotechnical Commission (2011)
4. European Commission: Proposal for a REGULATION OF THE EUROPEAN PARLIAMENT AND OF THE COUNCIL on the protection of individuals with regard to the processing of personal data and on the free movement of such data (General Data Protection Regulation), January 2012. http://eur-lex.europa.eu/legal-content/EN/TXT/?uri=CELEX:52012PC0011
5. OECD: OECD guidelines on the protection of privacy and transborder flows of personal data. Technical report, Organisation of Economic Co-Operation and Development (1980)
6. US Federal Trade Commission: Privacy online: Fair information practices in the electronic marketplace, a report to congress (2000)
7. Solovo, D., Rotenberg, M.: Information Privacy Law. Aspen Elective Series. Aspen Publishers, New York (2003)
8. Breaux, T.: Privacy requirements in an age of increased sharing. IEEE Softw. **31**(5), 24–27 (2014)
9. Reinfelder, L., Benenson, Z., Gassmann, F.: Differences between Android and iPhone users in their security and privacy awareness. In: Eckert, C., Katsikas, S.K., Pernul, G. (eds.) TrustBus 2014. LNCS, vol. 8647, pp. 156–167. Springer, Heidelberg (2014)
10. Deng, M., Wuyts, K., Scandariato, R., Preneel, B., Joosen, W.: A privacy threat analysis framework: supporting the elicitation and fulfillment of privacy requirements. Requirements Eng. **16**(1), 3–32 (2011)
11. Sheth, S., Kaiser, G., Maalej, W.: Us and them: a study of privacy requirements across North America, Asia, and Europe. In: Proceedings of the 36th International Conference on Software Engineering. ICSE 2014, pp. 859–870. ACM (2014)
12. Rost, M., Pfitzmann, A.: Datenschutz-Schutzziele - revisited. Datenschutz und Datensicherheit - DuD **33**(6), 353–358 (2009)
13. Bier, C.: How usage control and provenance tracking get together - a data protection perspective. In: IEEE Security and Privacy Workshops (SPW), pp. 13–17, May 2013
14. Zviran, M.: User's perspectives on privacy in web-based applications. J. Comput. Inf. Syst. **48**(4), 97–105 (2008)
15. Sheehan, K.B., Hoy, M.G.: Dimensions of privacy concern among online consumers. J. Public Policy Mark. **19**(1), 62–73 (2000)
16. Fhom, H., Bayarou, K.: Towards a holistic privacy engineering approach for smart grid systems. In: IEEE 10th International Conference on Trust, Security and Privacy in Computing and Communications (TrustCom), pp. 234–241, November 2011
17. Spiekermann, S., Cranor, L.: Engineering privacy. IEEE Trans. Softw. Eng. **35**(1), 67–82 (2009)
18. Breaux, T., Gordon, D.: What engineers should know about us security and privacy law. IEEE Secur. Priv. **11**(3), 72–76 (2013)
19. Tomaszewski, J.: Are you sure you had a privacy incident? IEEE Secur. Priv. **4**(6), 64–66 (2006)
20. Hoepman, J.: Privacy design strategies - (extended abstract). In: Cuppens-Boulahia, N., Cuppens, F., Jajodia, S., El Kalam, A.A., Sans, T. (eds.) ICT Systems Security and Privacy Protection. IFIP AICT, vol. 428, pp. 446–459. Springer, Heidelberg (2014)
21. Jones, R., Tahri, D.: EU law requirements to provide information to website visitors. Comput. Law Secur. Rev. **26**(6), 613–620 (2010)

22. Kung, A., Freytag, J.C., Kargl, F.: Privacy-by-design in its applications. In: IEEE International Symposium on a World of Wireless, Mobile and Multimedia Networks (WoWMoM), pp. 1–6, June 2011
23. Mulligan, D.: The enduring importance of transparency. IEEE Secur. Priv. **12**(3), 61–65 (2014)
24. Wright, D.: The state of the art in privacy impact assessment. Comput. Law Secur. Rev. **28**(1), 54–61 (2012)
25. Langheinrich, M.: Privacy by design–principles of privacy-aware ubiquitous systems. In: Abowd, G.D., Brumitt, B., Shafer, S. (eds.) Ubiquitous Computing (Ubicomp). LNCS, vol. 2201, pp. 273–291. Springer, Heidelberg (2001)
26. Otto, P., Anton, A., Baumer, D.: The ChoicePoint dilemma: how data brokers should handle the privacy of personal information. IEEE Secur. Priv. **5**(5), 15–23 (2007)
27. Masiello, B.: Deconstructing the privacy experience. IEEE Secur. Priv. **7**(4), 68–70 (2009)
28. Solove, D.J.: A taxonomy of privacy. Univ. Pennsylvania Law Rev. **154**(3), 477–560 (2006)
29. Wicker, S., Schrader, D.: Privacy-aware design principles for information networks. Proc. IEEE **99**(2), 330–350 (2011)
30. Sype, Y.S.V.D., Seigneur, J.: Case study: legal requirements for the use of social login features for online reputation updates. In: Cho, Y., Shin, S.Y., Kim, S., Hung, C., Hong, J. (eds.) SAC, pp. 1698–1705. ACM, South Korea (2014). Please check and confirm the inserted city name for Reference [30]
31. Mouratidis, H., Islam, S., Kalloniatis, C., Gritzalis, S.: A framework to support selection of cloud providers based on security and privacy requirements. J. Syst. Softw. **86**(9), 2276–2293 (2013)
32. Kalloniatis, C., Mouratidis, H., Vassilis, M., Islam, S., Gritzalis, S., Kavakli, E.: Towards the design of secure and privacy-oriented information systems in the cloud: identifying the major concepts. Comput. Stand. Interfaces **36**(4), 759–775 (2014)
33. Wright, D., Raab, C.: Privacy principles, risks and harms. Int. Rev. Law Comput. Technol. **28**(3), 277–298 (2014)
34. Pötzsch, S.: Privacy awareness: a means to solve the privacy paradox? In: Matyáš, V., Fischer-Hübner, S., Cvrček, D., Švenda, P. (eds.) The Future of Identity in the Information Society. IFIP AICT, vol. 298, pp. 226–236. Springer, Heidelberg (2009)
35. Feigenbaum, J., Freedman, M.J., Sander, T., Shostack, A.: Privacy engineering for digital rights management systems. In: Sander, T. (ed.) DRM 2001. LNCS, vol. 2320, pp. 76–105. Springer, Heidelberg (2002)
36. Alcalde Bagüés, S., Mitic, J., Zeidler, A., Tejada, M., Matias, I.R., Fernandez Valdivielso, C.: Obligations: building a bridge between personal and enterprise privacy in pervasive computing. In: Furnell, S.M., Katsikas, S.K., Lioy, A. (eds.) TrustBus 2008. LNCS, vol. 5185, pp. 173–184. Springer, Heidelberg (2008)
37. Hedbom, H.: A survey on transparency tools for enhancing privacy. In: Matyáš, V., Fischer-Hübner, S., Cvrček, D., Švenda, P. (eds.) The Future of Identity in the Information Society. IFIP AICT, vol. 298, pp. 67–82. Springer, Heidelberg (2009)
38. Antón, A.I., Earp, J.B., Reese, A.: Analyzing website privacy requirements using a privacy goal taxonomy. In: IEEE International Conference on Requirements Engineering, 23–31 (2002)
39. Antón, A.I.: Earp: a requirements taxonomy for reducing web site privacy vulnerabilities. Requirements Eng. **9**(3), 169–185 (2004)

40. Anton, A., Earp, J., Vail, M., Jain, N., Gheen, C., Frink, J.: HIPAA's effect on web site privacy policies. IEEE Secur. Priv. **5**(1), 45–52 (2007)
41. Miyazaki, S., Mead, N., Zhan, J.: Computer-aided privacy requirements elicitation technique. In: IEEE Asia-Pacific Services Computing Conference (APSCC), pp. 367–372, December 2008
42. Casassa Mont, M.: Dealing with privacy obligations: important aspects and technical approaches. In: Katsikas, S.K., López, J., Pernul, G. (eds.) TrustBus 2004. LNCS, vol. 3184, pp. 120–131. Springer, Heidelberg (2004)
43. Kelley, P.G., Bresee, J., Cranor, L.F., Reeder, R.W.: A "nutrition label" for privacy. In: Proceedings of the 5th Symposium on Usable Privacy and Security. SOUPS 2009, pp. 4:1–4:12. ACM (2009)
44. Kelley, P.G., Cesca, L., Bresee, J., Cranor, L.F.: Standardizing privacy notices: an online study of the nutrition label approach. In: Proceedings of the SIGCHI Conference on Human Factors in Computing Systems. CHI 2010, pp. 1573–1582. ACM (2010)
45. Lobato, L., Fernandez, E., Zorzo, S.: Patterns to support the development of privacy policies. In: International Conference on Availability, Reliability and Security (ARES), pp. 744–749, March 2009
46. Jalali, S., Wohlin, C.: Systematic literature studies: database searches vs. backward snowballing. In: Proceedings of the ACM-IEEE International Symposium on Empirical Software Engineering and Measurement. ESEM 2012, pp. 29–38. ACM (2012)

A Privacy Preserving Framework for Big Data in e-Government Environments

Prokopios Drogkaris[(⊠)] and Aristomenis Gritzalis

Systems Security Laboratory, Department of Digital Systems, University of
Piraeus, 18534 Piraeus, Greece
{pdrogk, agritz}@ssl-unipi.gr

Abstract. Big data is widely considered as the next big trend in e-Government
environments but at the same time one of the most emerging and critical issues
due to the challenges it imposes. The large amount of data being retained by
governmental Service Providers that can be (potentially) exploited during Data
Mining and analytics processes, include personal data and personally identifiable information, raising privacy concerns, mostly regarding data minimization
and purpose limitation. This paper addresses the consideration of Central
Government to aggregate information without revealing personal identifiers of
individuals and proposes a privacy preserving methodology that can be easily
incorporated into already deployed electronic services and e-Government
frameworks through the adoption of scalable and adaptable salted hashing
techniques.

Keywords: Privacy · Anonymity · Big data · Data mining · e-Government

1 Introduction

Transformation of Governmental electronic services through the exploitation of ICTs
has been an emerging task in the last decades often associated with the automation of
public services and heterogeneous information systems integration. While
e-government projects focused on operational efficiency, public service transparency,
participation, ministerial departments' collaboration, interoperability and exchange of
information, advances in Data Mining and analytics have expanded the scope of data
and information available for further processing [1]. Data are now available for analysis
in raw form, overcoming the restrictions of structured databases and enhancing abilities
to identify correlations and conceive of new, unanticipated uses for existing information [2].

Big Data however also means new challenges involving complexity, security, and
risks to privacy. The *data deluge* presents privacy concerns which could stir a regulatory backlash. In order to craft a balance between beneficial uses and individual
privacy, some fundamental concepts of privacy, including the definition of Personally
identifiable information, the role of individual control, and the principles of data
minimization and purpose limitation must be taken into consideration during the early
stages of adoption [3]. This paper addresses the consideration of central governments to
aggregate information, during data mining, without revealing personal identifiers of

S. Fischer-Hübner et al. (Eds.): TrustBus 2015, LNCS 9264, pp. 210–218, 2015.
DOI: 10.1007/978-3-319-22906-5_16

individuals and proposes a privacy preserving methodology that can be easily incorporated into already deployed electronic services and e-Government frameworks through the adoption of scalable and adaptable salted hashing techniques.[1] This approach has the advantage of coping with current electronic services provision as it does not substitute any of the existing identification schemes; it provides an additional level of anonymity which can be exploited during data mining.

The rest of the paper is structured as follows: Sect. 2 presents briefly potential applications of Big Data and Data Mining applications to e-Government environments along to emerging challenges related to users personal identifiers privacy; Sect. 3 presents our proposal while Sect. 4 discusses already proposed privacy-preserving data mining techniques. Finally, Sect. 5 concludes the paper providing directions for future work.

2 Big Data and Data Mining Applications and Challenges in e-Government Environments

Central Government provide a large variety of electronic services, which both produce and require massive amounts of data, often unstructured and increasingly in real-time. Big data analytics can improve efficiency and effectiveness across the broad range of government responsibilities, by improving existing processes and operations and enabling completely new ones. By incorporating structured and unstructured data from both internal and external sources, it can be empowered to present a much clearer citizen-centric picture and uncover invisible connections towards promoting transparency and effectiveness. Invisible patterns and useful information could be produced for Social Security frauds, overpayments, tax compliance and abuse. However, such data dissemination, even within the boundaries of central government, increases chance of compromising privacy sensitive data, which undermines trust of data subjects (e.g., users and citizens). Data disseminators are morally, ethically, and legally responsible for any misuse of the disseminated data [4].

2.1 Big Data and Data Mining

Big Data concern large-volume, complex, growing data sets with multiple, autonomous sources. With the fast development of networking, data storage, and the data collection capacity, Big Data are now rapidly expanding and has to be characterized by the volume, velocity, and variety of data that is generated. These constitute the 3Vs of big data [5]. Lately, two additional Vs have been proposed, namely Veracity and Value. Data Mining refers to the activity of going through big data sets to look for relevant or pertinent information and refers to operations that involve relatively sophisticated search operations that return targeted and specific results [6]. Data Mining is often

[1] This work has been supported by the national project "Secure and Privacy-Aware eGovernment Sevices – SPAGOS" (Grant Agreement 11SYN_9_2059), under "SYNERGAGIA 2011" programme, of the Operational programme "Competitiveness and Entrepreneurship".

treated in the literature as a synonym for Knowledge Discovery and Data Mining (KDDM) which highlights the goal of the mining process results [6, 7]. In order to acquire useful knowledge from data, the steps illustrated in Fig. 1 must be performed:

- *Step 1: Data Preprocessing.* Basic operations which include data selection, data cleaning and data integration;
- *Step 2: Data Transformation.* Feature selection and feature transformation operations to transform data into forms appropriate for the mining task;
- *Step 3: Data Mining.* Application of intelligent methods and representation techniques to extract valuable information.

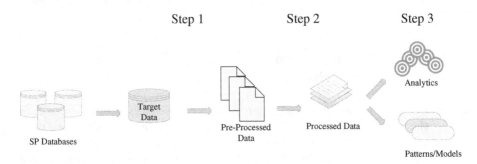

Fig. 1. Data mining and knowledge discovery process

2.2   Modern e-Government Environments Interoperability Frameworks

Modern e-Government environments have embraced the notion of interoperability and the deployment of e-Government Interoperability Frameworks (e-GIF), in order to enable the seamless flow of information across service providers and governmental departments. A general overview is presented in Fig. 2 while their main characteristics and components are presented below:

- *Central Portal*: A citizen portal that acts as the interface between users and ministerial departments. Its main purpose is to bring electronic services together providing a common interface between citizens and public sector, operating as a one-stop shop.
- *Uniform Registration and Authentication Procedures*: The registration and authentication procedures required for accessing the offered electronic services are provided through the Central Portal and Authentication Authorities operate under it's supervision where: the Registration Authority is responsible for the registration procedure and for maintaining a record of the services that a user may access, while the Authentication Authority is responsible for authenticating users and allowing them to interact with the Service Providers.
- *Assignment of Electronic Services to Distinct Trust Levels*: All electronic services offered through the Central Portal have been assigned to pre-determined levels of trust; these levels are understood as *"The level of confidence at an end-user's electronic identity along with the assurance that the security measures and*

procedures deployed to safeguard the access, the processing and the transmission of data are adequate" [8].

- *Per Sector or Uniform Identifiers*: Identification of users is performed either through a national unique identifier, where every user can be easily identified, irrespective of the requested service, and can also ease the exchange of information (interoperability) among different public departments, or through multiple per-sector identifiers, one for each sub-environment where each user can be uniquely identified through a sectorial identifier.

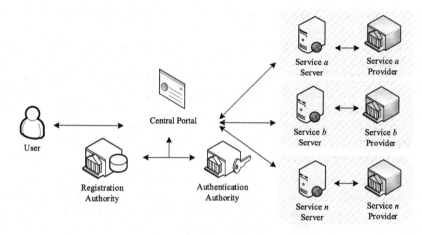

Fig. 2. e-Government central portal interoperability model

2.3   Privacy Preserving Data Mining

The appearance of Knowledge Discovery and Data Mining (KDDM) has revitalized concerns on secondary use of the personal information, and granulated access to personal information. As acknowledged in [9], the most realistic way to preserve privacy of information would be to encrypt it. Users wishing to access the data could be given decryption keys, and this could resolve all emerging privacy issues. Unluckily, this approach cannot not work in a Data Mining scenario, in which the information must be made available but the data subject to be kept anonymous. The key notion in this concept here is the one of utility [9]: *"the goal of privacy preservation measures is to secure access to confidential information while at the same time releasing aggregate information to the public"*, which constitute cryptographic approaches to privacy preservation challenging. In the most basic cryptographic scenario we always consider Bob and Alice as the two communicating parties and Malory as an adversary attempting to eavesdrop. In the context of Big Data and Data Mining, the adversary is the same as the recipient of the message, making security guarantees much harder to prove as privacy and utility are fundamentally in tension with each other. We can achieve perfect privacy by not releasing any data, but this solution has no utility [10].

The provision of governmental electronic services is necessary to comply with specific principles and obligations regarding protection of personal data. Normally these principles and obligations are imposed by the existing legal and regulatory framework and are based on the principles of purpose specification, fairness, minimality, accuracy, privacy and anonymity. A thorough description of these principles is provided in [8, 11] where it is also remarked that data controllers must comply with the privacy protection requirements and implement privacy protection based on them. Correspondingly, governmental Service Providers, and therefore the electronic services they offer, are obliged to explicit obligations related to the processing, retention and transmission of personal data submitted during services' provision. These obligations can be briefly summarized in the following key principles [7]:

1. *Notice/Awareness* – data subjects should be made aware of the nature of data processing;
2. *Choice/Consent* – data subjects should be allowed to choose how their own personal data is used;
3. *Access/Participation* – data subjects should have access to the collected data;
4. *Integrity/Security* – entities collecting data should ensure accuracy and secure the data from unauthorized access
5. *Enforcement/Redress* – there should be procedural measures in place to hold data collecting services, and therefore agencies, accountable for failure to address any of the aforementioned principles.

Even though the information discovered by Data Mining can be valuable, users are shown increasing concern on the privacy threats posed by Data Mining [12]. Individual's privacy may be violated due to the unauthorized access to personal data, the undesired discovery of one's embarrassing information, the use of personal data for purposes other than the one for which data has been collected, etc. The objective of Privacy Preserving Data Mining (PPDM) is to safeguard sensitive information from unsolicited or unsanctioned disclosure, and meanwhile, preserve the utility of the data. The consideration of PPDM is two-fold; First, sensitive raw data, such as personal identifiers (PII), should not be directly used for mining and second, sensitive mining results whose disclosure will result in privacy violation should be excluded [7].

3   Proposed Methodology

This paper proposes a privacy preserving methodology that can be easily incorporated into already deployed electronic services and e-Government frameworks through the adoption of scalable and adaptable salted hashing techniques on users' personal identifiers prior to their processing. Our proposal is based on the generic e-Government framework, as described in Sect. 2, in an attempt to ensure backwards compatibility with existing electronic services, procedures and normative regulations through the exploitation of framework's open architecture while taking into account the specific needs and requirements of Data Mining. Within the scope of this paper, we assume that the only information to be protected, prior to Data Mining, is Personal Identifiers (PII); however the proposed transformation can also be applied to other information, data or attributes related to each PII.

3.1 Framework Architecture

The envisioned approach pertains the addition of Anonymization Components, both at the back end of the e-Government environment i.e. each Service Provider, as depicted in Fig. 3 below. The newly introduced component is responsible for the preservation of anonymity of users through the transformation of their personal identifiers *PII* into an arbitrary size to digital data which can still distinguish one data subject from another but cannot be link backed to their real world identity. Such addition will allow for the creation of preprocessed data pools, ready to be released, where all Personal Identifiers are sanitized.

It should be noted that this addition does not affect the existing provision of electronic services and the deployed identification schemes; it provides an additional level of anonymity which can be exploited during Data Mining.

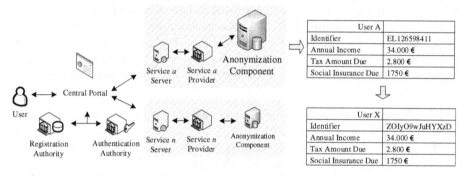

Fig. 3. Proposed methodology

3.2 Transformation of Personal Identifiers

Let's assume that User A has been assigned n personal identifiers (PII_1, PII_2 ... PII_n) and each one corresponds to an explicit SIItype, an object identifier that specifies the type of PII. Service Provider A creates a Salt value $Salt_{short}$ which even if it is kept secure it is inevitably considered as weak since it is used repeatedly for all identifiers processed. Assuming that F is a password stretching function [13], Service Provider calculates PII_{long} based on formula (1) and then $Salt_{long}$ based on formula (2). Even if Service Provider A can identify User A both through PII_1 and PII_2, and assuming it utilizes the same $Salt_{short}$, the outcome of formula (1), and correspondingly formula (2), for these two cases will not be same; PII and $SIIt_{ype}$ will still differ. Having calculated these two values, Service Provider A can then compute PII' based on (3) which can be submitted as pre-processed data to along the respective information.

$$PII_{long} = F\left(PII\|SIIt_{ype}\right) \tag{1}$$

$$Salt_{long} = F\left(Salt_{short}, PII, SII_{type}\right) \tag{2}$$

$$PII' = H \left(H \left(PII_{long} \| Salt_{long} \right) \right) \tag{3}$$

Service Provider A can now use PII', instead of PII, which can still distinguish User A among other users but cannot be link backed to her real world identity, and create preprocessed data pools where all Personal Identifiers are anonymized. The added value of this approach is that by using one $Salt_{long}$ value per Service Provider, it will allow for the update of all the information associated to the specific PII', thus moving towards a pseudonymization approach, rather than an anoymization one.

4 Related Work

A number of techniques have been proposed for modifying or transforming sensitive data in such a way so as to preserve privacy and are discussed in [14, 15]. Similarly to the transformation presented in Sect. 3.2, most methods use some form of conversion on the data in order to perform privacy preservation. Typically, such methods reduce the granularity of representation in order to reduce the privacy which eventually results in some loss of effectiveness of data management or mining algorithms. The most well perceived techniques [14], are:

- The *randomization* method where noise is added to the data in order to mask the attribute values of records [16, 17];
- The *k-anonymity* model and *l-diversity* where the granularity of data representation is reduced with the use of techniques such as generalization and suppression. [18].
- *Distributed privacy preservation*: In many cases, individual entities may wish to derive aggregate results from data sets which are partitioned across these entities. Such partitioning can be horizontal or vertical. While the individual entities may not desire to share their entire data sets, they may consent to limited information sharing with the use of a variety of protocols.
- *Downgrading Application Effectiveness*: In cases where, even the data are not available, the output of applications such as association rule mining, classification or query processing may result in violations of privacy [18].

5 Conclusions

Central Government expect Big Data to enhance their ability to serve their citizens and address challenges at national level; enhance transparency and participation, identify frauds and promote citizen oriented governance. The adoption of Knowledge Discovery and Data Mining techniques introduces new threats to privacy which could stir a regulatory backlash. This paper proposed a privacy preserving methodology which promoted the adoption of scalable and adaptable salted hashing techniques on users' Personal Identifiers prior to their Data Mining processing. It was based on a generic e-Government framework, in an attempt to ensure backwards compatibility with existing electronic services and infrastructures, while promoting the preservation of anonymity of users through the transformation of their PII into an arbitrary size to digital data. Our next steps, relate to the empowering citizens' to retain control over their personal information while using advanced governmental electronic services, through the adoption of Privacy Policies and Preferences XML documents.

References

1. Tene, O., Polonetsky, J.: Big Data for All: Privacy and User Control in the Age of Analytics, 239–272 (2013)
2. Kim, G., Trimi, S., Chung, J.: Big-data applications in the government sector. ACM Commun. **57**(3), 78–85 (2014)
3. Morabito, V.: Big Data and Analytics, 1st edn. Springer International Publishing, Switzerland (2015)
4. Bargh, M., Meijer, R., Choenni, S., Conradie, P.: Privacy protection in data sharing: towards feedback based solutions. In: Proceedings of the 8th International Conference on Theory and Practice of Electronic Governance, Guimarães, Portugal, pp. 28–36 (2014)
5. Xindong, W., Xingquan, Z., Gong-Qing, W., Wei, D.: Data mining with big data. IEEE Trans. Knowl. Data Eng. **26**(1), 97–107 (2014)
6. Lu, R., Zhu, H., Liu, X., Liu, J.K., Shao, J.: Toward efficient and privacy-preserving computing in big data era. Netw. IEEE **28**, 46–50 (2014)
7. Ganesh, D., Mahendran, S.: Security in data mining using user role based methodology. Int. J. Emerg. Trends Comput. Commun. Technol. **1**(2), 83–92 (2014)
8. Drogkaris, P., Geneiatakis, D., Gritzalis, S., Lambrinoudakis, C., Mitrou, L.: Towards an enhanced authentication framework for egovernment services: the greek case. In: Ferro, E., Scholl, J., Wimmer, M. (eds.) EGOV 20008 7th International Conference on Electronic Government, Torino, Italy, Trauner Verlag, vol. 1, pp.189–196 (2008)
9. Venkatasubramanian, S.: Measures of Anonymity. In: Aggarwal, C.C., Yu, P.S. (ed.) Privacy-Preserving Data Mining 1st edn. 34. Springer, Heidelberg (2008)
10. Dwork, C.: Differential privacy. In: Bugliesi, M., Preneel, B., Sassone, V., Wegener, I. (eds.) ICALP 2006. LNCS, vol. 4052, pp. 1–12. Springer, Heidelberg (2006)
11. Bélanger, F., Crossler, R.: Privacy in the digital age: a review of information privacy research in information systems, 1017–1042 (2011)
12. Brankovic, L., Estivil-Castro, E.: Privacy issues in knowledge discovery and data mining. In: Ustralian Institute of Computer Ethics Conference (AICEC 1999), Australia, pp. 89–99 (1999)
13. Kelsey, J., Schneie, B., Hall, C., Wagner, D.: Secure applications of low-entropy keys. In: Okamoto, E., Davida, G., Mambo, M. (eds.) ISW 1997. LNCS, vol. 1396, pp. 121–134. Springer, Heidelberg (1998)
14. Aggarwal, C., Yu, S.: A general survey of privacy-preserving data mining models and algorithms. In: Aggarwal, C.C., Yu, P.S. (eds.) Privacy Preserving Data Mining, pp. 11–52. Springer, Heidelberg (2008)
15. Verykios, V., Bertino, E., Saygin, Y., Theodoridis, Y.: State-of-the-art in privacy preserving data mining. ACM SIGMOD Rec. **33**, 50–57 (2004)
16. Agrawal, R., Srikant, R.: Privacy-preserving data mining. In: International Conference on Management of Data (SIGMOD), Dallas, Texas, pp. 439–450 (2000)

17. Agrawal, D., Aggarwal, C.: On the design and quantification of privacy preserving data mining algorithms. In: Aggarwal, C.C., Yu, P.S. (ed.) IGMOD-SIGACT-SIGART Symposium on Principles of Database Systems, pp. 247–255

18. Machanavajjhala, A., Gehrke, J., Kifer, D., Venkitasubramaniam, M.: L-diversity: privacy beyond k-anonymity. ACM Trans. Knowl. Discov. Data (TKDD) 1(1), 3 (2007)

Privacy Principles: Towards a Common Privacy Audit Methodology

Eleni-Laskarina Makri[✉] and Costas Lambrinoudakis

Department of Digital Systems, University of Piraeus, 18532 Piraeus, Greece
{elmak, clam}@unipi.gr

Abstract. A lot of privacy principles have been proposed in the literature with the aim to preserve users' privacy through the protection of the personal data collected by service providers. Despite the fact that there were remarkable efforts to gather all privacy principles and use them on a common privacy-by-design system, to the best of our knowledge, there is no published methodology that combines in a clear and structured way the existing privacy principles for supporting the design of a Privacy Preserving System. The absence of a widely accepted structured representation of the privacy principles makes their adoption or/and satisfaction difficult and in some cases inconsistent. Considering that privacy protection on its own is not an easy task for an organisation, the "scattered" privacy principles impose significant additional complexity. Consequently, very frequently organizations fail to effectively protect the privacy of their users. In this paper a structured privacy audit methodology that consists of discrete steps that organizations can follow for deciding or/and auditing the privacy protection measures is proposed. Every step is based on the significance of a privacy principle and on the sequence of the audit procedure.

Keywords: Privacy audit methodology · Privacy principles · Privacy protection

1 Introduction

Throughout the last decades the use of Internet has dramatically increased. More and more people use the Internet and its services on a daily basis in order to be informed, educated, entertained, etc. In order to utilize the online services, users reveal their personal information without considering, or just being unaware, of the consequences. As a result, very frequently the privacy of the users is violated since their personal data can be accessed by merely everyone and practically in every way. The meaning of *Internet Privacy* includes the way personal data are used, stored, processed, exploited from third parties etc. It targets to the protection of users against unwanted disclosure of their personal information.

One of the main user concerns is the absence of a privacy audit methodology and thus the uncertainty of whether the service providers protect their personal information adequately or not. On top of that the absence of a privacy audit methodology affects the service providers since they cannot be assured about the completeness and

© Springer International Publishing Switzerland 2015
S. Fischer-Hübner et al. (Eds.): TrustBus 2015, LNCS 9264, pp. 219–234, 2015.
DOI: 10.1007/978-3-319-22906-5_17

effectiveness of the privacy protection measures that they have adopted. In consequence, users' personal data is exposed to many different risks. Having a privacy audit methodology in place, helps users to trust service providers more and consequently use the offered services more.

Even though some steps have been taken towards a common privacy framework, only very few attempts have been made towards a structured privacy audit procedure. Such a procedure is proposed in this paper. To this direction, all privacy principles and requirements have been collected and classified in order to identify: (a) the way each privacy requirement can be satisfied and (b) the priority – sequence with which each privacy requirement should be addressed.

The rest of the paper is organized as follows: Sect. 2 provides an overview of the literature on the privacy principles used by public and private bodies. Based on the literature review, Sect. 3 presents the privacy principles that are the most widely accepted by the scientific community. Section 4 proposes a structured privacy audit procedure that can be followed by an organization to ensure the protection of users' privacy. Section 5 draws the conclusions giving some pointers for future work.

2 Literature Review

A lot of research effort has been invested in developing ways for protecting users' personal data. On one hand, many laws and directives, concerning users' privacy protection, exist in several countries, imposing to organizations that store personal data not to use them without first informing the users and obtaining their consent. On the other hand, there are a lot of public or/and private bodies, which are interested in protecting users' privacy and for that reason have published several privacy principles. At the same time, Privacy Enhancing Technologies (PETs), a variety of ICT measures that protect informational privacy by offering the technical means to protect user's personal data and thus to prevent unnecessary or unwanted processing, are utilised [9, 23]. Yet, both privacy principles and PETs cannot stand alone but are correlated and work on a supplementary basis.

It is many years ago that the protection of users' privacy became a concern and plenty of privacy principles have been established in order to avoid disclosure of personal data. Since 1980 [16], the OECD organization has defined a common privacy framework, which includes the most widely used privacy principles. The eight privacy principles, proposed in the '80 s, are still being utilised on the basis of privacy protection. Eminent scientists, such as Ann Cavoukian and her team [23] have relied on them to conduct their research and many organizations have applied them in order to ensure privacy protection.

These privacy principles have inspired a number of privacy legislations. In 1995, the European Commission (EC) introduced the Data Protection Directive (Directive 95/46/EC) [6, 7] in order to reinforce the data protection laws, aiming at the protection of individuals with regard to the processing of personal data and on the free movement of such data [6]. The OECD Privacy Principles (1980) and the Directive 95/46/EC (1995) were among the first serious attempts to protect users' privacy by imposing limitation to the ways that an organization can collect, store and process personal data.

In March 1996 [5], the National Standard of Canada "Model Code for the Protection of Personal Information" was developed based on the OECD Guidelines. Two extra privacy principles (consent and challenging compliance) have appeared for reinforcing the protection of personal information. In addition, the United States Department of Commerce developed Safe Harbor [19], a legal framework that allowed US organizations to comply with the EC Data Protection Directive [16]. Safe Harbor included privacy principles that have been based on the ones defined by OECD (1980).

Along with the privacy laws, directives and standards, there are certain organizations that try to support users' privacy protection. Based on the OECD Privacy Principles (1980), ISACA published the ISACA/OECD privacy principles, in 2009 [22]. Furthermore, ISACA proposed a list of sample privacy controls to protect and maintain the privacy of users' personal data. Other organizations such as ENISA [17] or IBM [11] have also taken steps towards privacy protection proposing appropriate mechanisms.

In 2011 [12], the International Organization for Standardization (ISO) and the International Electrotechnical Commission (IEC), provided a privacy framework based on eleven privacy principles that were the existing principles developed by a number of states, countries and international organizations. According to ISO/IEC 29100:2011, privacy principles should be used to guide the design, development, and implementation of privacy policies and privacy controls.

Over the years, the technological environment on which the privacy principles were applied has undergone significant changes, the most important of which were in the volume of personal data being collected, stored and processed. Furthermore, personal data are gradually becoming globally available while at the same time there are many more privacy threats. As such, for the existing more demanding technological environments, new privacy protection measures were necessary. The need to update the European Directive 95/46/EC led the European Commission to propose a major reform of the EU legal framework on the protection of personal data, in 2014 [8]. The new proposals reinforced the users' rights and at the same time dealt with the challenges of globalization and new technologies [18]. For the same reasons, in 2013 [21] OECD proposed supplementary privacy principles, adding eight more principles.

In parallel, there are several individual efforts from several countries and other public or private bodies. In November 2006, Ann Cavoukian [1], proposed the Global Privacy Standard (GPS), the aim of which was to create a common global privacy framework for the global protection of users' privacy. The GPS included ten privacy principles, which were derived from collective knowledge and practical wisdom of the international data protection community and was, therefore, the first team work towards a universal privacy framework.

Nowadays, privacy is a serious concern for both users and organizations. For this reason, many researchers support that privacy should be maintained throughout the entire lifecycle of an IT system. In other words, privacy should be considered from the design phase of an IT system until the end of its entire lifecycle. The notion of privacy-by-design as the philosophy for protecting privacy throughout the technological development process, from the conception of a new system up to its implementation, was strongly supported by Ann Cavoukian [4] and Jaap-Henk Hoepman [13, 14].

Despite the fact that there were remarkable efforts [1, 13, 14, 21] to gather all privacy principles and use them on a common privacy-by-design system, to the best of our knowledge there is no published methodology that combines the existing privacy principles for supporting the design of a Privacy Preserving System. One of the basic reasons for that is that the technological environment keeps changing all the time, something that makes it difficult for the organizations to adjust. Another possible reason is that the volume of information is huge and hardly manageable. Furthermore, the current information systems require global availability of personal data in order to operate. In addition, the threats in privacy have increased and organizations cannot catch up with them because of their rapid transformation. All the above are some of the most important reasons why current privacy principles are essential, yet somewhat outdated. Therefore, organizations are still failing to apply effective privacy protection mechanisms.

Furthermore, the literature review has revealed that so far there has been no attempt to provide a roadmap on how the existing privacy principles should be addressed (i.e. are some principles more important than others? is there a specific order that someone should try to satisfy them and in that case what is that order? etc.) for facilitating the design of systems that are indeed consistent with the privacy principles. Although there is extended literature about different privacy principles and their definitions [8, 12, 18, 21], there has been no reference as to which principle should be applied first, which should follow or which could be used as input to others.

The absence of a widely accepted structured representation of the privacy principles makes their adoption/satisfaction difficult and in some cases inconsistent. Considering that privacy protection on its own is not an easy task for an organisation, the "scattered" privacy principles impose significant additional complexity. Consequently, very frequently organizations fail to effectively implement the privacy principles and thus to protect users' personal information. Now, more than ever before, the need for creating a structured roadmap for the fulfilment of privacy principles is absolutely necessary.

The aforementioned structured roadmap could be also capitalized as the basis of an auditing methodology for the use of PETs by an organization. The need for a common privacy audit methodology is not new, since in 2004 a team of scientists [15] have highlighted its absence. Nevertheless, until today, no considerable effort has been made towards this direction.

3   Privacy Principles

The protection of users' personal data and therefore their privacy is a fundamental human right. As mentioned in the previous section, many countries, as well as public and private bodies, have made significant effort to protect this right by defining privacy principles that should be followed by organizations that process personal data. The eight privacy principles, which were first defined in 1980 [16], were adopted by many countries and the public or private bodies. Despite the fact that some bodies have tried to expand them with additional privacy principles, the newly introduced principles have not been adopted yet, due to the lack of time to become widely accepted.

The most common and widely accepted privacy principles [10, 16] will be used in our research work to propose a structured privacy audit methodology.

- *Purpose Specification Principle*: The personal data should be collected and used only for the specified purposes. The user should be notified for the reason his personal data is collected and used.
- *Collection Limitation Principle*: The personal data should be collected with lawful and fair means. In this way, only the necessary data will be collected without redundant personal information. Also, the data collection should take place under the user's consent.
- *Data Quality Principle*: The personal data should be accurate, complete and kept updated. The information quality should be maintained throughout the whole process of collection and use of personal data.
- *Use, Retention and Disclosure Limitation Principle*: The personal data should be used only with the user's consent or under the authority of law. The use of personal data should be limited without disclosing or making it available for any reason other than the purpose of the collection.
- *Security Safeguards Principle*: The personal data should be protected by applying security safeguards. In this way, the personal information will be protected from security and privacy threats.
- *Openness Principle*: The practices, policies, processes and procedures concerning the users' personal data should be easily accessible and transparency should be maintained in every stage of its collection and use.
- *Individual Participation Principle*: The owner of personal data should participate in the process of its collection and use. The user should have the right to intervene wherever necessary other than in the case where that it is prohibited by the law.
- *Accountability Principle*: A data controller should be accountable for being in accordance with protection mechanisms which give effect to the above principles.

The above privacy principles are among the most widely adopted ones [10, 16] for the protection of personal information. As it was mentioned in the previous section, there are no better practices or guidelines or no such structured procedure for applying them either from the organization's perspective or from the user's perspective.

Some good practices and advices on how the privacy principles should be accounted during the design of a system can be found in blogs, fora and websites [20]. However, the information remains "scattered" and not yet official. It is therefore really difficult for both an organization and a user, to determine the effectiveness and consistency of the employed privacy protection mechanisms. The existence of a structured procedure can help the organizations apply the privacy principles and, at the same time, help the users to ensure that their personal information is secured. What is more, such a structured procedure can help Privacy Auditors to audit if privacy is effectively applied. Auditing is one of the most important processes in an organization, since it can affect its reputation either positively or negatively. As a consequence, it can either increase users' confidence or users' insecurity.

4 A Privacy Audit Methodology

4.1 From an Organization's Perspective

Towards the definition of a privacy audit methodology, the existing privacy principles have been classified in four levels based on their significance and on the sequence that the audit procedure should take place. Each level is associated with a *"Step"* of the audit procedure. All the steps should be followed in strict order since failure to audit any step automatically means that the remaining steps cannot be audited either, as all steps are interdependent.

The proposed methodology consists of four auditing steps. Each auditing step includes one or more privacy principles and is depicted in hierarchy. The auditing results of each privacy principle can be used as input for the auditing of some other privacy principle in the same or in the next step. The solid arrows between different steps symbolize the input from a privacy principle to another in the next auditing step. At the same time, it has been identified that there is need for certain privacy principles to be maintained throughout the entire auditing procedure.

STEP 1:

- **PRIVACY PRINCIPLE:** Purpose Specification **(PP-S1-1).**
- **PREREQUISITE PRIVACY PRINCIPLE:** -
- **DESCRIPTION:** The first auditing step includes the "Purpose Specification Privacy Principle" (Fig. 1). When an organization wishes to protect the users' privacy, the first step is to clearly define and explain the purpose of collection and use of personal data. To do so, the documents presented in the privacy audit checklist are essential. Therefore, when a privacy auditor wishes to audit if an organization applies the principle, he/she should ask for all the documents, which specify the purpose listed in Table 1.

STEP 2:

- **PRIVACY PRINCIPLE:** Collection Limitation **(PP-S2-1).**
- **PREREQUISITE PRIVACY PRINCIPLE:** (PP-S1-1).
- **DESCRIPTION:** The first privacy principle that belongs to the second auditing step is the "Collection Limitation Privacy Principle" (Fig. 1). When an organization wishes to protect the users' privacy, it has to limit the data collection and use. Having defined the purpose of data collection and use in the previous step, the organization is obliged to collect and use only the necessary data needed for its services. To do so, the documents presented in the privacy audit checklist (Table 2) are essential. Consequently, if a privacy auditor wishes to audit if an organization applies the principle, he should ask for all documents and means of data collection limitation, as listed below, that are used by the organization. If the "Purpose Specification" principle has not been audited, the auditing of "Collection Limitation" cannot be accomplished.

- **PRIVACY PRINCIPLE:** Data Quality **(PP-S2-2).**
- **PREREQUISITE PRIVACY PRINCIPLE:** (PP-S1-1).

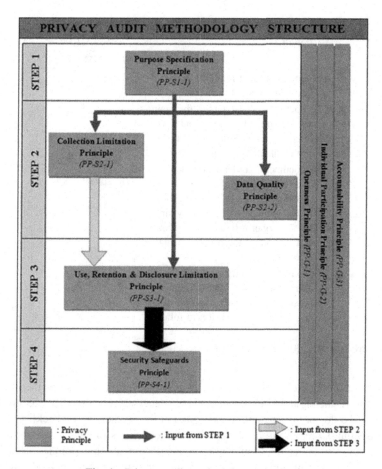

Fig. 1. Privacy audit methodology structure

- **DESCRIPTION:** The final privacy principle of the second auditing step is the "Data Quality Privacy Principle" (Fig. 1). The organization is obliged to keep the personal data of its users accurate, complete and up-to-date to the extent that this is necessary for the purpose of the data collection and use. To do so, the documents presented in the privacy audit checklist (Table 3) are essential. Therefore, if a privacy auditor wishes to audit if an organization applies the principle, he should ask for all documents, means and policies, which the organization uses to maintain the quality of personal data. If the "Purpose Specification" principle has not been audited, the auditing of the "Data Quality" principle cannot be completed.

STEP 3:

- **PRIVACY PRINCIPLE:** Use, Retention and Disclosure Limitation **(PP-S3-1)**.
- **PREREQUISITE PRIVACY PRINCIPLE:** (PP-S1-1), (PP-S2-1).
- **DESCRIPTION:** The third step of auditing includes the "Use, Retention and Disclosure Limitation Privacy Principle" (Fig. 1). This time the organization has to

Table 1. Privacy audit checklist for "Purpose Specification"

PRIVACY PRINCIPLE	EVIDENCE	ASSESSMENT			ACTIONS
		M	NM	PM	
Purpose Specification	The document that refers to the general purpose of the organization.				
	The document that refers to the main and specific aim for personal data collection either before or at the time of data collection.				
	The documents, brochures, videos, advertisements, conference workshop proceedings, notifications via the application, and everything else the organization uses to inform the users about the purpose of data collection.				
	The existence of privacy icons that inform the user about the purpose specification privacy principle and obligate the organization to follow it.				

M: Met, NM: Not Met, PM: Partially Met

limit the use, retention, and disclosure of personal information so as the individual should have the right to intervene wherever necessary (except if that is prohibited by law). To do so, the documents presented in the privacy audit checklist (Table 4) are essential. Consequently, if a privacy auditor wishes to audit if an organization applies the principle, he should ask for all documents and policies used by the organization to limit the use, retention, and disclosure of personal information. If the "Purpose Specification" principle and the "Collection Limitation" principle have not been audited, the auditing of the "Use, Retention and Disclosure Limitation" principle cannot be accomplished.

STEP 4:

- **PRIVACY PRINCIPLE:** Security Safeguards (**PP-S4-1**).
- **PREREQUISITE PRIVACY PRINCIPLE:** (PP-S3-1).
- **DESCRIPTION:** The fourth auditing step includes the "Security Safeguards Privacy Principle" (Fig. 1). For the protection of users' privacy the organization has to employ security safeguards against loss or unauthorized access, destruction, use, modification or disclosure of data. To do so, the documents presented in the privacy audit checklist (Table 5) are essential. Therefore, if a privacy auditor wishes to audit if an organization applies the principle, he should ask for all documents and policies used by the organization to apply security safeguards. If the "Use, Retention and Disclosure Limitation" principle has not been audited, the auditing of the "Security Safeguards" principle cannot be achieved.

Table 2. Privacy audit checklist for "Collection Limitation"

PRIVACY PRINCIPLE	EVIDENCE	ASSESSMENT			ACTIONS
		M	NM	PM	
Collection Limitation	The document that refers to the purpose of data collection.				
	The documents, brochures, videos, advertisements, conference workshop proceedings, notifications via the application, and everything else the organization uses to inform the users about the purpose of data collection.				
	The document that refers to the policies and procedures, used by the organization to handle and collect the information.				
	The document that refers to the user's consent.				
	The document with the organization policies and procedures, concerning the destruction of personal data, when it is not useful anymore.				
	The appropriate technical means used by the organization's systems to minimize personal data.				
	The lawful and fair means used by an organization in order to collect the data. It includes the physical presence of the auditor during the operation of systems or subsystems. The means can either be technical or not.				
	The organization's privacy policy.				
	The existence of privacy icons that inform the user about the collection limitation privacy principle and obligate the organization to follow it.				

M: Met, NM: Not Met, PM: Partially Met

Global Principles. The privacy principles that follow have not been classified in any of the four auditing steps since they have been considered to be applicable throughout the entire auditing process (Fig. 1). As a result they have been considered as "Global" privacy principles, applying to all audit steps, and they should be strictly checked during the audit process. In practice, the usability of these global principles is that they add to the audit controls of each distinct audit step (i.e. for the principle "Collection Limitation" of step 2 (PP-S2-1) on top of the audit controls listed in Table 2, the auditor will need to check the global principles as well).

Table 3. Privacy audit checklist for "Data Quality"

PRIVACY PRINCIPLE	EVIDENCE	ASSESSMENT			ACTIONS
		M	NM	PM	
Data Quality	The document that refers to the purpose of data use.				
	The appropriate technical means used by the organization's systems to audit if the personal data is kept accurate, complete and up-to-date.				
	The document with the organization policies and procedures, concerning the restoration and update of the personal data.				
	The organization's privacy policy.				
	The existence of privacy icons that inform the user about the data quality privacy principle and obligate the organization to follow it.				

M: Met, NM: Not Met, PM: Partially Met

Table 4. Privacy audit checklist for "Use, Retention and Disclosure Limitation"

PRIVACY PRINCIPLE	EVIDENCE	ASSESSMENT			ACTIONS
		M	NM	PM	
Use, Retention & Disclosure Limitation	The document that refers to the purpose of the personal data use.				
	The document with the organization's policies and procedures, concerning the limitation of the use, the retention and the disclosure of user's personal data.				
	The document that refers to the user's consent.				
	The organization's privacy policy.				
	The existence of privacy icons that inform the user about the use, retention and disclosure privacy principle and obligate the organization to follow it.				

M: Met, NM: Not Met, PM: Partially Met

- **PRIVACY PRINCIPLE:** Openness (**PP-G-1**).
- **DESCRIPTION:** When an organization wishes to support openness, it has to make available to users all policies, practices and procedures about personal information. To do so, the documents presented in the privacy audit checklist (Table 6) are

Table 5. Privacy audit checklist for "Security Safeguards"

PRIVACY PRINCIPLE	EVIDENCE	ASSESSMENT			ACTIONS
		M	NM	PM	
Security Safeguards	The document that refers to the physical, administrative and technical measures that the organization applies. For all these measures, the privacy auditor should check the premises, the employees and the technical means used by the organization.				
	The employees' training program.				
	The document with the organization's policies and procedures, concerning the employment of security safeguards for the protection of personal data.				
	The organization's privacy policy.				
	The existence of privacy icons that inform the user about the security safeguards privacy principle and obligate the organization to follow it.				

M: Met, NM: Not Met, PM: Partially Met

essential. Therefore, if a privacy auditor wishes to audit if an organization applies the principle, he should ask for all documents and policies used by the organization to keep its services transparent in and inform its users. If the prerequisite privacy principles are not met, auditing of the "Openness Privacy" principle cannot be accomplished.

– **PRIVACY PRINCIPLE:** Individual Participation **(PP-G-2)**.
– **DESCRIPTION:** The second global principle is the "Individual Participation" (Fig. 1). When an organization wishes to support individual's participation, it should allow users to access and modify their personal information. To do so, the documents presented in the privacy audit checklist (Table 7) are essential. Therefore, if a privacy auditor wishes to audit if an organization applies the principle, he should ask for all policies and procedures used by the organization to help users access their personal data. If the prerequisite privacy principles are not met, auditing of the "Individual Participation" principle cannot be accomplished.

– **PRIVACY PRINCIPLE:** Accountability **(PP-G-3)**.
– **DESCRIPTION:** The final global principle is "Accountability" (Fig. 1). When an organization wishes to be reliable, it should be accountable for complying with measures, which give effect to the privacy principles stated above. To do so, the documents presented in the privacy audit checklist (Table 8) are essential.

Table 6. Privacy audit checklist for "Openness"

PRIVACY PRINCIPLE	EVIDENCE	ASSESSMENT			ACTIONS
		M	NM	PM	
Openness	The document that refers to the purpose of data collection.				
	The document that clearly expresses the policies, practices and procedures for the management of personal information.				
	The technical or other means that the organization uses to inform the users about the management of personal data. The privacy auditor should check the means in practice.				
	The document stating the way in which policies, practices and procedures for the management of personal information are made public. The privacy auditor should control the ways of publication in practice.				
	The document with the steps that inform a user about all policies, practices and procedures for the management of personal information (on user's request).				
	The organization's privacy policy.				
	The existence of privacy icons that inform the user about the openness privacy principle and obligate the organization to follow it.				

M: Met, NM: Not Met, PM: Partially Met

Therefore, if a privacy auditor wishes to audit if an organization applies the principle, he should ask for all policies and procedures used by the organization so as to be reliable towards users. If the prerequisite privacy principles are not met, auditing of the "Accountability Principle" principle cannot be accomplished.

4.2   From a User's Perspective

Protecting user's personal data should always be of interest to the organization. The user should always have the right to be informed about the protection mechanisms in place, as well as about the personal data and the documents the organization uses.

To be more specific, in order for the user to trust the organization and the services offered, it is essential that he will be given the right to get any information he needs in

Table 7. Privacy audit checklist for "Individual Participation"

PRIVACY PRINCIPLE	EVIDENCE	ASSESSMENT			ACTIONS
		M	NM	PM	
Accountability	The Privacy Officer and the employees who are responsible for the management of personal information.				
	The training program of Privacy Officer and employees.				
	The policy about the responsibilities of the Privacy Officer.				
	The supplementary policies and procedures that the Privacy Officer has created.				
	The organization's privacy policy.				
	The existence of privacy icons that inform the user about the accountability privacy principle and obligate the organization to follow it.				

M: Met, NM: Not Met, PM: Partially Met

regard with the collection, processing and storage of his personal data, as well as the way the organization complies with the main privacy principles. Indicatively, from the user's perspective the following cases should be supported by the organization: (Fig. 2)

– The first case is when the user wishes to be informed about the audit procedure followed by the organization. In this case the organization should allow the user to get information about all the documents, means and policies or practices that are used in order to collect and process his personal data. The user should have access to all or to selected documents with the audit information of privacy principles. These documents should be offered in a user-friendly way, so users can easily access them at anytime.

– The second case is when the user wishes to contact the organization in order to get further information. The organization should provide an appropriate user-friendly way to receive user requests and provide them with the necessary clarifications. The idea behind that interaction, between the organization and the user, is to support the necessary transparency that the user needs in order to decide if he will proceed utilizing the services offered by the organization or not.

– The third case is when the user is not interested in the details of the auditing procedure but he simply needs some assurance that his personal data are secure. To achieve that the organization could employ the following privacy audit icons that will visually inform him that the organization has been audited by an appropriate auditing body.

Table 8. Privacy audit checklist for "Accountability"

PRIVACY PRINCIPLE	EVIDENCE	ASSESSMENT			ACTIONS
		M	NM	PM	
Individual Participation	The document that refers to the policy which informs the users on the personal data that the organization collects.				
	The document that refers to the user's consent.				
	The policy that refers to the period of time in which the organization should respond to the users' requests concerning the access to the corresponding personal information.				
	The policy that refers to the way third parties manage the users' personal data and how the users can have access to them.				
	The policy that refers to all exceptions of denying access to users' personal data.				
	The complaint procedures.				
	The identification procedures.				
	The organization's privacy policy.				
	The existence of privacy icons that inform the user about the individual participation privacy principle and obligate the organization to follow it.				

M: Met, NM: Not Met, PM: Partially Met

Fig. 2. Privacy principle icons

5   Conclusions and Further Work

Driven by the most widely used privacy principles, which have been either introduced by countries or by public/private bodies, this paper presents a structured privacy audit methodology that consists of discrete steps that organizations can follow for protecting or/and auditing the privacy of their users. Every step is based on the significance of the privacy principle and on the sequence of the audit procedure.

Currently, we are in the stage of applying the proposed privacy audit methodology to a real environment in order to validate its correctness and effectiveness, as well as its importance for both organizations and users. Furthermore, we are in the process of integrating this work with a privacy requirements elicitation methodology, in order to develop a uniform environment that system developers can utilize for both identifying privacy requirements and then audit their correct implementation.

Acknowledgements. This work has been partially supported by the Research Center of the University of Piraeus.

References

1. Cavoukian, A.: Creation of a Global Privacy Standard, November (2006). http://www.ipc. on.ca/images/Resources/gps.pdf
2. Cavoukian, A., Taylor, S., Abrams, M.E.: Privacy by Design: essential for organizational accountability and strong business practices, Identity in the Information Society, Springer (2010). http://link.springer.com/article/10.1007/s12394-010-0053-z
3. Cavoukian, A.: The privacy payoff: how building privacy into your communications will give you a sustainable competitive advantage. In: International Association of Business Communicators International Conference 2008, New York, June 24, 2008. http://www.ipc. on.ca/images/Resources/2008-06-24-IABC-NYC.pdf
4. Cavoukian, A.: Privacy by design – the 7 foundational principles, Technical report, Information and Privacy Commissioner of Ontario, January 2011. (revised version)
5. Canadian Standards Association, Model Code for the Protection of Personal Information, A National Standard of Canada, Canadian Standards Association, March 1996. http://www. rogerclarke.com/DV/CanModel.html
6. Le Métayer, D.: Chapter 20 - Privacy by Design: A Matter of Choice, Data protection in a profiled world, Springer, (2010). http://link.springer.com/chapter/10.1007/978-90-481-8865-9_20
7. Directive 95/46/EC of the European Parliament and of the Council, The European Parliament and the Council of the European Union, October 24, 1995. http://eur-lex.europa. eu/LexUriServ/LexUriServ.do?uri=CELEX:31995L0046:en:HTML
8. Directive of the European Parliament and of the Council, European Commission, Brussels, March 12, 2014. http://www.europarl.europa.eu/sides/getDoc.do?pubRef=-//EP//TEXT+TA +P7-TA-2014-0212+0+DOC+XML+V0//EN
9. van Blarkom, G.W., Borking, J.J., Olk, J.G.E.: PET, Handbook of Privacy and Privacy-Enhancing Technologies, The Case of Intelligent Software Agents, 2003, ISBN 90-74087-33-7. http://www.andrewpatrick.ca/pisa/handbook/Handbook_Privacy_and_PET_ final.pdf

10. Generally Accepted Privacy Principles (GAPP) (2010). www.aicpa.org/privacy, https://www.cippguide.org/2010/07/01/generally-accepted-privacy-principles-gapp/

11. Karjoth, G., Schunter, M., Waidner, M.: Privacy-enabled Services for Enterprises, IBM Research, Zurich Research Laboratory (2002). http://www.semper.org/sirene/publ/KaSW3_02.TrustBus-final-2002-05-01.pdf

12. Information technology — Security techniques — Privacy framework, International Standard, ISO/IEC 29100:2011(E) (2011)

13. Hoepman, J.-H.: Privacy Design Strategies, May 7, 2013

14. Hoepman, J.-H.: Privacy Design Strategies, October 25, 2012

15. Konstantina, K., Stefanos, G., Konstantinos, M.: Towards a Privacy Audit Programmes Comparison Framework. Springer-Verlag, Heidelberg (2004)

16. OECD Privacy Principles, OECDprivacy.org (1980). http://oecdprivacy.org/

17. Privacy, Accountability and Trust – Challenges and Opportunities, ENISA, February 2, 2011. https://www.enisa.europa.eu/activities/identity-and-trust/library/deliverables/pat-study

18. Reform of data protection legislation, European Commission, (2012). http://ec.europa.eu/justice/data-protection/

19. Safe Harbor Privacy Principles, issued by the U.S. Department of Commerce, July 21, 2000. http://www.export.gov/safeharbor/eu/eg_main_018475.asp

20. The 10 Privacy Principles of PIPEDA, PrivacySense.net. http://www.privacysense.net/10-privacy-principles-of-pipeda/

21. The OECD Privacy Framework, OECD (2013)

22. Tommie, W.: Singleton, IT and Privacy Audits. ISACA J. 5, 2009

23. Wang, Y., Kobsa, A.: Privacy-Enhancing Technologies (2008). http://www.cs.cmu.edu/afs/cs/Web/People/yangwan1/papers/2008-Handbook-LiabSec-AuthorCopy.pdf

Author Index

Printed in the United States
By Bookmasters